In August  volunteered to g... ...an.

With 100... ...was transferred from
training as a fighter pilot to a top-secret naval
base. There, for the first time, he saw the suicide
weapon in which he had volunteered to die.

It was a torpedo, 54 feet long and carrying
3,000 pounds of high explosive in the warhead
at its nose.

It could run at 40 knots underwater—faster
than any ship.

And it would be guided to a direct hit on a
U.S. warship by a human pilot who would die
in the blast.

Yutaka Yokota, who miraculously survived
the war, tells how he learned to operate his
suicide torpedo and describes the farewell
ceremony in which a man is dedicated to death.
Most important, he succeeds in conveying to
American readers an understanding of men like
himself who deliberately accepted annihilation
in the hope of defeating us in World War II.

MORE BALLANTINE WAR BOOKS
YOU WILL ENJOY

Suicide Submarine!

(Formerly THE KAITEN WEAPON)

---

by Yutaka Yokota,

**FORMER PETTY OFFICER IN THE
IMPERIAL JAPANESE NAVY**

WITH JOSEPH D. HARRINGTON

BALLANTINE BOOKS • NEW YORK

PRINTED IN THE UNITED STATES OF AMERICA

First Edition: May, 1962
Second Printing: July, 1966

BALLANTINE BOOKS, INC.
101 Fifth Avenue, New York, N. Y. 10003

☐ FOREWORD ☐

I had already written a book, in Japanese, about my experiences, several years before I was introduced to Mr. Harrington, who was seeking out ex-Navy men. Impressed with his profound knowledge of Japanese naval activities in the war, I agreed to furnish him material from the four notebook diaries I had filled while on active service. I am happy that our collaboration has resulted in this manuscript, which will acquaint Americans with a Japanese military secret so well-guarded that many of my countrymen still have no knowledge of it. Perhaps our story will also help Americans understand what sort of men their naval sons and brothers fought.

YUTAKA YOKOTA

Chofu, Tokyo-to, Japan
December, 1961

In gathering material for this work I was helped tremendously by Mr. Masaru Fujimoto, managing editor of *Mainichi Daily News*, a leading English-language newspaper in Yokota's country. Japanese does not translate easily into English. Much has to be interpreted and explained, together with the background behind a particular phrase or thought. This is singularly important when trying to relate the tale of men so staunch that they could volunteer for deliberate death in their country's behalf, then maintain a peak level of determination for many months before getting into action. Such an action is not easily explained.

Masaru Fujimoto was born in America, and educated at the University of California (Berkeley campus). He was a staff member of the American Embassy in Tokyo on December 7, 1941, and for nearly twenty years has been a working newspaperman in Japan, the U.S. and Europe. Having moved back and forth between the Oriental and Occi-

V

dental worlds, he is particularly well-equipped for the ticklish task of explaining either to the other.

This book could not have been written without the interest, aid and encouragement of a person like Masaru Fujimoto. Because of him I have grown to understand the Japanese people a little, respect them a lot, and perhaps have given a few of them some small idea of my country and people. I have also made a friend for whom I have much affection. If the great gap between America and Asia is ever truly closed, the credit will belong to men like him.

JOSEPH D. HARRINGTON

East St. Louis, Illinois
December, 1961

◘ CONTENTS ◘

▣ DEDICATION ▣

For Gini, who brought me coffee in quantity, and for Sheila and Polly, who made sure their playmates avoided "that corner" of our basement where the working papers for this book lay in crazy disarray.

1 ☐ I Volunteer for a "No-Return" Mission

"All hands fall out in front of the main hangar for general formation!"

I cursed the loudspeaker. It was always beckoning me to do this, or do that. Only one thought comforted me through all the months I had been at Tsuchiura Naval Air Station. If I could continue just a short while more in my flight training, and graduate, I would soon be rid of that loudspeaker. It would be an aircraft carrier for me, and an airplane of my own. I'd have a new enemy, the Americans, instead of that black box on the wall.

I ran out of the barracks and took my place in formation. The entire Thirteenth Flying Class was falling in, all two thousand of us. I came rigidly to attention, letting my eyes move only enough to see our base commander, Captain Kenjiro Watanabe, stride towards a raised platform. He was a stern-looking, straight-backed man, the model of what we felt every Imperial Navy officer should be.

Silence was complete as Captain Watanabe began to speak. At first I thought it would be another of the many pep talks we were used to receiving from our instructors, but the serious look on Captain Watanabe's face convinced me it would not be, especially with his brown skin looking a little pale. He faced the sea of white uniforms, which had gathered on the run from all parts of the base, and began to speak.

"It grieves me very much to tell you this," he said, "but the news from our Navy comrades on the front lines is not good. The material difference between the enemy's power and ours is growing ever greater." The August sun that makes the Kanto Plain of Japan so unbearable in summertime was beating down on us, and I could feel a trickle of sweat run down the center of my back, but I hung on each word. This was the summer of 1944, and Captain Watana-

9

be's opening words did not catch us by surprise, for we had heard of our Navy's severe defeat off the Marianas just two months before. Our defense forces on Guam and Saipan had been wiped out, and in a sea battle we had lost the air-craft carriers *Shokaku, Taiho* and *Hiyo,* together with over four hundred planes. Our training had been speeded up after that, and we expected to graduate well ahead of schedule.

"In spite of the gallant fight our countrymen have been making," said Captain Watanabe, his voice growing sadder with each word, "the enemy's power grows ever greater. Saipan is in enemy hands, and we are having great difficulty getting supplies to our forces at Rabaul.

"We must face the raw truth now, about what is happen-ing. Japan has suffered defeats. Too many defeats. Our country cannot afford any backward steps, any more re-treats. If we continue to give ground, what do you think our final fate will be? So, we depend on men like yourselves not to give ground. We depend on you to drive the enemy back. The hopes of every man, woman and child in Japan rest in you."

Captain Watanabe paused a long time then, as Japanese do when wishing to draw complete attention to the next thing they plan to say. "In this time of serious crisis," he then said, "our naval scientists have developed a new weapon. Nothing like it has ever existed before. Once it is put into use, it can overwhelm the enemy and win a victory for our beloved country. It has been tested, and we are positive it will be effective. What we need now are men who will operate this weapon for us."

Again he paused a long time, then went on. "I realize," he said, "that all of you men have a great love for flying. You have worked and trained long and hard for just one purpose, to fly into combat against the enemies of Japan. That is why it is so difficult for me to ask you to cut short your flight training and volunteer to man this new weapon. But I would not for one moment consider asking you to make such a sacrifice, if I were not convinced of this weapon's tremendous value. It can change the course of the entire war, once it goes into action!"

The strong discipline instilled in us during our time at Tsuchiura relaxed for a few seconds as a great murmur of curiosity arose. A man near me turned and said, *"Nandai,*

Yokota? What is it, Yokota?" Then Captain Watanabe's deep, clear voice brought us back to attention again.

"If any man among you burns enough with the desire to save his country, to board this new weapon and take part in our great offensive against the approaching enemy, he may volunteer. I cannot tell you any more about it, except that it will have more power than any airplane you might fly. Now, listen carefully to what I say next. Your squadron leaders are to hand each of you a piece of paper. If you are particularly anxious to volunteer for this new weapon, write your name and squadron number at the top of the paper, and make *niju maru*, two circles, below it. I repeat, two circles if you are really eager to go. If, however, you do not have a truly deep desire to go, but are willing to make this sacrifice for your country if called upon, inscribe only one circle. This is most important, so I repeat . . . two circles if you feel very strongly that you must go, but only one circle if you are merely willing to do this duty. Those who don't want to go at all, but wish to continue with flight training, are to destroy their papers."

More murmuring from the two thousand men in ranks made one think of a soft wave breaking on the shore in the moonlight. But again, Captain Watanabe's crisp voice brought us out of our wondering.

"One last thing must be added," he said, "before the papers are handed out. I must tell you that this weapon is of such a nature that whoever mans it on a mission against the enemy is not expected to return alive. He will surely be able to inflict a great hurt on our enemy during his mission, but he will give his life in doing so. Therefore, think carefully before you decide. Be absolutely sure you want to go, before volunteering. Most of all, be sure you will not be concerned later with what you leave behind. Your minds will have to be absolutely clear at all times, so you will be able to give full concentration to the job ahead of you."

Papers were handed out, and the ranks broke then, men moving off slowly to whatever they had been doing before the call to general assembly. Some returned to the flight line, and others to classrooms, where we had been getting twenty hours of academic training each week. I started back for the barracks and, while covering the few hundred meters from the hangar, listened to the remarks of my comrades.

"The captain must be *kichigai!* He's crazy if he thinks

men will volunteer for something he tells us nothing about, except that we will die!"

"Will we go immediately to the front lines?"

"What a chance for glory! How proud your parents and friends would be!"

"I'm tearing up my paper! I have a sweetheart, and I want to marry her when this war is over."

"Should I make one circle, or two? I wouldn't want anyone to think I had no *Yamato damashii*. My patriotism is as great as any man's."

"I know I'm making two circles! Think, what an adventure! One's name would appear in history books. *Tenno-Heika* himself might even send a personal memorial to your father and mother. It has happened before, you know."

The remarks passed straight through my head without stopping, for I already knew what I was going to do. I had made up my mind just as soon as Captain Watanabe finished addressing us. During his talk I felt my blood heating. His words about Japan's defeats had stirred me up. The round-eyes of America, England and The Netherlands had tried to choke my country to death, and forced us into war. It was all right for American and British troops to be stationed in China for protection of their national interests, but when Japan did it, she suddenly became everybody's enemy. Captain Watanabe's remarks about what Japan's final fate might be had sent courage up into my stomach. No one had ever defeated my people, and no one ever would if I could help it. Our land destroyed, all its culture gone—no! It would not take a memorial from the Emperor to my family to influence me. As soon as we got to the barracks, I would mark my paper with two circles and pass it to my squadron commander. At that point, I began walking a little faster. With luck, I would have the honor of being the first in my squadron to volunteer.

For the rest of that day and night, our quarters were like an aroused beehive. Everyone was speculating about what this new weapon might be. All agreed it really must be a very powerful one, to be kept so secret. At Tsuchiura, as at every place where military men are stationed, a secret usually leaked out one way or another. But not this time. We had had no hint of anything at all, until the call to assemble before the hangar. Perhaps, we told ourselves, the secret was so great that even Captain Watanabe did not have full information.

There was no playful wrestling or judo practice or practical joking in our barracks that night. Even the loudmouths, who bored us with telling of the feats they would accomplish in the air against the enemy, were quiet for a change. They spoke softly and seriously. And the quiet men among us were more quiet than ever.

I lay in my hammock and looked at the ceiling, taking little part in the discussions, though they continued long after lights were out. My paper, with two large, black circles on it, had been turned in. Now I reflected on my decision.

All my life I had wanted to fly for the Imperial Navy. The great aircraft carriers in Tokyo Bay had always been a beautiful sight to me. Like thousands of other Japanese boys, I burned to be a naval officer, stern and commanding in bright whites, a sword of authority at my side. I had, in fact, taken the nationwide competitive examinations for admission to Etajima, the naval academy, twice. The first time I had passed the written examination, but failed the physical. Not willing to give up, I tried again the following year, but was again turned down, simply because I had a few teeth missing. Requirements for admission to Etajima were very strict, and great numbers of young men who were almost perfect physical speciments were turned away each year because of some minor flaw. Mine had been the lack of just three teeth. No one who wore glasses was considered at all, of course, and all young men were envious of anyone who even advanced far enough to be examined at all.

In 1943, having just turned eighteen, I gave up hope of getting into Etajima and, enrolling in cadet pilot school, was sent to Tsuchiura, one hour's train ride northeast of Tokyo. My missing teeth were overlooked, and my eyesight was perfect. Now, after nearly a year of training, I had decided in an instant to throw away my dream of becoming a carrier pilot. I had volunteered for this mysterious new weapon. What was it? Would I be successful using it? Would I really be able to do more for my country with this weapon than at the controls of an airplane? These thoughts were topmost in my mind as I drifted into sleep.

The next morning, I raced with others to the board where the loudspeaker announced the names of accepted volunteers had been posted. My name was on the list, and my heart nearly burst with joy. I would man the new weapon! I would meet the enemy! No doubt about it. I stood straight and proud as barracks mates pounded fists into my shoulder blades and shouted, *"Yokattana, Yokota!"* As I accepted their congratulations, a strange feeling came over my entire body. I have never been able to describe it accurately. It was as though I had stepped out of one body into another, and was looking at the first. Perhaps this is how all men feel who have learned there will soon be no life left in the body they have inhabited for years. The feeling passed quickly, however, being replaced by impatience. How soon would we see this new weapon? How long would we train in it? When would I go up against the enemy? I didn't want to wait very long.

Only 100 men were selected from those who volunteered, and the small number surprised me, for spirit was so high among men at Tsuchiura that I was sure many hundreds more must have volunteered. For nearly a year we had been undergoing severe training and indoctrination, to build a strong spirit in us. Physical exercise sessions were long and arduous, and every man was in the best of health. We thought nothing of standing in the snow, going through Swedish calisthenics, while clad only in *fundoshi*, the white loincloth worn as underwear in Japan. We built our muscles with cross-country races and six-mile rowing competitions. I had thrived on this part of the training, for in Middle School I had always been very active in athletics. My love for sports, in fact, had cost me the three teeth that prevented me from entering Etajima.

At every stage in training, our instructors reminded us of our national duty. All were demanding, and nearly all pushed us to the limits of physical and mental endurance. Too, as each bit of bad news about the Combined Fleet seeped into Tsuchiura, the voices of instructors became harsher. More and more often they spoke through clenched teeth.

"To win, in war, is not enough! You must overwhelm and down the enemy completely!"

We were caught up in this spirit, especially since the faces of officers grew grimmer each day.

"Should the need for it come, one should give his life for the Empire gladly!"

"If in doubt as to whether you should live or die, it is always better to die!"

"Don't waste your life! Death must have a purpose. Do not accept death unless, by dying, you can hurt the enemy severely!"

Such phrases as these, spoken many times a day by instructors and officers, repeated often over loudspeakers, and posted everywhere on walls and bulletin boards, even in the washrooms and toilets, helped fill us with steel. And dozens of times each week one heard the words of Meiji, grandfather of our Emperor, repeated with vehemence. "Death has only the weight of a feather, but duty is as heavy as a mountain!"

Senior officers had pored over the list of volunteers all night, we were later told. They based their selections on three basic qualifications:

1. Is this man exceptionally strong physically, and has he a powerful will?
2. Is his fighting spirit high, and has he shown great sense of national responsibility?
3. Does he have a minimum of family responsibilities, or none at all?

No married men were selected, only men who would have little or no tendency to look behind them. I am sure that family played an important part in my being selected. My mother had died when I was five years old, so I wouldn't be worrying for her sake. And my father had another son, as well as two daughters. I was the youngest of four children, a position not meriting much concern in Japan. If I died, my older brother Hiroshi could carry on the family name. If anything happened to him, it was always possible that my sisters Chiyoe and Toshie might have husbands who were willing to be adopted by my father. An adopted groom would become a Yokota, and thus carry on the family line. I am sure that the officers who chose the volunteers must have felt that loss of a youngest son was not too much of a sacrifice to make for the Emperor when a father still had three other children.

There was a lot of excitement after the names of accepted volunteers were posted. Not all my friends congratulated me, however. A lot of them rushed off to find our squadron leader and protest their not being chosen. During the dragging weeks that followed, they asked again and again for their names to be added to the list. I was proud of my friends, and of the Tsuchiura training that could make so many men fight and argue when refused the chance to die for our country. But it did them no good. The list was to contain 100 names only, as ordered by higher command. It stayed at that figure.

On graduation day, when others were deemed ready for training in aircraft of the Fleet, our group of 100 marched in a double file through their ranks, led by Lieutenant Komatsu. Great cheers went up as we passed. Even cadets with whom some us had had quarrels of long standing, or even fist fights, joined in the noisy send-off. We boarded a train and headed south, passing through Tokyo without an idea of our destination. The air of secrecy was still heavy as we went through Yokohama, and when we noticed the train did not veer down the Miura Peninsula to the great naval base at Yokosuka, near the mouth of Tokyo Bay, we began speculating. By the time we reached the Sagami Bay resort town of Atami, and sacred *Fuji-san* was looming up to our right, we had decided we were headed either for Kure, the giant naval arsenal on the Inland Sea, or for the big base at Sasebo, on the southern main island of Kyushu.

We rode the train most of that day and all the next, our constant speculation as to what the secret weapon might be keeping us awake most of the time. Darkness covered us as we finally left the train and boarded Navy trucks. In a little while we were stopped at the entrance to a barracks. A few minutes later we were all in hammocks and fast asleep, exhausted from our trip and the tension. The following day we discovered that we were indeed at Kure Naval Arsenal, where the headquarters of the Sixth Fleet, Japan's submarine force, was located.

That day we spent like tourists, looking around here and there. On the following day, about noon, Lieutenant Komatsu came and gathered us in a circle about him.

"I want to thank all of you," he said, "for being so orderly during our movement here. I have to return to Tsuchiura now, so I wanted to say goodbye. No one here has told me what kind of a weapon you have volunteered for, but I know you will serve Japan bravely and gallantly.

"Another 100 men are coming from the naval air base at Nara," he said, "so show them a good example by living up to the memories of the many brave men who trained at Tsuchiura. Your future commander is a man I know very well. He expects big things of you, for I have told him you are the pick of Tsuchiura's best men."

He spoke all of these words in a low voice. When he finished there were tears in his eyes, and some of us were crying. Lieutenant Komatsu was our last link with Tsuchiura, where some of the world's best pilots had slept in the barracks we used.

That afternoon we were ordered to take our belongings on board two launches. For me, it was the first time aboard any kind of naval craft, unless the rowing races at was in charge of us, but said nothing much until we were Tsuchiura, were counted. A young officer, Ensign Miyake, was in charge of us, but said nothing much until were were under way for more than an hour. The stifling air of secrecy, which had started with Captain Watanabe's speech, still hung over everything.

Finally, Ensign Miyake stood up and spoke to the group in my launch. "Attention, men!" he shouted at the top of his lungs, though it was a small launch and we could hear him perfectly well. "We are headed for Otsujima Island, just off Tokuyama City!" This was, as most of us knew, in Yamaguchi Prefecture. "I have only been to Otsujima once before!" he continued in a high, shrill tone. "It is a special base for secret weapons! Dozen of naval officers have already been there for weeks, training! We will join them soon, and they will instruct us! You and I will all soon be members of their special attack groups! That means that from now on we will all be brothers!"

This ensign must be just out of Etajima, I told myself, for he acted like every other new officer I had met during my year of service. One would think he was standing on the stage of a giant Tokyo auditorium, he screamed so loud.

"Do you understand?" he shouted.

"Yes, sir, we do!" came the answer, several pranksters shouting their response even louder than the question.

There was little more said by him during the journey. My mind filled again with the thought that I was giving my life for my country. I had no regrets, though. Whatever lay ahead of me would fill my family with pride when they finally received news of the manner of my death, for Japanese history, music and literature are rich in stories of heroes who died defending their country and its ruling family. Every schoolboy knew most of the names by heart, much as American boys can name famous frontiersmen. The *samurai*, with his quiet, polite ways and unending courage meant to us what cowboys mean to American youths.

I especially had no regrets about leaving Tsuchiura. Though I was a good student pilot, the atmosphere there was always tense. In spite of Japan's great need for replacement pilots, no let-down had been made in training standards. Only your best was good enough. Flight and ground instructors were just as demanding as they had been during peacetime, when only a small percentage of entrants completed flight school successfully. Meanwhile, while under training, the slightest wrong word, or gesture could be reason enough for an instructor to recommend immediate expulsion. Most of us found the strain very difficult to bear, so I was not too unhappy about leaving the place, except for separating from good friends.

Several hours passed before we reached Otsujima, and our first impression was not favorable. Inside the sheltering breakwater lay two very old submarines, and as we approached the pier we could see two large black buildings that resembled airplane hangars. Our launches tied up, and we formed two ranks on the pier as an officer came out of one of the buildings and addressed us.

"Are you the men from Tsuchiura?" he called out when he stood before us.

We had been fired up by Lieutenant Komatsu's and Ensign Miyake's words. "Yes, sir!" we shouted simultaneously.

"Well, you certainly seem filled with enthusiasm!" he said, "I am your new commanding officer, Lieutenant Commander Itakura. From now on you will be in my charge. I have been told you have been selected from more than a thousand volunteers at Tsuchiura. That is good. I want you to devote yourselves to your new work with all your strength." With that he said something to Ensign Miyake, and walked back toward the building.

How much alike do naval officers speak, I told myself. Every officer, beginning with Captain Watanabe, had ended every address to us in a similar way. "Work with all

your might!" or "Give your very best effort!" or something like that were always the last words spoken.

Still, a tense feeling came over us as he spoke, for he
seemed so different from the officers at Tsuchiura. They
had been training officers. Now, at Otsujima, we would be
among combat officers. We were, in fact, combat people
ourselves now. We could see a distinct difference between
training people and combat people in our first few minutes
at Otsujima, just by the calm but swift way people moved
around. Just from the way they looked at us, we knew
they considered us equals. At Tsuchiura, one referred to his
squadron commander as *Oyaji,* as father. The executive
officer was *Ofukuro,* mother. And the senior petty officer
in charge was *Aniki,* our big brother. Though discipline
was severe, for they treated us as very strict parents might,
with swift punishment for carelessness or wrongdoing, they
still looked closely after our personal needs, especially when
we fell sick or were injured. It was not unusual for a
squadron chief to spend the night in sick bay by the side
of one of his men. Nor was it unusual for a senior petty
officer to give that same man a severe beating two weeks
later for something he'd done wrong. Lieutenant Commander Itakura seemed, by contrast, remote from us, and
it would be some time before we realized that this was
because he did not look upon us as little brothers, but men
with whom he would fight, side by side.

We started moving off the pier then, in two files, and
marched about fifty meters to where one of the buildings
stood. On its door, in large Kanji ideographs, was a sign
saying, "No admittance except by special permission of
the Navy Minister."

The new weapon was in there! I was sure of it. Ensign
Miyake went through the door, then came back when he
noticed no one was following him. "What's the delay?" he
shouted. "Break ranks and follow me!" No one moved,
but all eyes swung to the ominous sign. Ensign Miyake
laughed then and, for the first time since we'd met him,
spoke in a normal voice. "Don't worry about that," he said,
"If you did not already have permission of the Navy Minister, you would be nowhere near this island."

We moved through the small doorway a few at a time.
The first thing I saw when I got inside the building was
a long, fat, cigar-shaped object, resting on two big blocks.

I knew at once what it was, by the periscope jutting from its top—a torpedo which would carry a man. So that's what our highly secret new weapon was! I, Yutaka Yokota, had volunteered to become a human torpedo!

2 □ I Learn About My New Weapon

All about the inside of the building I could see men working, quietly, urgently. Groups of oil-stained mechanics moved about, and I was struck by the sight of young officers, all of whose eyes shone with a bright light whenever they looked at or touched one of the giant torpedoes. Most of them had beards, which surprised me much. Few Japanese men, except the Ainu from Hokkaido, our northernmost main island, can cultivate a really handsome chin growth. Only elderly men usually grow them. I thought these beards, thin and scraggly as they were, must be some kind of brotherhood sign. A sort of symbol, or bond, between the men who would take this terrible weapon into action. Then I remembered they were probably all submarine sailors, since the secret weapon was a torpedo. Perhaps they just got out of the habit of shaving while on sea patrols.

When the hundred of us were inside the building, Lieutenant Commander Itakura called to us. "Gather around me!" he ordered, waving us with his hand toward the nearest torpedo. "You men will be boarding this weapon before long," he said. "You will train in them until you have become experts in handling them. Then you will take them to sea and help overwhelm our enemies."

Our new commander paused, then went on. "We call this new weapon *kaiten*," he told us, "but for the sake of complete security it is always referred to as *maru roku kana-mono*—Circle Six Metal Fitting. That way, whenever it shows up in my messages, correspondence or requisitions, no one but certain members of the High Command and Sixth Fleet submarine staff will have any idea of what it is. Strangers will assume it is some kind of spare part, or shipboard equipment. They will have no idea of what we are doing here, and our activities cannot leak out to the enemy. As you no doubt have already determined for yourselves, this is a human torpedo, capable of carrying

21

one man, its pilot. It is faster than any warship afloat, so nothing will be able to escape it."

Itakura's eyes bored into ours then. "All of you volunteered to come here," he said, "so you must have expected something of this nature. Still, all of you were training to be pilots, and you may be disappointed that this has not turned out to be an air weapon. I can understand that, so, if any of you change your minds, see me before the day is over. I will make sure you are returned to flight training, with no question asked."

Some of us looked at one another. We said nothing, but I could read the minds of my comrades as well as my own. Was this officer crazy? Did he think we had come all the way from Tsuchiura just for a sightseeing tour? We had volunteered to give our lives! The manner of dying did not matter, so long as we could, as Captain Watanabe promised, overwhelm the enemy. I personally had felt, since arriving at Kure base, that the new scientific invention would be some kind of water weapon, and was still willing to go.

"One more thing," said Lieutenant Commander Itakura, "I want you to know that, although I am your commanding officer, I am also a *kaiten* pilot. I, too, will be going out to attack the enemy in one of these. Some of you may be on the same mission with me."

His voice became very sober. "A few days ago," he said, "a man named Hiroshi Kuroki, one of the inventors of this weapon, was killed in a training accident. We found his will in the *kaiten* when we recovered it. It is an inspiring document, a source of hope and confidence for all of us. I trust that you men will train hard, and do your jobs well, so that Kuroki will not have died in vain."

There they were again! The typical officer's closing words. But this time they carried more weight than ever. My commander's voice was calm and even. No shouting for him, to fire up the blood. His voice gave you confidence, instead of seeking to inspire you. After all, when a man stood before you, having promised to give his life in your service, there wasn't much point in urging him to do his best. Lieutenant Commander Itakura was simply asking us to exert all efforts to master the techniques of handling this new weapon, so we would be experts when it came time to take it out. That way, the enemy was bound to suffer sure death at the same time we met ours.

Lieutenant Commander Itakura stopped talking. He searched every face. He was looking to see if anyone's determination had lessened, after learning what the new weapon was. I glanced to either side of me, and thought my comrades looked as calm as any men could. I made sure my face was calm, too, as his glance moved along to me. What he saw must have satisfied him, for he smiled and said, "That is all for now. I just want to introduce your squadron commander to you."

A short, but very tough-looking officer then stepped forward. "I am Lieutenant, junior grade, Chosa," he said. "I will be responsible for the Tsuchiura detachment while you are taking training." I was much impressed by this man. Although small in stature, he was very broad-shouldered and looked like a pocket-size *sumo* wrestler. You could see large muscles bulging beneath his shirt and trousers. He did not raise his voice when speaking to us either. His very presence commanded attention. He was like a rock, and I felt that others as well as I were pleased this man would be our leader. Nothing reassures a military man so much as a leader who exudes authority from every pore. I knew right then I would obey his every command promptly, and try to act at all times in such a way that my behavior would reflect favorably on him. He was the kind of man I would want to be if I ever became an officer.

No chance of that happening, of course. My life would be ended before very long. If I were to become an officer, it would only be through the Imperial Navy's double promotion system, which applied after death to men who performed outstanding feats for our country, like the midget submarine men who had gone to their deaths at Pearl Harbor three-and-one-half years before. No one in the Japanese Navy ever received medals while he was still alive. It was a tradition. Some people objected to this, and at one time there was much protest because the High Command refused to consider special commendations for flyers who had fought through the East Indies, Malaya, the Philippines, New Guinea and the Solomon Islands. The reason was, simply, that it had never been done before for living men, so it would not be done now. Throughout the entire Pacific war, not one Japanese sailor or officer was decorated for bravery. A Japanese Navy man, whether he be seaman or admiral, was expected to fight, and die if necessary, for his country simply because that was his duty. He fought to preserve his country, or to defeat her enemies, but not for any medal or glory. The privilege of fighting, and dying, was considered reward enough. Perhaps this is one of the things that has always made it so difficult for Westerners to understand us Japanese. I am sure that volunteering for *kamikaze* duty, or *kaiten* duty, must be another. However, it has always been the Japanese way.

Thus started my first day at Otsujima, one of Japan's most secret bases during the war. It was never referred to as anything but "Base P" and, since the great torpedo was referred to only as Circle Six Metal Fitting, only a handful of our 75,000,000 countrymen knew where we were and what we were doing. My mail came in and went out through Fleet Post Office, Kure, like that of men in air squadrons and fighting ships. As far as anyone I wrote to was concerned, I was still in flight training, somewhere else than Tsuchiura. I never told anyone differently.

Throughout the rest of that first day we were free to look around and do as we pleased, provided we did not get in the way. I was surprised to see that our new quarters were furnished with *tatami*, the rush straw mats still used in nearly every Japanese home. There were no *futon*, though, the thick Japanese comforters that serve as mattress and bed cover at night, being rolled up and tucked away in a cabinet each morning. Throughout my Navy training, I had always slept in a hammock, and I smiled, seeing the *tatami*. It would not be easy, getting used to sleeping on the floor again.

During that first day, and later, we learned how the *kaiten* came to be. Translated literally into English, "*kaiten*" means "*sky change*," but it has a much fuller meaning in Japanese. *Kaiten*, in our connotation, means to bring about a tremendous change in the way things are going, to make a radical reverse in affairs. The weapon was given this name by its inventors, so its development needs some explaining.

At the time of the Battle of Midway, in June, 1942, Ensign Sekio Nishina and Lieutenant, junior grade, Hiroski Kuroki were pilots of midget submarines. All Japan, thanks to the much-publicized double-promotion of midget submarine men lost in the Pearl Harbor attack, felt that such craft played an important part on the war's opening day. They were considered very valuable weapons. Admiral Isoroku Yamamoto, Commander-in-Chief of the Combined Fleet, had a large number of midget submarines with him when he sailed against Midway with an armada of nearly two hundred ships. They were loaded into the seaplane tenders *Chiyoda* and *Nisshin*. After the island of Midway was captured, these were to be hoisted out of their mother ships and based at Midway, or nearby Kure. (This was a very small island, in English spelled, but not pronounced the same as our great naval base on Japan's Inland Sea.) *Chiyoda* and *Nisshin* did not see any action at Midway, for they were many miles to the northwest of where all action took place, held back with Admiral Yamamoto's main body, which included the super-battleship *Yamoto*, the greatest warship ever built.

Everyone knows, of course, that Japan lost four very valuable aircraft carriers in the battle for Midway. They were *Soryu*, *Hiryu*, *Kaga* and *Akagi*, these last two having been converted from battle cruisers in the late twenties, as had been the *USS Lexington* and *Saratoga*. Had we taken Midway, midget submarines would have been part of its defenses, nearly two dozen of them ready to sortie out and sink any enemy warships that came to bombard for a counter-invasion.

With the loss of the four carriers, the plan to take Midway was a failure. Our top naval leaders were horrified, and an all-out attempt was made to withhold this news from the Japanese people. Except for a few top officers, no one from the Midway force was allowed to go ashore in Japan on their return to port. All hands, including even some admirals, were restricted to their ships for nearly two months. By that time, word of the horrendous loss had leaked out, and was being passed around the country by word of mouth. Still, our government waited a long time before releasing any news, even though it had been broadcast from the U.S. many times.

The sinking of those four carriers became of special concern to Kuroki and Nishina, for they were men of much intelligence as well as high spirit. Though they were submarine men, they knew the Imperial Navy placed most of its trust in naval air warfare. All strategy was planned on the principle that our Navy pilots, the best trained in the world, capable of carrying out their missions by day or blackest night, in any kind of weather, would control the air above the scene of any sea action or amphibious movement. This they had done through all of the Imperial Navy's early successes. But now the initiative was gone with those four carriers. American shipbuilding would soon give our enemy the balance of power, unless something could make up for those four missing flattops.

Nishina and Kuroki knew that their chosen weapon, midget submarines, had many limitations. They were battery-powered, which limited their speed. Actually, they were very small submarines, which carried just two torpedoes. They were very vulnerable when discovered and attacked, for they could not seek deep waters, like regular submarines, or move about quickly enough to dodge depth charges. They could neither run away from, or pursue, an enemy. They could only be used along Japan's or enemy shores, and it took a terribly long time for a submarine to surface, embark a midget submarine crew in their vessel, and get them away to their target. What was needed in their place was something much faster, easier to launch, with much more power, and with a much better chance of really hurting the enemy. Many enemy carriers had to be sunk to keep the odds in favor of Japan's Imperial Navy.

The two young officers pondered the problem a long time, then came up with their basic idea. A human torpedo! That was the answer! Such a thing could be released more easily from the deck of a submarine than a midget craft carrying two or three men. A submarine might carry up to six such torpedoes, accessible from within the hull. She could creep close to enemy anchorages undetected and loose her missiles into a thick fleet of warships. With skill and good fortune, such attacks, repeated again and again, might sink enough carriers and battleships to redress the balance in the Pacific.

Two vital requirements would be accuracy—that would be provided by the human pilot—and high speed. The enemy, even if he should somehow sight this torpedo, must not be able to dodge it, or run away from it. Finding volunteers to man the weapon would be no problem, the officers knew, for the national spirit was strong. Didn't everyone revere the famous Three Bombs, the Army men who ran forward and blew themselves up to make a hole in enemy defenses early in the China Incident? Their action let Japanese forces swarm through to victory over a strongly entrenched force. Surely the Navy could do as well as the less popular Army! Having decided upon the basic weapon, Nishina and Kuroki now sought some means of building and designing it.

Fortunately for them, the Japanese Navy possessed at that time the world's largest, fastest and most powerful torpedo. No other country ever developed anything like the oxygen-powered Model 93, sweeper of the seas. This torpedo, which struck terror into the American Navy again and again during the campaign for the Solomon Islands later, was developed by Japan alone. It was perfected by my "copycat" countrymen when neither Great Britain nor the United States, considered far more advanced technologically, could bring anything comparable into being. Its story deserves telling here.

In 1922, when the Washington Naval Disarmament Treaty was signed by Great Britain, the United States, Japan, France and Italy, our top naval strategists were distressed. Our diplomats agreed to keep our capital ship tonnage down to 60 per cent of that allowed Great Britain or the U.S. They felt that this allotment, which gave our two greatest competitors in naval strength better than three to one odds against Japan in case of a war, was not sufficient strength for defending the homeland. These worried men gained little public sympathy for their thoughts, however. The world was at peace, and Japan had been awarded a mandate over the Pacific Islands. These would help with the country's overpopulation problem, and were a significant source of the revenue Japan needed for buying vital imports. Also, the country was in the middle of a great business boom, and prosperity was enjoyed nearly everywhere. No one had much enthusiasm about paying more taxes, just to increase the strength of our Navy. This view was universally prevalent. Big armies and navies only lead to big wars, people said. Japan is enjoying friendly relations with nearly all countries. Why disturb things? So the protests of senior naval officers were stifled under sighs of contentment.

But our strategic planners did not give up. If they could

not have a navy of quantity, they meant to have one of quality. Top quality. They would modernize the Imperial Japanese Navy to such a degree that, ship for ship and man for man, it would be the world's best! Each warship would be made the equivalent of two! A modernization program was started. Old battleships were pulled into shipyards and almost completely reconstructed. *Hiei, Haruna, Kirishima* and *Kongo* were so improved that their top speeds were better than thirty knots, nearly half again that of the fastest American battleships. Great emphasis was placed on naval aviation and on night battle training. High-speed maneuvers, in total darkness, were practiced over and over again, though they cost much through collisions and loss of planes and men. The world's first design for assisting pilots to make carrier landings at night by use of varying lighting arrangements and mirrors was developed and placed aboard the old aircraft carrier *Hosho*. World War II was already over before the British developed something similar and let America copy it. Everything that was possible was done, but members of the Naval General Staff felt they needed just one more thing, something that would give them assured superiority over any enemy that steamed toward Japan's homeland.

Our naval ordnance technicians thought they had the answer in the oxygen-propelled torpedo. They had been experimenting with such a torpedo during World War I and the years following. Torpedoes in those days were propelled by steam, and it was generally considered that the steam-driven torpedo had been brought to its peak of performance. But oxygen was another matter altogether. Naval experts knew that a torpedo propelled by oxygen could have a far greater range and speed than a steam-driven one. It could also carry a larger warhead, and would leave no wake. It could be the perfect underwater weapon.

But oxygen presented grave problems. It was very difficult to handle. In both Japan and Great Britain experimental oxygen-powered torpedoes had blown up without warning, killing torpedomen and technicians. This discouraging feature, coupled with the fact that funds for research kept decreasing, led to shelving of the oxygen torpedo project indefinitely. For three years, after 1924, nothing was done on it.

Then, during 1927, a report was mailed to Tokyo that changed things radically. It was the custom, according to the Washington Treaty, for naval inspectors to visit the shipyards and warships of other treaty nations, to assure themselves that all were living up to the agreement. A Japanese naval inspector was at Portsmouth, England, in 1927, and had satisfied himself the British were keeping their word. While touring the battleship *HMS Rodney,* however, he noticed an odd-looking apparatus on one of her decks. His experienced eye told him at once it was an oxygen generator, but he pretended to give it little notice. A few days later he heard that the *Rodney,* which had torpedo tubes mounted below her waterline like many other battleships of her day, was going to run a torpedo test. He managed to be inside Portsmouth Naval Base on that designated day, and what he saw made him hasten to his lodgings and write an urgent report to the Navy Ministry in Tokyo. "The battleship *Rodney,*" part of it read, "has tested oxygen-propelled torpedoes!" This portion of the message was enough to impel Japanese naval officials into immediate action. Funds were diverted from other sources, and our surprised ordnance technicians found themselves hastily dusting off old plans and under orders to make all possible speed with tests.

By 1933, these men had brought to the fleet-testing stage a giant torpedo, 24 inches in diameter, nearly 30 feet long, and weighing 6,000 pounds. It was able to carry more than a thousand pounds of high explosive in its nose, just about twice that of American and British torpedoes. Development problems were encountered along the way, but they were solved. Fuel lines, very angular at first, were redesigned until they contained only gentle curves, for it was discovered that oxygen tended to "mass" at sharp turns, and start heating up. A problem in oil stains, caused by lack of care in torpedo assembly, was eliminated by cleaning all fuel lines with a special potassium compound during assembly, and keeping them sealed thereafter. The combination of massing and overheating was, in the opinion of our experts, why oxygen torpedoes had been blowing up without warning. The heated oxygen sparked the oil, which detonated oxygen under pressure, they said. They must have been correct, for Great Britain never solved the explosion problem. She gave up experimenting with oxygen torpedoes and settled for the slower but stable steam-driven ones, at just about the time Japan's experts achieved success. America, aware of the failures of the British, never gave oxygen torpedoes serious attention.

A great deal of testing was given the Model 93 torpedo before naval leaders in Japan were satisfied with it. Dozens of obsolete warships and merchant ships were sent to the bottom in secret firings held far out to sea, away from prying eyes. These tests provided power, speed and range data. The island of Oshima, well south of Tokyo Bay, provided the perfect place for checking the Model 93's depth-setting mechanism. Though Oshima was a popular tourist spot—known especially for the active volcano Mihara, into which troubled lovers often leaped—one side of it was a sheer, deserted coastline which rose up sharply from the sea. Torpedoes fired against these perpendicular cliffs could not be heard elsewhere on the island, and Navy divers went to recheck every shot, to make sure it struck at the distance below the surface for which it had been set.

The most dramatic test was when the old battleships *Aki* and *Satsuma* were used for targets. Just as the American pilot Billy Mitchell proved the airplane's worth by sinking two large captured German warships in the Atlantic Ocean with aerial bombs, our torpedo tacticians used two heavy warships to impress our strategic planners. Japan profited from Mitchell's example; my countrymen always having been most receptive to new ideas and concepts which other nations sometimes ignored.

It took exactly three torpedoes to sink *Aki* and *Satsuma*, and prove the Model 93's might. Orders came down to equip all destroyers and cruisers with this "Long Lance" that could strike from beyond the range of a battleship's guns. Maximum range was 21 miles, maximum speed an incredible forty-nine knots! By the end of 1938 all Japanese destroyers, as well as both light and heavy cruisers, were equipped with the Long Lance, and not a foreign nation was the wiser. Torpedo petty officers and torpedo officers were thoroughly impressed with the need for absolute secrecy, and the oxygen-manufacturing machines mounted in their ships were always described to shipmates and visitors as "special air generators."

Long Lance's first wartime use struck a blow at four nations at once. During the Java Sea Battle, in February,

1942, a combined force of American, British, Dutch and Australian warships that tried to intercept a guarded convoy heading south to invade Java was shattered. Eight of the fourteen enemy ships fell victim to the Long Lance.

At Savo Island, which we Japanese call the First Battle of the Eastern Solomons, a force of our ships under Rear Admiral Gunichi Mikawa, although far outnumbered and outgunned, surprised and sank four heavy cruisers, *USS Quincy, USS Vincennes, USS Astoria* and *HMAS Canberra*. Three of these were crippled by Long Lances which put their power plants out of commission, then smashed into the sea by gunfire and more torpedoes. Altogether the Model 93 Long Lance sank or badly damaged nearly thirty enemy cruisers and destroyers during the first two years of war, and was responsible for finishing off *USS Hornet*, an aircraft carrier. It might have done far more harm than this, too, but our Navy, bit by bit, lost many of the ships that carried this weapon into battle. Most were lost to enemy bombers.

So it was that Nishina and Kuroki, searching for the weapon they needed, found the main part of it right at hand. At Kure Naval Arsenal they consulted with a very ingenious man named Hiroshi Suzukawa, who is now chief technician with the Canon Camera Company, in Tokyo. Mr. Suzukawa, then a Navy employee, looked over the rough sketches they presented him and was at once interested. Working together in every spare moment during the remaining months of 1942, the three men finally drafted plans for a one-man torpedo, so designed as to be quickly released from the deck of a submerged submarine. Their hopes soared with each movement of their drawing pencils, for Japan at that time had over ninety submarines. What destruction these could wreak on an enemy fleet, with four or five or six *kaiten* mounted on each deck! The final design drafted by Kuroki, Nishina and Suzukawa was, like their earlier ones, built basically around the Model 93 Long Lance. It proposed removing the warhead, then inserting a pilot's compartment aft of it before reassembling the big torpedo. A periscope, seat and set of controls would be in this added chamber.

By January, 1943, the completed plans were ready. The enlarged Model 93 was now much thicker than its original 24-inch diameter. Also, it had grown from 30 feet in length to 54, but it would carry a monster charge—3,000 pounds—of high explosive in its nose, 5 times that of the enemy torpedoes! Calculations showed that the *kaiten* would be able to make 40-knot speed, and run for one hour. Range could be increased by sacrificing some explosive power, but Kuroki and Nishina would not consider this alteration at all. They felt that a 40-nautical-mile range was sufficient for the kind of operation they had in mind, especially since a 3,000-pound warhead would surely sink any warship in the world. Nothing afloat could withstand such a hit in its vitals. If the Model 93 Long Lance could break the back of a heavy cruiser, as it did two months before in the battle off Tassafaronga, in the Solomons, surely the new weapon, three times as powerful, could do the same to a battleship or aircraft carrier.

Kuroki and Nishina, overjoyed at its possibilities, now called their invention *kaiten*, for they had very high hopes it would make a great change in the way the Pacific war was going. The Americans had invaded Guadalcanal and, though our fleet had inflicted much damage on theirs, clung tenaciously to their foothold. During the last five months of 1942, Japan lost two battleships, many cruisers and destroyers, and an aircraft carrier, *Ryuho,* in attempting to regain full control of the Solomons. Things could not be allowed to continue this way. America's industrial machine could build warships much faster than Japan's, and in greater numbers. Japan would have to sink enemy ships faster than they were built, so as to stop the enemy from advancing. Especially aircraft carriers, for without them the Americans would have no air cover for further amphibious movements.

But the young inventors got nowhere with their plan. The Naval General Staff refused even to look at diagrams and sketches of a weapon so fantastic. Kuroki and Nishina argued their plan with everyone they could engage in conversation. "We do not understand why our scheme is rejected," they would say. "It fits precisely into the great general plan around which our Navy has trained for more than ten years! Haven't we always assumed that any enemy fleet approaching Japan would have to come by way of the Mandated Islands? Haven't we assumed the enemy would need islands in the Marshalls, Carolines and Gilberts, for bases? It must be obvious that the American fleet will have to use atolls for anchorages, for their westernmost large base is at Pearl Harbor!

"Now, then, if the American fleet anchors in such atolls, what better weapon is there than a *kaiten* for attacking these task forces? Just four submarines, carrying four *kaiten* each, could be on the enemy before he suspected their presence, launch *kaiten*, and retreat. The *kaiten* would penetrate the atoll, and sixteen enemy ships would be sunk at one blow. Imagine trying to dodge a weapon that is faster than any ship, especially when you are in a crowded anchorage. Our weapon could reverse the way this war is going. We could still win it!"

It was no use. High officials would not give them a chance to explain. So Nishina and Kuroki kept working with Mr. Suzukawa, refining their sketches, making small improvements in design, and submitting one set of proposals after another. Finally, in desperation, they resorted to a device much used throughout my country's history—they submitted a petition *written in their own blood!* Among Japanese, who are very romantic-minded, writing in your own blood, whether it is a petition, a threat or a love poem, is proven evidence of the purest sincerity. This method worked for the inventors. Eight months after sending their original set of plans through the chain of command, they were given the special assignment of building a prototype, under one condition. It must not be a suicide weapon. It must have an escape device so that its pilot, once he had it heading straight for the enemy, could get out safely. In February, 1944, the Naval General Staff finally approved their prototype design, nearly twenty months after the two young officers first had the original idea for it and thirteen months after they first asked permission to work on such a weapon.

Everything was handled in fullest secrecy. The hidden base at Otsujima was set up, and a few officers assigned to assist Nishina and Kuroki. However, by June, 1944, only a few *kaiten* had been built. The Naval General Staff, deeply immersed in a grand plan for ending the war with one overwhelming smash at the enemy, seemed to lose interest in the *kaiten*.

The Marianas campaign, however, changed their attitude radically. Our campaign in New Guinea had been going badly, with much loss suffered whenever we tried to reinforce our garrison there. The Solomons had long since been lost, and the enemy was in the Marshalls and Gilberts. Finally, on June 15, 1944, he invaded Saipan. This was the moment our Naval General Staff had been waiting for, for they had a plan that would give the American Navy such a blood bath that American citizens would demand an immediate end to the war.

The plan was called *A-Go*. It called for a mighty force of carriers, battleships and cruisers to sortie from the Philippines as soon as the enemy had set foot on Saipan. Our carrier planes would wipe out enemy air cover and sink the enemy's carriers, by making shuttle runs. Our fighters and bombers would take off, strike the enemy, land in the Marianas, refuel and rearm, strike the enemy again, and fly home to their carriers. Then they would repeat the process, as long as was necessary.

But the plan went awry when American submarines sank two of our carriers, *Taiho* and *Shokaku*, before these ships even got within striking range of the Americans. A third carrier, *Hiyo*, was sunk the next day when enemy carrier planes counterattacked. The loss of over four hundred Japanese planes in that engagement is usually referred to by Americans as the "Marianas Turkey Shoot," and much false credit is usually given to American aviators. Actually, nearly half of our lost planes either went down with the carriers or were ditched at sea when they had no place to land. Also, because loss of *Taiho's* and *Shokaku's* planes to the American submarine torpedoes sent our remaining planes into battle against overwhelming odds, the American aviators had an easy time of it.

I mention this because the remarkable work by American submarine men finally made the Naval General Staff think of its own submarine men. A frantic order was sent out to produce *kaiten* on crash priority. A second order told lesser authorities to start recruiting pilots for them, at once! Thus it was that we 100 men of Tsuchiura came to be at Otsujima.

Not all this was learned the first day, of course. Only a little of it. My comrades and I were too busy enjoying what we hadn't had for a long time—a leisurely, hot Japanese bath. At Tsuchiura the bathing facilities were never adequate for the increasing number of men accepted for pilot training. It was always rush in, rush out, at the bathhouse. That long hot bath was something a cadet often missed more than anything else after leaving home for the Navy.

We stripped, doused ourselves with scalding hot water, and sat around, soaping up generously. Then we doused ourselves again with water, removing all soap. After making sure we were perfectly clean, we lowered ourselves into *ofura* filled with steaming water, easing down until it came to our chins. Aaaah, what a treat! Since there was no call for our services, we carried out Lieutenant Chosa's order to "take it easy for the day," soaking, chatting and singing.

It was 8:30 P.M. before I was finally out of the Otsujima bathhouse and ready to go to bed. I settled down at last, deep in reflection. So, the *kaiten* was the weapon in which I would die! My world had certainly changed in the past few days. Since joining the Navy, I had often considered that I might have to die. Every Japanese man had such thoughts. But now that I had actually seen my "coffin," I began thinking of friends like Tanaka, Okamura, Miyamoto, Koizumi, and others who had chosen to stay with airplanes at Tsuchiura.

What was my father, in Tokyo, doing right now? And my sisters, who had been two mothers to me for more than twelve years? They had worked so hard with my upbringing. What would they say if they knew I would sleep this night at a secret base on the Inland Sea, getting ready for training as a human torpedo?

How soon would it be before I could go out on a mission? What a great feeling of power! As a pilot, I might have been given fighter plane duty. In battle I might down one, or maybe two, of the enemy. But as a *kaiten* man I would down an entire ship. I would be powerful as a ship myself! When my weapon struck, it would down the enemy by the hundreds. But, at that very moment, I would explode with them. Bits and pieces of me would probably go flying through the air. The thought was a horrifying one.

But I had no time for such thoughts. My country was in grave danger. Our force on Attu, in the Aleutians, had been wiped out to the last man. Countrymen had died in battle, and of hunger, disease and exhaustion in the southern Pacific regions. The Americans were on Saipan, and making plans for further advances against my homeland. What would become of Japan if a *"kaiten,"* a great change, were not made? Three thousand years of culture would be destroyed. No, I must defeat the foreigners! Japan must not come under the heel of *gaijin!*

I would make myself very skilled at operating my *kaiten,* when I was assigned one. I would learn its every mechanism. I would work until superiors said I was the best *kaiten* man at Otsujima. Then I would go into battle and destroy the enemy. That was important thing, to preserve my native land. Downing her enemy would do it. And my death would be nothing. It was merely something that would happen as I did my part to help Japan live forever.

3 ▣ The First Kaiten Mission

"All hands arise!"

I woke without trouble, well rested. After all my contemplation the evening before, my slumber had been dreamless.

I responded quickly to the loudspeaker, from force of habit. Inside three minutes the entire Tsuchiura group was in ranks outside our barracks. From where we stood, we could gaze out on the waters of Tokuyama Bay. We enjoyed the sight of it, and the cool morning breeze, as we jumped through calisthenics. When we were through, Lieutenant Chosa spoke.

"Well, men, now that you've been here one day, what do you think of your new life?"

No one answered, but we all smiled or grinned. Our presence, after being given several opportunities to withdraw, was answer enough.

"At this moment," he said, "we have only thirty *kaiten* pilots in training. That's because we have only six *kaiten* on hand."

A groan of dismay went up from us. With only six *kaiten* available, it would be forever before we even were trained, not to mention selected for a mission.

The officer read our groan correctly. "Don't worry," he said. "There will soon be sufficient *kaiten* for all, now that they are in mass production. Until they are plentiful, however, you can best use your time by learning everything there is to know about them. Our chief maintenance officer will start you out today with a lecture on the Model 93 torpedo. I will see you tonight, because today I am scheduled for *kaiten* training in the bay.

"The recreation facilities here are very scant," he said, "for we have no motion pictures. There's no place on the island to go, and no women, so it may not prove very entertaining for you. But the food here is very good, better than most bases. And we have an excellent canteen, with

37

many hard-to-get items. All the cigarettes you want, for instance. And candy. If you desire anything else, I have been instructed to get it for you, so please let me know your desires."

He left then, and we marched off to breakfast, talking about how we would probably be so wrapped up in the *kaiten,* how it worked, and discussing how soon we would be trained and sent on missions, that there would be no time for boredom.

After breakfast, Lieutenant Commander Itakura came into our barracks. We all sat down on *tatami,* and it reminded me of temple school, with everyone listening to the teacher. Our commanding officer used a blackboard and chalk to bring us up to date on how the war was going. He gave us many shocking pieces of information, especially about the Sixth Fleet, our submarine force. Once it stood among the world's finest, but it had been cut down terribly. Only a few of the large, fleet-type, cruising submarines were left. These were the only ones with the range necessary for *kaiten* operations.

"I know you have always had pride in our Navy," he said, "and I assure you it has fought well everywhere. Nevertheless, the tide of war has turned against us. Again and again the enemy has been able to range forces of ships and planes against us in overpowering strength. His ships can open fire at greater distances, and much earlier than ours, because of his superior radar. He sights our ships and planes before they sight him.

"Our gunners and torpedomen are at least as good as his, and perhaps better, for the Imperial Navy trained seven days a week for many months of the year. But guns and torpedoes are no good until you are at close range. That's what radar does for the enemy. Even Musashi Miyamoto, the greatest swordsman who ever lived, would be helpless against a man throwing a spear from five meters away."

Confidence was draining from us. "There is still hope, though," said Itakura. "When the American fleet moves closer to Japan, we will attack it with 'seeing' torpedoes. You, and men like you, will be the eyes of the greatest sea weapon ever devised. If each one of you scores a hit, what do you think the result will be? Even America, for all her industry and riches, cannot afford the loss of 100 warships.

"There is one thing I want to add before you start your

classes. We once made a mistake, in underestimating our enemy's will. We did not think he would fight so hard. Well, he does fight hard. His fighting spirit is strong. Like you, he loves his country, which is why he fights so hard for her. Therefore you must love your country even more, so you can fight even harder, and defeat him. Although you have *Yamato damashii,* Japanese spirit, your enemy has national spirit, too. Yours must be stronger than his!"

He left, and we went to our first class. During that second week of September, 1944, and for weeks afterwards, our lives followed the same daily pattern. In the mornings we had lectures on the Model 93 torpedo, how it was steered, and how to maintain it. As time went by, we studied the *kaiten,* too, and saw how the Long Lance principles were worked into its design. We had "cockpit" drills, such as we were used to back at Tsuchiura, during which we familiarized ourselves with *kaiten* controls and instruments. Each afternoon we worked as crewmen and assistants on torpedo boats. These towed *kaiten* into the bay, acted as "target" and mother ships for them, and recovered them at the end of a training period. It was hard work, but we enjoyed it, for we were learning much about the *kaiten* while waiting for one of our own.

The evenings were the most interesting times, for that was when round-table discussions of each day's operations were held. The *kaiten* was a new weapon, and only a few men had experience with it in the water. Every bit of information they gathered while actually operating *kaiten* had to be shared.

Two days after starting our classes, the Tsuchiura group was allowed to sit in at a seminar. Lieutenant Commander Itakura called it to order about 7:00 P.M.

"This is our seventh seminar," he said, "and I am sure that our new men will learn much from you who have taken the *kaiten* out. Before we start, however, I'd like to introduce the officers here. My executive officer will be first."

A second officer stood up. "I am Lieutenant Mizoguchi," he said. "When I was in my final year at Etajima, we welcomed a new class aboard. I felt toward them as younger brothers, and did my best to help them train. In welcoming you here, I again have that feeling. I will do anything I can to assist you, and hope all of you will join us in establishing worthwhile traditions at this base."

Other officers spoke in turn, making similar speeches, and creating a warm feeling in us. We felt more like equals than inferiors—comrades, who had been accepted. It was much different treatment than we had ever received before in the Navy.

Then the last officer stood up, and I gasped at the sight of him. He had extremely long hair, an oil-stained, messy uniform, and a dirty face that looked drawn and tired. How did he get in here, I asked myself. Surely, he could not be a naval officer! He looked like a vulgar person, with no standards of dress or cleanliness. But he had fierce, bright eyes, and as he looked out upon us I told myself that whoever this man was, he would throw himself, body and soul, into whatever he undertook.

When he spoke, his voice was very gentle. "I am Sekio Nishina," he said, and hesitated before going on. So this was one of the *kaiten's* inventors! It was hard to believe, for he looked more like a dreamy poet than anything else. "I am happy to meet you," he said, "and hope all of you will have as great a spirit as my dear, intimate friend, Lieutenant Hiroshi Kuroki." Kuroki, we knew, had died on September 6, when his *kaiten* went out of control and stuck fast in the bottom of the bay. "Although I may not be with you long, because I hope for the honor of going on the *kaiten's* first mission, I will do my best to teach you everything I can in the time remaining to me."

He bowed, sat down, and the seminar started. First to report was Ensign Hideichi Utsunomiya, destined to fight and die with one of our *kaiten* groups, in an attack. "Here is a chart of my operation today," he said, drawing on the blackboard. He outlined for us the courses and speeds he had followed, and how he occasionally had checked his position with a quick look through the periscope. Next was Lieutenant, junior grade, Katsumi Murakami. He explained how he had to make many adjustments to the controls of his *kaiten,* which had tended to give him trouble when diving and ascending. He also covered his cruising, navigation and "attacks" on his mother ship, the torpedo boat. More pilots followed him, and a long discussion followed, filled with suggestions for improving the *kaiten* itself and individual performances in it. It was 10:30 before the meeting closed.

All the way back to the barracks I was bubbling with

excitement. I had not understood a great deal of what had been said during the seminar, but all of it intrigued me. Especially the calm voices of the pilots, as each told of maneuvering his craft. Imagine, I said to myself. Each of those men had actually been sealed into his craft! He started his motor, was cast loose from the torpedo boat, and operated independently, like a fish. He cruised, dived, surfaced, hovered just underwater, and made runs on the mother ship. He did all of these things alone, with no one to help him if he read his instruments wrong. It sent a tingle through me, to realize that *kaiten* piloting was much like flying, but far more dangerous. If something went wrong in the air, you might have a chance to coast down to an emergency landing. In a *kaiten*, though, there were only the watery depths below you.

Impatience gripped the entire Tsuchiura group as our training continued. Some of our afternoons were spent inside the big black buildings now, instead of out in the torpedo boats. We went through the simulated motions of being sealed into our *kaiten* and running practice exercises. Being closed in was an eerie feeling, but one got used to it quickly. Keeping track of instruments took time to learn, however, and some of us felt pretty ridiculous on learning, after we got out of a *kaiten*, that our simulated run had missed its target by hundreds of meters. Meanwhile, we kept asking our instructors when more *kaiten* would be delivered, so we could begin water training. "Pretty soon," they would say. "It shouldn't be long now." But we were still waiting for more *kaiten* to be delivered for us when the first mission was officially announced.

Morale at Otsujima soared with this news. Americans had landed in the Palau Islands during my first month at the base, and our intelligence section interpreted this as preparation for a thrust into the Philippines. It followed the enemy's strategy of seizing one island, then using it as a base to jump off for another invasion nearer to Japan. They also seized Ulithi Atoll, in the Carolines, a deepwater anchorage where an entire fleet could assemble, so it was known that a major landing would soon be forthcoming. It had to be stopped. A *kaiten* attack would help.

Twelve men were selected for the honor of making this first *kaiten* strike. Besides Nishina, Murakami and Utsunomiya, there were nine more: Lieutenant Yoshinori Kamibeppu; Lieutenant, junior grade, Kentaro Yoshimoto; Lieutenant, junior grade, Hitoshi Fukuda; Lieutenant, junior grade, Kazuhisa Toyozumi; Ensign Taichi Imanishi; Ensign Akira Sato; Ensign Kazuhiko Kondo; Ensign Kozo Watanabe; and Ensign Yoshihiko Kudo. The training of these officers was intensified. They were given maximum opportunities for building themselves to a peak of efficiency. I can truthfully say that, because of their being first, they were probably the fittest of any men who ever went to battle in *kaiten*.

A special ceremony was conducted during the afternoon of November 7, 1944. American troops were then already ashore in the Philippines, and our fleet had suffered another disaster in the waters around those islands. In five days nearly thirty of our warships had been sunk, including the great *Musashi*, sister ship to the mighty *Yamato*. Four carriers had gone down, including *Zuikaku*, from whose deck had flown planes for the Pearl Harbor attack. Twenty cruisers and destroyers were lost in the same general engagement. Nearly stripped of sea defense, Japan was in a truly perilous situation. It would take a tremendous blow to stop the enemy now, for the Naval General Staff's plan *Sho-go*, a pincer movement to shatter the enemy's amphibious landings on the island of Leyte, in the Philippines, had resulted in our fleet being smashed. The only bright spot in the entire proceedings was the inauguration of the airborne Special Attack Force, the *kamikaze*, under Vice Admiral Takejiro Onishi. Named for the "divine wind" typhoon which destroyed the Mongol fleet of Kublai Khan in 1281 when he sought to invade our country, these special attack planes had been successful from the start. On October 25 they sank two American light carriers and damaged six others, as well as lighter warships. What they could do, the *kaiten* could do.

So Vice Admiral Shigeyoshi Miwa, commander of the Sixth Fleet, was very optimistic as he spoke to us that day, pointing now and then to the fleet submarines I-36, I-37 and I-47, which were in the bay nearby. Each of these ships would carry four *kaiten* to Ulithi Atoll, northwest of the Palaus, where the enemy based much of his fleet when it was not on the offensive. There our *kaiten* pilots hoped to carry out the plan of sinking major enemy ships at anchor.

Four *kaiten* had already been installed on each submarine. Ship's colors were flying at each submarine's stern, and on their conning towers were painted our Rising Sun flag. Each conning tower also carried the crest of the great Kusunoki family, famed throughout the ages in Japan. Composed of two Kanji ideographs, *kiku* (chrysanthemum) and *sui* (water), this crest stood for the highest in ideals and loyalty, exemplifying the great determination of all *kaiten* to preserve Japan, in the person of its Emperor.

All Japanese history books tell the story of Masashige Kusunoki. All Japanese children know, almost as soon as they can read, of our country's greatest hero. The name has stood for six centuries as a symbol all good Japanese could engrave on their hearts. In very early times Japan had not been ruled by emperors, but by a series of military leaders called *shogun*. This name had first been given to a general for defending Japan from invasion, and meant "barbarian-conquering leader." As the years moved past, our emperors each had one such *shogun*, who was responsible for our island empire's defense. In time, however, *shogun* became hungry for power, and eventually assumed so much authority that they were responsible for internal peace and order, as well as defense from external enemies. Most *shogun* after the first one, Yoritomo Minamoto, proved to be tyrants. It was only a step from defending the country to controlling it, and our imperial families were practically kept prisoner at Nara and Kyoto, our ancient capitals. There they concerned themselves with developing the delicate and intricate culture of art, literature and manners we inherited. Meanwhile, *shogun* attended to more and more "details not worthy of our Emperor's attention."

Our national belief always was that our sun-goddess ancestor, Amaterasu, had entrusted three special treasures, known as the Sacred Regalia, to her descendants. Whoever held these, she promised, would alone have authority from her to rule Japan. In the fourteenth century our Emperor Daigo II, a cultured, intelligent man, decided that he, the ruler, should rule. The *shogun*, suspecting this, ordered Daigo II to turn over the Sacred Regalia, which had always been retained by the imperial family. Daigo II refused at first, then appeared to relent, but he provided the *shogun* three counterfeits, and hid the real ones. For this the *sho-*

gun exiled the Emperor, and took control of the country.

It was then that Masashige Kusunoki, a feudal lord most loyal to his Emperor, and who also felt that the Emperor should rule, came to Daigo II's aid. He raised an army, defeated the *shogun*, and put the Emperor back on the throne. Several years later, however, because Daigo II was foolish and gave high posts to idle courtiers rather than those who fought for him, treachery toppled him and another *shogun* took power. Kusunoki, although he knew his ruler had been foolish, again fought to restore him, but this time he was defeated, dying in battle. His last words were, "I wish I had seven lives to give for my Emperor." They had been repeated in songs and stories ever since that time, further increasing in popularity from 1868, when a national revolution overthrew *shogun* for all time, bringing Emperor Meiji, grandfather of our *Tenno-san* to the throne and true power in what is called The Imperial Restoration.

After a salute to the massive Imperial Navy flag flying above him, and a deep bow toward the ruler's residence in Tokyo, Admiral Miwa turned to face the Kikusui Group, as Nishina and his eleven comrades were called. They stood in a single row before the admiral, spotless in their best uniforms. He presented each of them a short sword, an important symbol for Japanese fighting men. In ancient Sparta, it is said, each mother handed her son his shield when he went forth to his first battle, and spoke the words, "With it or on it!" He was supposed to come back, victorious, carrying the shield, or be carried back on it, dead, if he were defeated.

The short sword meant the same thing in Japan. A man must either fight honorably to victory, or use the short sword to commit *seppuku*, which Westerners call *hara kiri*, as atonement for failing. Once this sword was presented, a life was pledged for the Empire, either through battle death or disembowelment. We were proud of these men as each bowed and accepted his sword, for we knew those blades would never taste blood. Those twelve men would fight through to the enemy, and take him down with him.

The officers held a party for the *kaiten* pilots that night. Wearing light green pants with brown shirts and navy blue neckties, they sat in places of honor. All had packed their belongings for shipment home. These packages, which included cuttings of hair and fingernails parings, so relatives would have "remains" for an honorable burial, bore on their outsides such sayings as, "Japan—God's Land Eternal," and "Loyalty to His Majesty Forever." After opening remarks by high-ranking officers, Lieutenant Kamibeppu spoke for the *kaiten* men.

"We are determined to destroy the largest enemy ships we can find," he said, "and on the eve of our departure we are grateful for all you have done for us. We wish all of you the best of health, and the best of good fortune." *Sake*, a gift from the Emperor, was then poured, and Admiral Miwa offered a toast to the mission's success.

All enjoyed a fine, traditional Japanese festive meal of *tai* (redfish), dried seaweed, rice, and *kachi kuri* (victory chestnuts). These chestnuts are always served on an occasion where wishes for success are in order. Our *sumo* wrestlers today eat them on the eve of a great national tournament. Throughout Japan in late 1944, there was a shortage of everything, because many of our merchant ships had been sunk by American submarines. But canned fruit and other hard-to-get items were plentiful. *Sake* flowed freely, the "Navy March" was sung over and over again, and tears at the forthcoming departure of beloved comrades were many. Anyone who thinks we Japanese are a stoic, unemotional race, should have been at Otsujima that night, or with me on other occasions between then and the war's end.

At the height of the party Lieutenant Sekio Nishina slipped away and came to see the Tsuchiura group. He wished us the best of luck, asked us again to train hard for victory, and shook everyone's hand personally before he left.

At 8:00 the following morning a band played our national anthem *"Kimigayo."* Its words, "May Thy reign last one thousand, eight thousand, generations," must have been inspiring to men who were going out to die that the Emperor's reign should not end. They made a deep bow before a shrine constructed especially for *kaiten* men. Each man had an officer's sword at his right side and gripped the short sword in his left hand. Lieutenant Nishina also carried the ashes of his dead friend, Lieutenant Kuroki, in a small box. These would go into the *kaiten* when he manned it for attack, so that both friends could still carry out the first mission together. All went aboard their submarines then, and at 9:00 the I-36 led the way out of the harbor. I-37 and I-47 slowly followed the flagship of the Kikusui Group, and many of us trailed them on torpedo boats and smaller craft, shouting and waving our caps around our heads in the naval farewell gesture. The first *kaiten* mission was on its way.

The three submarines broke company not long after leaving port. I-37 would proceed towards Kossol Passage, in the Palaus, and attack enemy shipping there. I-36 and I-47, meanwhile, would head for Ulithi. There they would attack the American fleet at anchor, launching their *kaiten* through two different entrances to the atoll's giant lagoon. I-37 was fated not to reach her destination. Despite having six lookouts on the bridge at all times when surfaced, she was picked up by the sonar of the American destroyer *Nicholas* on the evening of November 12. In a sudden attack, the enemy caught I-37 before she could dive deep and take evasive action. She was sunk with all hands, before Murakami, Utsunomiya, Kamibeppu, and Kondo ever had a chance to strike at the enemy.

I-47 was under command of Lieutenant Commander Zenji Orita, one of Japan's best submarine captains. He steamed smoothly for his destination, making twenty knots on the surface until within range of enemy patrol planes. He then ran submerged by day, surfacing at night to charge batteries and receive radioed information from Sixth Fleet headquarters at Kure. His ship and I-36 were working in close cooperation with reconnaissance planes from Truk Island. They would provide reports on the enemy shipping at Ulithi.

The *kaiten* men enjoyed their trip with Captain Orita, and were particularly fascinated with the submarine's toilet, a complicated arrangement of valves and handles that could truly embarrass the man who did not know how to operate it properly, or was careless in doing so. I-47 had one bad scare when heavy seas appeared to be giving the *kaiten* a beating. Several crew members, who had grown devoted to the four heroes, dashed impulsively out on deck amid the washing waves and checked the weapons' lashings. Nothing was found wrong, and all hands relaxed. One of the heroic repairmen was Petty Officer Oka, who was also a talented artist. En route to Ulithi he painted an excellent picture of an American aircraft carrier, breaking in half and sinking as a *kaiten* exploded in its vitals. Lieutenant Nishina, Lieutenant Fukuda and Ensign Sato were happy to autograph it for him.

Good news came by radio to I-36 and I-47 on November 17. The day before a high altitude reconnaissance plane from Truk had made a report on enemy ships present at Ulithi. The enemy fleet was massed inside the lagoon, in three groups. "To the north there are about 30 ships, including 3 battleships," the report read. "In the central anchorage there are about 100 transports and other auxiliary types, in two sections. To the south there are about 50 warships. These appear to be the task forces. They include battleships and carriers."

"That is too bad!" said Nishina when he read the report Captain Orita showed him. "All those ships, nearly 200, and we have only eight *kaiten* for our attack. What a chance this could have been!"

But there was a good reason why only two submarines had been sent to Ulithi: those were all the Sixth Fleet could spare for the mission. Japan had gone to war with a powerful submarine force, but this had been reduced radically by the excellent tactics and equipment of the Americans. They had placed high emphasis on submarine and anti-submarine warfare, right from the start, while the Sixth Fleet in the Japanese Navy was nearly always treated like an orphan. Furthermore, our submarines had never been used in packs, like those of Germany and America, so our underseas ships were picked off, one by one.

On November 18, while just fifty miles west of Ulithi, Captain Orita surfaced so the *kaiten* could be given a final check. All four were found in good working order. At noon of the next day, he was maneuvering his submarine as close as one mile from the atoll's southern entrance. At midnight, a half-moon having sunk below the horizon, *kaiten* men on I-47 began making final preparations. They packed their spare uniforms and other belongings, together with last-minute written messages. Lieutenant Nichina and the others gave Captain Orita their wills, and all four men wound *hachimaki* around their heads.

The *hachimaki* looks like a white bandana. It is worn to signify relentless determination, and tradition says it was first worn by the famous Forty-seven *Ronin*, centuries before. On almost any given day a *kabuki* play is presented somewhere in Japan that retells part of the heroic action of these men. All forty-seven were *samurai*, whose master was tricked by a jealous rival into drawing his sword while on the Yedo palace grounds. This grave insult to the *Shogun* could only be atoned for by giving one's life, so the *daimyo* these forty-seven men served had to commit *seppuku*. Thus the retainers became *ronin*, master-less *samurai*, but they made up their minds to avenge their lord's death, no matter how long it took. In order to accomplish this they scattered and tried to act as little like men of nobility as possible. One deliberately became a drunkard and purposely acquired a reputation as a useless man. Another sold his daughters, a most shameful thing for a *samurai* to do. The awful sacrifices made by each man have provided a comfortable living for an untold number of Japanese playwrights, novelists, poets, street-walking storytellers and, lately, television producers.

Several years after their lord's death, having convinced all who knew them they had given up the *bushi do*, the way of the *samurai*, and had become insignificant *heimin*, or commoners, they suddenly met in Tokyo on a prearranged date, all armed and armored. Winding *hachimaki* around their heads, they quickly broke into the palace at night, and slew the treacherous lord who had caused their master's death. Then they marched at once to the grave of their deceased master, knelt down, and disemboweled themselves. Their combined graves are a landmark and tourist spot in Tokyo today.

This story gives an idea of what winding a *hachimaki* on one's head means to a Japanese. It shows that nothing will keep you from a victory. You can see *hachimaki* today in Japan when school-children are having a field day of competitive games and races, when union members are picketing during a strike, or when angry university students are protesting against something that offends them. It means to us what "never-say-die" means to Anglo-Saxons.

Ensigns Sato and Watanabe boarded their *kaiten* from the deck of I-47 at midnight, while it was surfaced, for only those of Nichina and Fukuda had access tubes to them from the submarine's interior. Later, all *kaiten* could be reached through access tubes, and the submarine could stay beneath the surface. Captain Orita dipped I-47 beneath the waves then and maneuvered until he was just off Ulithi lagoon's southern entrance. Sato and Watanabe sat in their *kaiten* for three hours, their only contact with the world two telephone cables. At 3:00 A.M. Nishina, dirty and untidy as ever, climbed through a tube into *kaiten* No. 1, the post of honor, followed by Fukuda, who manned *kaiten* No. 2.

Each *kaiten* had been bound in its place by four cables. Two of these were loosened from on deck while I-47 had been surfaced at midnight. The other two could be released from inside the submarine. At 4:00 Captain Orita glided into firing position guided by the twinkle of welding torches on enemy ships seen through his periscope. All four *kaiten* men reported, "Ready in all respects" over their telephone lines.

"Kaiten Number One, stand by to start your engine!" said the captain.

"Standing by," came Lieutenant Nishina's soft voice over the circuit. With the ashes of his fellow inventor, Kuroki, beside him, Lieutenant Nishina was about to see their two-and-one-half year dream fulfilled.

The third cable on No. 1 *kaiten* was loosened. "Start your engine!" said Orita.

Inside the submarine, a motor sound could be heard.

"Engine started."

"Ready?"

"Ready!"

"Go!"

The fourth cable was loosened. It was 4:15, November 20, 1944. Captain Orita, peering through his periscope, could see just a trace of bubbling water for a moment, as Nishina's *kaiten* moved off. Final checks of position, depth and the course Nishina was to follow had been made. He was now on his run-in, under orders to penetrate as deep into the anchorage as he could before raising his periscope and selecting a target for attack.

Ensign Sato left at 4:20, followed by Watanabe and Fukuda at five-minute intervals. The second and third *kaiten* were to get inside, then move off to the right and left, respectively. Fukuda was to attack when just inside the lagoon. This, it was hoped, would throw the enemy into a panic, when ships began exploding at widely separated points. The last words heard from *kaiten* men in I-47's conning tower were Fukuda's, *"Tenno heika banzai!"* Long live the Emperor! In the great tradition of Masashige Kusunoki, the Kikusui Group was giving its lives to preserve the throne.

The four *kaiten* were swimming toward their targets now, each craft making better than 30 knots, and each seeking a target 1000 times as large as itself. Though Kuroki and Nishina had designed into the *kaiten*, as ordered by the Naval General Staff, a device which could cast the pilot free while he was still 150 feet short of the target, no one intended to use it. And no one ever did, in all the *kaiten* missions carried out. A man could only be positive of a sure hit when he met sure death. Abandoning the *kaiten* might allow it to go off course. The best method was to take it in, all the way.

Captain Orita felt the I-47 bob upwards as the twelve tons of weight left its deck. He broached slightly and submerged again on a southeast heading, planning to surface shortly before 5:00, the time at which all *kaiten* were expected to hit, including those from I-36, off to the northeast. The captain wanted to be on deck, watching through large binoculars, rather than looking through his small night periscope. He wanted definite confirmation of hits, to take back to Japan with him.

At 5:00, I-47 was again on the surface. It was predawn twilight and the crew was edgy, for daylight came quickly in the South Pacific. One, two, three minutes ticked past. Then another. And another. Then, at 5:07, a reddish orange flash blossomed above Ulithi Atoll, in the center of the enemy fleet. A direct hit!

"Congratulations, Nishina!" shouted the captain, for flames were well within the lagoon, where the inventor of the *kaiten* was supposed to be.

At 5:11, another great flash appeared. A second hit! I-47's crew went wild, shouting and laughing. Then they snapped to diving stations, for Orita suddenly spotted an American destroyer. The big sub was rigged for depth charges, but none came, so Orita soon surfaced again, just in time to greet the sunrise. He could see the enemy destroyer moving away from him, making for the Ulithi entrance just used by the *kaiten* pilots. At 5:52, one more great explosion was heard, and reported by I-47's sound room as coming from the atoll. At 6:00 Captain Orita ordered a minute of silent prayer for the four who had just laid down their lives. Then he dipped his ship beneath the waters and steamed away at a quiet two knots, making a wide circle around the southwest part of Ulithi Atoll, and headed for home. Throughout I-47 men were alternately cheering and crying, happy for the successful warriors, yet saddened by their deaths.

I-36 was not as lucky. Lieutenant Commander Teramoto sent Ensigns Imanishi and Kudo into their *kaiten* from the deck shortly after midnight. At 3:00 Lieutenants Yoshimoto and Toyozumi mounted their craft through access tubes. Everything seemed to be going well until I-36 had reached the point designated for launching, just off the eastern entrance to Ulithi.

There, at the moment set for firing, *kaiten* No. 1 and No. 2 were found stuck fast in their racks! They could not be freed after their engines had started. All hands cursed this ill fortune, and cursed even louder on hearing that No. 4 was leaking badly. The only man who could be sent off was Ensign Imanishi, in No. 3. He moved away at 4:54, while the telephone sets in I-36's conning tower were flaming with the language of Yoshimoto, Toyozumi and Kudo, who grew more desperate with each unsuccessful attempt to free their weapons. Danger from counterattack was now imminent, and Captain Kiyotake Ageta, who was riding in I-36 as commander of the Kikusui Group, cancelled the mission. I-36 moved out to sea, surfaced, took *kaiten* pilot Kudo on board from the deck, and submerged again, shutting off all motors so that atoll explosions might be heard. At 5:45 one explosion was heard, and at 6:05 another. There were still hopes among the three disappointed *kaiten* men that Captain Teramoto might surface I-36 and try to repair the *kaiten* so they would have a chance at the enemy, but American defense forces prevented that. Several ships raced from the lagoon's eastern entrance at top speed and began spraying depth charges everywhere. Apparently they thought the torpedoes had been regular ones, fired from a submarine close to the eastern entrance. They wanted to get her before she could escape. More than one hundred depth charges were dropped, but none came near I-36.

Still, she had to stay submerged nearly nineteen hours, and air in her really became foul. Finally Captain Teramoto decided to risk enemy detection, for he had to get his batteries charged and relieve the crew's exhaustion. At twenty minutes before midnight he surfaced; I-36 was not spotted, so he ran northward on the surface as fast as he could. He cleared the area without further incident.

I had left Otsujima four days before I-36 and I-47 had made their attacks. With half of the Tsuchiura detachment, I had been ordered to Hikari, somewhat closer to Kure. The *kaiten* program was going ahead faster, now that more weapons had been delivered, and at Hikari, a partially complete naval arsenal considered the largest in the Orient, more men could be trained. It was at Hikari that we heard the news of the Kikusui Group's success. I felt very sorry for Kamibeppu, Kondo, Murakami and Utsunomiya, who had died in I-37 before they had a chance to strike at the enemy, but I sucked in my breath with a deep gasp and uttered the oft-spoken Japanese saying, *"shikata ga nai!"* Nothing could be done. It was fated that some *kaiten* men would not reach their targets. I could only hope that later attacks would do even greater damage to the enemy, to make up for these losses.

I-36 and I-47 returned to Kure on November 30, having stopped at Otsujima en route. On December 2, a special meeting was held on board *Tsukushi Maru*, flagship of the Sixth Fleet, to study results of the attack at Ulithi. Over two hundred people were present, including high-ranking officers from Tokyo and Japan's leading experts on submarine warfare and *kaiten* tactics.

The meeting opened at 10:00 A.M., and more than one officer wiped his eyes as Lieutenant Commander Orita told of the brave spirit shown by Nishina, Sato, Watanabe and Fukuda through every moment of the Kikusui's mission. Much discussion took place, after which Lieutenant Commander Gunichi Sakamoto of the Sixth Fleet staff summarized the results. He noted that I-47 had seen two giant columns of fire, and that I-36 had heard explosions. He then described the plan of attack and the courses and speeds each of the five *kaiten* men had been instructed to follow. Then he displayed photos taken by reconnaissance planes from Truk on November 23, three days after the mission had been carried out.

"We can estimate from this," said Lieutenant Commander Sakamoto, "that Lieutenant Nishina sank an aircraft carrier, as did Lieutenant Fukuda and Ensign

Imanishi. Ensigns Sato and Watanabe sank a battleship apiece!"

The meeting broke up in bedlam, everyone shouting, congratulating and cheering the *kaiten* plan. This was repeated at Otsujima, and again at Hikari. There nearly two hundred *kaiten* pilots, instructors and trainees were gathered, for a detachment from Nara had finally arrived to join my group. Three aircraft carriers! And two battleships! That ought to give the enemy something to worry about!

I said a short prayer, giving thanks for the success of Nishina and the others. The *kaiten* was now a proven weapon. It had shown what it could do. If luck smiled on me, I too would strike such a blow at our nation's enemy. I, too, would send a carrier to the bottom of the sea!

4 □ My First Kaiten Ride

Joy at the news about the Kikusui Group's success kept us buoyant at Hikari for weeks. All of us were in extremely high spirits, even though it would be a long time before any of us went out on a mission. A number of men at Otsujima were fully trained. They would go out first, we were sure. This turned out to be true. The next mission, the Kongo Group, sailed from Otsujima. This was to be a much more ambitious strike than the first. Six submarines, I-36, I-47, I-48, I-53, I-56 and I-58, would be used. A total of twenty-four *kaiten* would be borne by them, and a grand plan was devised for hitting the enemy simultaneously, at scattered points. After what had been accomplished at Ulithi it was felt that another success, more widespread, and happening all on one date, might rock the enemy and halt his advance long enough for the Japanese Navy to catch its breath. Then our leaders could prepare for the one great pitched battle they had always sought.

According to the plan, Kongo Group would attack the enemy at not less than five different points. Lieutenant Commander Zenji Orita, whose I-47 had done so well with the Kikusui Group at Ulithi, would head for Hollandia, New Guinea, where the campaign had been going very badly for Japan.

I-56, commanded by Lieutenant Commander Masahiko Morinaga, was destined for the Admiralty Islands, west of New Britain, where the Americans and Australians were supposed to have a large group of ships moored. Like I-47, this submarine would carry four *kaiten*.

Lieutenant Commander Iwao Teramoto, with four *kaiten*, would take I-36 back to Ulithi, for a second attack on this target. Another target, which had gone unscarred during the Kikusui mission because I-37 was sunk en route, would receive the attention of I-53, under Lieutenant Commander Seihachi Toyomasu. Lieutenant, junior grade, Hiroshi

Kuzumi, a Naval Academy man, would lead the four *kaiten* strike group.

Lieutenant Commander Mochitsura Hashimoto, who would later win fame by sinking the U.S. heavy cruiser *Indianapolis* and also have the unusual experience of being a witness at the court-martial of her American captain, commanded I-58. On board her would be four *kaiten* led by Lieutenant, junior grade, Seizo Ishikawa, another Etajima graduate.

The sixth *kaiten* group would also be led by an Etajima man, Lieutenant, junior grade, Kentaro Yoshimoto. Three other *kaiten* men would be with him on I-48, commanded by Lieutenant Commander Zenshin Toyama. The first five submarines were to hit their targets on January 11, 1945. The sixth, I-48, would keep the pressure on and the enemy confused by making her attack on Ulithi, greatest island anchorage in the Pacific, nine days later.

Much had happened since the Kikusui operation. The enemy had taken Mindoro Island in the Philippines and was expected to follow this with another thrust, much farther north in the chain of islands. Since the Kikusui operation, too, a pair of valuable submarines had been lost, I-46 and I-365. Our *kamikaze* pilots in the Philippines were still doing much damage to the American fleet, but their effect was growing less as great swarms of U.S. planes, launched from aircraft carriers, made sweep after sweep over the Philippines, destroying many of our planes before they could get off the ground.

Meanwhile, enemy submarines roamed freely off our shores, thanks to the neglect of antisubmarine warfare on the part of our Naval General Staff earlier in the war. The great Japanese feats of 1941 and 1942, when our submarines shelled the American coast, sinking ships almost within sight of land, and even sending an airplane twice to bomb Oregon forests, had all been for nothing. The Americans accented sub-hunting, while our top planners de-emphasized it. As a result, our underseas fleet had shrunk almost to nothing, while the enemy's grew ever more powerful.

Of the twenty-four *kaiten* sent out with the Kongo Group, only fourteen were launched at the enemy. Lieutenant Commander Orita kept his score perfect by getting away all four *kaiten* into Humboldt Bay, New Guinea, after dodging a destroyer and patrolling seaplanes while making his final approach. The four *kaiten* pilots, Lieutenants Kawakubo and Hara, and Petty Officers Muramatsu and Sato, were later credited with one large vessel sunk apiece, this being judged by the large columns of fire seen by Captain Orita and his gunnery officer some fifty minutes after the first *kaiten* was launched. I-47 then had to run for her life, but later, on surfacing, she heard the enemy sending out frantic "Submarine present!" signals to all ships nearby.

Lieutenant Commander Hashimoto approached Apra, Guam, safely, and sent away all four *kaiten*. Led by Lieutenant Ishikawa, Ensign Kudo and Petty Officers Mori and Mitsueda were later credited with sinking an escort aircraft carrier and two large transports.

In the Admiralties, Captain Morinaga showed much skill in making an undetected approach with I-56, but then he ran into trouble. The enemy had very cleverly laid anti-submarine nets, far out from where their ships were moored, and these were so well-placed that I-56 could not penetrate them. Captain Morinaga tried over and over again—I-56 once even stuck fast in the nets—but finally he had to give up, and call off the attack. His *kaiten* pilots, Kakizaki, Maeda, Furukawa and Yamaguchi, of whom you will read more later, hoped he would find other targets for them to attack, but had to return, full of sadness, to their home base.

I-53 had very bad luck. Lieutenant Commander Toyomasu again proved the skill of our submarine commanders by moving into firing position off Kossol Passage, in the Palaus, where enemy shipping was thick. Then, just as he was ready to fire, Ensign Kuge's *kaiten* would not start. Still fuming over this, the captain fired Ensign Kuzumi's weapon, which mysteriously exploded almost immediately after it was free of the submarine. The final pair of *kaiten* worked all right. Ensign Ito and Petty Officer Arimori were later credited with a large transport apiece.

Lieutenant Commander Teramoto got a bad scare while approaching Ulithi. I-36 ran up on an underwater shelf and hung there, an easy target for any ship that detected her. But she was able to get off, and this time all her *kaiten* worked. The official judgment of her effort was that four ships, including a battleship and a fleet tanker, had been sunk.

Of I-48 no news was ever received. She was sunk on January 22, 1945, by American destroyers off Ulithi. Since I-36 had done so well, however, and since I-48 was not sunk until two days after the proposed date of her attack, it was assumed that all four *kaiten* were launched and had scored hits.

Again, Sixth Fleet termed the overall attack a signal success, though a valuable submarine had been lost. We at Hikari felt sorry for the men in I-48 if they had been sunk, like *kaiten* men in I-37, without making an attack. I could only pray that when my time came I would get a chance to steer straight into the enemy and do him even greater damage, to make up for the loss of such fine men.

All this news didn't come to me until February, of course. Meanwhile I had been studying hard, impatient for the day when I would start underwater training in a *kaiten* of my own. I had left Otsujima four days before the Kikusui Group had made their November 20 attack, and had been hoping ever since that I would be selected for a mission. But no one could be selected, of course, until he had proven himself proficient through lengthy training. By the middle of December, it looked as though my chance would never come. I wished I were back at Otsujima. There, at least, the atmosphere would be some compensation for not being selected. At Otsujima, it was only on rare occasions that a person was punched or slapped for making a mistake or being forgetful. I put this down to the fact that most Otsujima people were submarine sailors. Like submarine sailors all over the world, they had a special code of their own. Officers were most friendly toward the enlisted men, especially the petty officers, with whom they had sailed. And the petty officers were friendly, not domineering. They tried to teach, not drive. All of them had displayed a friendly attitude toward us men from Tsuchiura. The entire island base was—there is no other way to describe it—like one big house with one big family in it.

So we had all fallen into gloom when it was announced some of us were to be sent to a new *kaiten* base which was being opened up at Hikari. Nobody wanted to go, of course, so we had to draw lots to see who would depart for this new base.

My division lost. When the boat which was to take us there failed to appear on October 15, we were overjoyed.

Perhaps the orders had been changed! It was not to be so. Next morning all forty-eight of us were on our way, and in two hours were at Hikari. Our first moments there gave us an impression of what the place would be like.

We left the launch, formed ranks, picked up our belongings, and were sauntering leisurely toward headquarters building when an officer intercepted us.

"How sloppy!" he shouted at us, "Go back to the dock and do that all over again!"

We ran back, formed ranks again, and returned on the run, staggering under our burdens.

"That's better!" the officer shouted. "I hope you'll remember the lesson well. From now on, when something is not done properly you can expect to do it over and over again until you do it right!"

But the next bit of news he gave us wiped out our bitter first experience at once. "You men have already had enough basic training," he said, "so we plan to start some of you on water training immediately. Tomorrow! Meanwhile, you can get settled in your new quarters. I am Lieutenant Keisuke Miyata. I am the executive officer of this base. You will meet some of the other officers later."

Our new quarters pleased us still more. They were excellent. The rooms were airy, and the furnishings really surprised us. At Tsuchiura we had slept in hammocks, and at Otsujima on *tatami* mats. But here they had Western-style beds! It was like living in a great modern hotel with all facilities. Maybe Hikari wouldn't be so bad after all!

That evening, all hands were summoned to assembly, and our new officers were introduced to us. By now we were completely at ease. The speeches were just like those we had heard many times before, so there was no great excitement about the meeting. Too, we had begun to realize that our time at Otsujima had made us as familiar with *kaiten* as the men who stood before us. We had, after all, been *kaiten* trainees many weeks longer than these men even though we had not yet been in the water aboard one. The abrupt greeting of Lieutenant Miyata was forgotten in our growing feeling of superiority. All we could think about was that these long-winded speeches were keeping us from the evening meal. That launch trip had made us very, very hungry.

But there was one good laugh. One of the last officers

to get up had a short stick in his hand. He pointed it at us and said, in a voice that he made very deep, coming out of the bottom of his chest. "I am Ensign Mamoru Miyoshi. People around here call me 'Miyoshi Seikai-Nyudo'!" All hands burst into uncontrollable laughter. This man had such baby face and all of us knew from our history books that Miyoshi Seikai-Nyudo was the strongest man who ever lived, the founder of one of Japan's most popular sports—*sumo* wrestling. This slight, five-foot-six-inch officer, standing there before us and trying to make himself about three times as big as he actually was, made a hilarious sight.

We set about our work with a will the following day, our eyes shining with optimism. There were more than 70 *kaiten* at Hikari and, though there were 200 trainees, we of Tsuchiura felt it would not be long before we would be going out into the bay in a weapon. Half of the *kaiten* people were newly arrived from Nara, and we surely had more experience than they. Though I had not yet ridden, even as a "passenger," my chances looked good. Discounting the 100 from Nara, that left 70 *kaiten* for 100 men. It shouldn't be long now, we told one another.

But it didn't work out that way. Despite the fact that there were six dozen *kaiten* on hand, only a dozen or so men could be trained daily, half in the morning and half in the afternoon. The reason for this was the shortage of technicians. We had only about forty-five maintenance specialists who knew about the Model 93 torpedo and *kaiten*. The *kaiten* themselves were brand new, and it took a team of seven technicians to check and test each one, get it ready for a student, then recheck it, test it and recharge the oxygen tanks after he had finished his period of water instruction. This process took four or five hours from the time a *kaiten* was rolled out until it was placed on chocks again. So despondency once more swept through our ranks. It looked as though the enemy would be steaming across the Inland Sea before we got a shot at him.

American submarines also played a part in slowing our rate of training. They had by now sunk hundreds of our ships, including many of the fat tankers that hauled oil from the Netherlands East Indies to Japan. Each *kaiten* was mothered by a high-speed torpedo craft, something like the American PT boat, while cruising in the bay. These fast vessels used high-octane gasoline, which was becoming harder and harder to get. Our commanding officer reminded us many times that people all over Japan, even the military, were beginning to depend on horse-drawn and ox-drawn wagons, as well as charcoal-burning motor vehicles, for transport. "Get the most out of each minute in the water," he would say. "Our torpedo boats cannot be allowed to cruise indefinitely. These days, one drop of high-octane gasoline is as precious as a drop of human blood!"

So it was that on the evening of December 22, when I saw my name posted on the headquarters bulletin board for water training, I couldn't believe my eyes. I looked again. Yes, there it was—Petty Officer Yutaka Yokota, *Kaiten* No. 27—scheduled for the following morning. My moment had finally arrived! The first tests would check me for attitude and technique in handling the weapon. If I passed them, I would be eligible for further training, and later selection for a mission. I ran back to my room to break the news to my best friend, Petty Officer Yoshihito Yazaki. He had had his first water training in a *kaiten* the day before. I fired question after question at him, until finally he raised his hands in protest.

"Easy, easy, Yutaka," he said. "Hearing things from me will do you no good. One has to learn about *kaiten* himself. Each one has certain little characteristics of its own. You have to master them yourself. I cannot help you there." He did help me, though, in drawing up the chart I'd be using in my underwater navigation. On it I plotted courses, speeds and, most important, the number of seconds I'd run on each leg of my route. It was 11:00 P.M. before we went to bed. As we undressed Yazaki warned, "Don't foul up, Yokota. If you do, they'll really squeeze you at the next seminar. They love to ride people who make sloppy runs." With that, he fell asleep.

But I couldn't sleep. I kept thinking of all the details that had to be considered. Did my flashlight have fresh batteries? I couldn't afford to be without emergency lighting if I lost illumination in my weapon. And what about my stop watch? When was the last time I had it tested for accuracy? If it were wrong, I could smash into a rock and sink like a stone. All my earlier training would have been for nothing.

Then I thought about my will. In case something should

happen to me underwater, I wanted to leave some final words behind. I'd better make sure I had some pencils and paper.

All these thoughts and others crowded my mind. Finally I could no longer bear it. I got up and started going through my belongings. If anything did happen to me, it would not do for anyone to find them in a mess when he came to ship them home to my family. I looked into my seabag, and what I saw horrified me. The top half of it was filled with dirty clothes, a most disgusting sight. Whatever had happened to the spruce Cadet Pilot Yokota of Tsuchiura? While in flight training I, like all others, had been required to keep every item of clothing immaculate at all times. I scrubbed my soiled clothes each night, so my belongings would be ready for full inspection next day. But I had grown so sloppy in the relaxed atmosphere of Otsujima. What a pig! I hurriedly rummaged through my clothes, intending to take the dirty ones at once to the washroom and scrub them white. Petty Officer Ozawa, awakened by my bustling about, peered over the top of his bedding at me angrily.

"What in the name of heaven are you doing, Yokota?" he said in an urgent whisper, speaking softly so as not to waken anyone else. "I thought you were scheduled for water training tomorrow. Get to bed! You'll need the rest."

"I can't sleep, Ozawa," I said. "Look, will you do me a personal favor? If anything happens to me tomorrow, will you straighten out my things? I'll let you have anything you think worth keeping, if you'll do that for me. There are four or five dirty *fu* in here. Will you wrap them in something and throw them away, so I won't be ashamed in memory before the others?"

Ozawa burst into a loud laugh at the thought of throwing away my *fundoshi,* the wrap-around loincloth we used for underwear. "Don't be so dramatic!" he said in a voice I was sure would wake all hands. "You are only going four or five miles into the bay. Nothing will happen!" He buried his head under his blankets again, and I felt pretty foolish. I gave up, stowed everything in my seabag, and jumped into bed.

Next morning, right after breakfast, I rushed to the *kaiten* shed on the waterfront. There was mine, No. 27, resting on a rack. Ensign Iwao Kitagawa, the chief maintenance officer, was there, too. "Are you going to ride this one?" he asked me.

"Yes, sir," I said, coming briskly to attention.

"You've got a good one, then," he said. "The engine is in perfect condition. You'll have to be careful, though. They are all the same when they arrive here new. The valves are always a little tight."

"How tight, Sir?" I asked. Tight valves meant that control would be jerky, instead of smooth.

"Oh, not too bad," he said, with a soothing smile. "I think you'll be able to operate them without too much trouble. Just don't get too anxious. Now, get in and give your *kaiten* a check."

My *kaiten*! I hastily mounted, and climbed through the upper hatch. This was a method of escape, designed into the weapon on orders of the Naval General Staff, but none of us had ever discussed even the possibility of using it. Every one of us intended to ride our *kaiten* right into the target.

All the controls were bright and gleaming with newness. The lights worked perfectly, but there was grease everywhere. Mechanics must have used plenty of it on the valves and fittings. I found that it took much effort to operate the various controls, but felt the *kaiten* was in satisfactory shape for a thirty-minute run. Now I had to report to the base commander. I climbed out, told Ensign Kitagawa I was satisfied with the weapon, and looked for the senior officer. I found him on the steps of the headquarters building.

"Sir!" I shouted, trying to show how great was my eagerness, "Petty Officer Yokota is ready for test run! *Kaiten* is No. 27! Operation area is No. 1 Area! Speed will be limited to twenty knots! Duration of test will be thirty minutes! Purpose will be to train in diving, ascending and underwater navigation! Launching hour is 0830!"

"Your first test?" he asked.

"Yes, Sir!"

"Visibility is not so good today," he said, "so be very observant when you check the surface on rising. Have you examined your *kaiten*?"

"Yes, Sir!"

"Which boat will escort you?"

"Torpedo Boat 220, Sir! Ensign Tsuboi in command!"

"Very well. Carry on."

I ran back to my *kaiten* and looked out over the bay. He was right about the visibility. Fog cut it down considerably. Perhaps the sun would burn that away. But the water was almost slick, ideal for *kaiten* operations. It looked cold out there, though. That started me thinking once more about possible failure of my *kaiten*. I wouldn't want to leave it in such frigid water.

Maintenance technicians started hauling my *kaiten* from the shop to the pier, and from then on my attention was focused upon it. Torpedo Boat 220 was alongside the dock, awaiting my weapon. I climbed once more through the upper hatch and felt a very short moment of fright when it closed over me. I turned on the lights, gave all meters and gauges a second quick check by eye, then worked the periscope. The men who designed the *kaiten* left little room for movement. I am a relatively small man, but even I was cramped inside it.

Directly before my face was a single-eyepiece periscope and its pair of handles. To my right was a crank for raising and lowering the periscope. Overhead on the right was the valve for controlling speed, by regulating the flow of oxygen to the mighty engine astern of me. I released the starter bar, then opened the fuel valve. Overhead on the left was a crank for controlling the angle of my weapon's diving planes. They would regulate my rate of descent or climb underwater. On deck to my left was a valve for letting in sea water. That was necessary for maintaining stability as I used up the oxygen that served as fuel. At my right was the rudder control lever used in steering left or right. When sent on a mission, that would be last control I touched as I straightened out on a final course headed dead for an enemy ship.

A man had to have about six hands for operating a *kaiten*. And about the same number of eyes for watching its control panel. There was an air-driven gyrocompass, a clock, a depth meter, a fuel gauge and an oxygen pressure gauge to keep an eye on, and that periscope was close by, always ready to gash your skull if you moved too suddenly or knocked into some underwater object. Bandaged heads were a frequent sight at Hikari.

While I waited for a hoist to lift my *kaiten* off its dolly, I hummed and sang to myself. It helped overcome my nervousness and, since no one could hear me from outside, I found it a fine way to relieve tension. Soon I felt myself being lifted into the air. I could tell when my *kaiten* touched the water, too. Waves lapped along its sides. I heard the scrape of cables across my weapon as helpers lashed it to the side of Torpedo Boat 220.

Then three knocks sounded on the upper part of the hull, to ask if everything was all right inside. I knocked in answer to them, showing that all was well. The torpedo boat's engines sent vibrations through the *kaiten* as we moved out into the bay. Before long we arrived in position to start the training session. One more set of knocks sounded on the hull. That meant I was to be launched in ten more seconds. I counted to ten slowly, let out my breath, and reached behind me to give the starting lever a mighty shove. I was off!

That first time, I was to practice smooth ascents and descents, and then a little underwater navigation. So, after cruising on the surface several seconds, I remembered about high-octane gasoline being so valuable, and set to work. I set the *kaiten* for a four-degree down angle and submerged. I watched the depth gauge . . . thirty feet . . . Forty-five feet . . . sixty feet! "That's much too fast, Yokota!" I shouted to myself in the tiny chamber and began to level off as best I could. The controls were all stiff. Either they wouldn't respond at all, or else they responded too much when I gave a mighty twist or pull. I leveled off, finally, at seventy-five feet, though awkwardly. Thank heaven, I told myself! Another fifteen feet and I'd have rammed into the bay's muddy bottom, perhaps for good.

But now my weapon, over-controlled, was rising at an angle of three degrees. The diving plane control was sticky, and I was not able to flatten out the climb angle right away. I was disgusted when my depth gauge fell off to zero. I knew I was sticking above the surface, for the men in the torpedo boat to see and laugh at. I was supposed to keep a steady depth of no less than fifteen feet, dipping down from that level and rising up to it.

I looked at the stop watch I carried, then at my compass. I was supposed to be working a dead reckoning navigation problem as well, holding proper course and speed so that I would come about and return to my starting place within a given time. After I was confident I had reasonable con-

trol of the balky *kaiten*, I made another dip and another
ascent. This time I was determined to level off properly
at fifteen feet and hold at that level. This was the depth
at which *kaiten* attack ships, so as to hit them in their vitals,
below the waterline.

When I thought I was steadied at fifteen feet, I raised
my periscope for a look around. This stuck on me, too, and
I had to use plenty of muscle to get it up. By the time I
peered through it, a chance glance at my depth meter
showed me at a level of only six feet. I sticking up above
the surface again!

In my lap was a towel. Sweat had broken out all over
me, running down from my forehead into my eyes. I wiped
it off and began talking to myself. "Take it easy, Yokota!"
I said, angrily. "You're doing everything wrong! If you
continue this way, you will soon be finished as a *kaiten*
pilot! They'll never let you ride one again!"

I forced myself to relax and concentrate on doing things
with great deliberation and care. A glance through the periscope helped me. The island of Ushijima, at the outer edge
of Hikari Bay, was off to the left, twenty degrees from
my bow. If I continued straight ahead until her summit
was directly to my left, I'd be at the proper point for
making a wide circle to go back. This time I would do
things right, I told myself.

I submerged again. The controls were acting a little
better, and I was able to level off smoothly at thirty-six
feet. I eased the *kaiten* up to fifteen feet again, proper cruising level. From this depth a pilot could raise his periscope
just above the waves for a quick look around. Theoretically,
his mother submarine would line up on a course, and each
kaiten man would check his own compass heading. In the
conning tower, officers would plot out each man's attack
for him. If an enemy were heading toward the submarine
at such a speed and on such a course that she would pass
the submarine on its right, her officers would calculate a
course for a *kaiten* man that would help him intercept her.
He might receive word, for instance, to "Go right thirty
degrees on leaving the submarine. Make speed of twenty-
five knots, for twelve minutes and thirty seconds." He
would do that, then poke up his periscope for a look. If
all went well, he would be looking right at the enemy,
who would then be four to five hundred yards away. He

could steer straight for the enemy's vitals then, at top speed of forty knots.

I dipped, rose, dipped, rose, and things appeared to be much improved. I wondered what it would be like if I pushed the *kaiten* to her maximum speed. I increased the oxygen flow a little and thrilled at the sudden surge of power behind me. I increased it more. And still more! The great rumble astern of me had every bone in my body quivering. What a thrill! About thirty seconds had passed since my last submerging, and I eased up my periscope to check Ushijima's position. She should be almost exactly ninety degrees to my left now.

I looked. Nothing but ocean! I turned the periscope more to the left, and more, until it was over 100 degrees from the bow, nearly twisting my head off as I jammed forward in the tiny cockpit. Still nothing! I must be very far beyond Ushijima. I was well beyond my turning point!

I immediately dipped down again and began a one hundred eighty-degree turn to the left, watching my compass carefully. I was more than halfway through the turn, making only fifteen knots now, when I suddenly remembered something. Ensign Tsuboi had wanted me to make a careful check of this particular *kaiten's* performance. He had told me to time a fifteen knot, one hundred eighty-degree turn, and I had forgotten to do it. Panic seized me. What would he do when I told him I had forgotten to time the start of the turn? Then I had an idea. I would time the last half of the semicircle, multiply the time by two, and report that figure to him. He might not know the difference. Anyhow, it would be better than no report at all.

I looked at my stop watch, to get a timing start, and my whole world collapsed around me. For some unknown reason, the thing had stopped running. I couldn't give Tsuboi any time at all now. The only thing to do was straighten out on my new course, and try to count seconds to myself. After a while I'd surface, hoping I'd arrived back where I started from.

That's what I did. When I surfaced, I returned the starting bar to its original position. That was supposed to stop the engine. But it didn't! I had absolutely no idea what to do next, so I began twisting the fuel valve. When that was closed, the engine would die for lack of oxygen. The valve, which had worked so smoothly when I toyed with it, urging the *kaiten* to greater and greater speeds, now chose this moment to stick on me. It took the last ounce of my strength to close it, and when I did I slumped in my seat, exhausted.

At that moment I heard two loud gunfire reports. The warning signal! I became filled with fright once more. The mother torpedo boat fired guns when its blind-navigating *kaiten* seemed to be in danger. What had gone wrong for me now?

I cranked up my periscope as quickly as I could, peered through it, and recoiled. The viewing field was filled with rocks! There, not fifteen feet away, lay Hikari Harbor's breakwater! I was about to crash into it. My *kaiten* could crumple or spring a leak. I might sink, drowning before anyone could get to me.

I closed my eyes and waited, expecting the crash, not even thinking to use my upper escape hatch. But all that happened was a very gentle bump. Turning that fuel valve to shut off the oxygen had probably saved my life. Luck, just luck, had preserved me. I had no idea at all of where I was when I had surfaced.

I sat in my seat, feeling my *kaiten* bob up and down in the wash of the bay off the breakwater. Soon the torpedo boat approached, and I could hear men scrambling over the top of my *kaiten*, and felt the rumble later of a winch as it tugged me to the side of the boat. When I felt it bump against Torpedo Boat 220's side, I opened my top hatch, climbed out, and stepped aboard. Ensign Tsuboi was waiting for me. His face was tight as I addressed him, so I made what I thought was a bold move, trying to bluff it out.

"First test run completed, Sir," I said, "Nothing was out of order." Maybe he hadn't seen anything. I might still get away with it. I saluted, and started to walk aft.

"Wait!" he shouted.

I turned around, making a look of wonder fill my eyes. "Yes, Sir," I said. "What is it, Sir?"

"What was the purpose of your test run, Petty Officer Yokota?" he asked, the words grating through his clenched teeth.

"To maintain proper depth for attack, Sir. To keep at proper level so an enemy would not detect me."

"What? Do you think your work out there would let

you get within a mile of an enemy? You looked like a dolphin! What do you think would happen if you did that before the enemy? His guns would sink you in an instant!"

I could say nothing, and stood there, my eyes downcast. I had been found out. Now I waited for the awful words that would expel me from the *kaiten* program.

Surprisingly, Ensign Tsuboi's voice softened. "Since this is your first time," he said, "you were probably nervous. I will let it pass. But, mind you, just this once! You were far off your course, and you were lucky to stop when you did. Otherwise you would be a dead man now, and we would have one less *kaiten*."

I walked aft then, thanking the stars for my luck. When I put on that burst of speed underwater, just for a thrill, I must have let my weapon wander off-course. Then, when I came about, I was heading straight into the breakwater, instead of past its end.

My room was the place I wanted to be right now. That half-hour in the *kaiten* had sapped all my energy. My muscles were sore, and every nerve was tipped with fire. That had been a close call with Ensign Tsuboi, and my mattress felt good when I dug my face into it, hoping someone would call me for the noon meal. Never again would I trifle with a *kaiten*! I could have been dismissed from Hikari for my foolishness. If that happened, I would have had to slink back to Tsuchiura, where men would talk behind their hands about me.

5 ▣ Undeserved Punishment, and Sweet Revenge

After supper that night, all of us were in our barracks. Some men were playing chess, some were munching on the candy so plentiful at our canteen, and others were smoking the cigarettes so few persons in Japan could obtain in those days. A few were soaking themselves luxuriously in hot baths and some were, as usual, discussing the *kaiten*. I was the center of an attentive group, having had my first run that day, and I was telling several friends in great detail of my narrow escape. The tale grew more and more exciting each time I repeated it for a newcomer to my narrow circle of listeners.

Then Petty Officer Shigeyuki Kobayashi, who was duty man that night and had just taken a report to the instructors' quarters, stopped just inside our dormitory on his return and shouted in a very loud voice, "All members of the First Division! Assemble outside the instructors' quarters!"

What could they want, we asked one another? Were we in for another of the many pep talks we'd been getting since our arrival at Hikari? These officers weren't anything like those at Otsujima. They treated us like children. And discipline was most severe. In spite of the better quarters and our congenial division officer, Ensign Miyoshi, most of us would have preferred to be at Otsujima.

"I wonder what's going on?" said Petty Officer Nagata.

"I don't know," said Kobayashi, "but I can tell you one thing. They all looked pretty angry out there!"

The seven instructors responsible for our training lived together. Why they wanted to see us we did not know, but it could not be for anything pleasant. Especially if, as Kobayashi said, they all looked angry.

"Is Ensign Miyoshi with them?" asked someone else. We hoped he would be. Especially if they planned some kind of punishment. All of us had liked Miyoshi since the time he introduced himself and got such a big laugh from everyone. He was the youngest of the seven officers, but somehow seemed older, in spite of having such a youthful face. He had a very strong sense of right and wrong and was full of honor. Also, he took a deep personal interest in every one of us. In a few weeks he had come to know, through quiet questioning, all about every one of us, and we were sure that he would handle any necessary personal affairs with great tact and feeling after we had gone out on a mission. If there was to be punishment, Ensign Miyoshi would take our side if he felt we were in the right.

"He was in the quarters," Kobayashi said, "but he was in bed. Come on, now. All of you better hurry. It won't do to keep them waiting much longer."

In a few moments all of us were lined up outside the instructors' quarters. The roll was called, and two men were found missing, Tsuda and Ishibashi. Kobayashi put his head in the door and reported this. We could hear Ensign Inouye shouting at him.

"I told you everyone, *bakayaro!*" he screamed. "And I mean everybody! Find those other two! Get them here at once!"

No Japanese calls another stupid if he wants to retain his friendship. The very fact that Ensign Inouye used this expression in talking to a man with whom he might die in a *kaiten* attack someday showed us how upset he was. We now knew for sure we were in for something truly unpleasant. We had to find those other two men, and fast. The longer those officers had to wait, the angrier they would get, and the worse our punishment would be. Kobayashi, I, and two other trainees fell out of ranks and ran back to our dormitory. We found Ishibashi right where we expected to find him, soaking in a deep tub of hot water, singing at the top of his lungs.

"Ishibashi!" I shouted. "Get out of there, quick! All the other are lined up outside the instructors' quarters. It looks like we're getting it."

"Getting what?" he asked, interrupting his roaring for only a moment.

"It's the instructors!" I said. "The junior officers. They've got us all lined up. And they're all very, very angry."

Ishibashi gave a long sigh, rose to his feet, and began toweling himself slowly. *"Hayaku!"* I shouted, urging him to greater speed. "And do you know where Tsuda is?"

"In the other bathhouse," Ishibashi answered. "I could hear him a little while ago.

I ran to the bathhouse used by the maintenance men. There I found another happy singer, roused him from his hot bath, and kept hurrying him along as fast as I could. Soon we were all lined up again where we were supposed to be. It struck me for a moment that I might be the cause for all of this. Ensign Tsuboi had told me he'd talk to me later when he excused me on the torpedo boat. Perhaps he meant to shame me in front of everyone for my silliness in the *kaiten* that afternoon.

Six officers came out then, all ensigns. Ensign Narumi led, followed by Inouye, Kajima, Toyama, Tsuboi and Ikegaki. All had dark frowns lining their faces, and I knew at once it wasn't my fault we were lined up. Six officers couldn't be that angry at just one man for a poor showing in training.

"Don't you have any respect for officers?"

It was Ensign Narumi shouting. His voice echoed down the corridor. I knew what was coming now. A beating. I'd heard that tone of voice often enough at Tsuchiura to know what it meant. One of us had done something. What it was, I had no idea, but as usual the Imperial Navy principle of mass punishment was going to be applied. When one erred seriously, all paid. That way, many officers felt, the rest would later punish the responsible man most severely themselves. He would not repeat his offense, and discipline would be strengthened. I was resigned to what was coming, but bursting with curiosity to know what the punishment was for.

"One of you men," shouted Ensign Inouye, taking over, "at the seminar held two nights ago, called Ensign Toyama *donguri* and also said he was 'pop-eyed' when he made a small error in statement! Now, who was it? Who said those things? They were heard, and we want to know who said them! Speak up! Speak up!"

Ah, wakatta! Now I understood! Two days before, during a session of water training, Ensign Toyama's *kaiten* had plunged to the bottom of the bay. Our training *kaiten* carried water instead of high explosive in their warheads, and the way to get out of an emergency situation like that was to turn a special valve that released compressed air into the warhead and blew the water out. The empty warhead would then act like a buoy, bringing the *kaiten* to the surface. But when Ensign Toyama tried this standard procedure, nothing happened. He had to tap on the hull of his weapon until the mother torpedo boat located it. Then a diver was sent down to attach a hoisting line, after which one of our boats pulled the *kaiten* to the surface and took it aboard.

Ensign Toyama scurried from the weapon and told an exciting tale of his experience. He repeated it to many people that day. But that night, at the seminar, he was exposed. Everyone thought he had been stuck fast in the mud and for that reason could not surface. But the technicians, making a routine check of his *kaiten*, reported that his engine had never been started. Therefore he had not dived to the bottom, as he described it. but settled down slowly. He should have been able to rise again, quite easily, but the technicians also found his blow valve closed! And his fuel valve open! The blow valve and fuel valve were very close together in a *kaiten*, but all of us had been so drilled that we could reach for the correct control without even looking at it. The full truth of the matter was that he simply lost his head. He had tried to open a valve that was already open, and the wrong one, at that!

Now, our evening seminars were not always completely serious. Perhaps it is that way with men who are so dedicated. Sometimes the seminars were a lot of fun, as when we teased a friend about a small mistake he made. That night we saw our chance to get even with Ensign Toyama, who was often hard on enlisted men. We meant to roast him good.

Petty Officer Nobumichi Sakamoto was the first to ask questions. He asked them slowly, then faster and faster, pinning Ensign Toyama down to where he was shown to have made a serious error in elementary *kaiten* knowledge. Watching it was like viewing one of those American motion pictures where the lawyer twists a courtroom witness all around with many changing questions. We enjoyed every second of Sakamoto's thrusting performance and could hardly wait our own turn in firing questions at this haughty young martinet.

By the time we were through, Ensign Toyama's face was as red as an over-ripe tomato. But, instead of admitting his mistake and letting the seminar go on, he rose to the bait as we were sure he would. He denied his error and kept putting the blame on the maintenance men or the men who manufactured his *kaiten*. This we knew to be ridiculous, for we had all watched the technicians at work and knew what care they took with each weapon. We kept pressing him until he finally looked around him, helpless, hoping someone would come to his aid. We let up on him then. We'd had more than enough satisfaction.

Later, walking back through the darkness to our barracks, someone, I don't know who, remarked on what a *donguri* he was, and how his eyes had nearly popped from his head as he got more and more upset. In Japanese, *donguri* means "acorn" or "nut." Some words have a universal meaning. All the way to the barracks there was laughing, with several unidentified people repeating *"donguri-san"* and "Mister Pop-Eyes." Apparently some officer had overheard the remarks.

"You men of the First Division are just a little too fresh!" Ensign Inoye continued. "All the time boasting that you are Tsuchiura men!" This was certainly true. We had a great tradition at Tsuchiura. Japan's greatest naval aces had trained there, among them Saburo Sakai and Hiroyoshi Nishizawa. During our training we'd had hopes of scoring dozens of kills as they had, and we built a very strong spirit in ourselves. It carried over when we left the place, making us determined to show all Japan what Tsuchiura men could do. Perhaps we were just a little overbearing at times, but we had good cause to be proud.

"Another thing!" said Ensign Inouye. "You are always talking about how much more experienced you are than anyone else, just because you had a few weeks training at Otsujima before coming here! Well, you are still enlisted men. Perhaps you have been spoiled, and have forgotten your places. Well, we are now going to give you a good reminder of the fact that we are your superiors, and that we will be respected. No enlisted man can call an officer contemptuous names and expect to go unpunished. Form two ranks! Quickly! Facing each other!"

We did as he said. It was a direct order, and there was no way out of it. Ensign Inouye walked with quick strides to the left-hand end of the row, and I sighed inwardly when he appeared in the corner of my eye. When such beatings were administered in the Japanese Navy, it was always better for you if you were at the far end from where the punishers began. That way, when the officer or petty officer reached you, his hand was sore from hitting everyone else. His arm was tired, too. The blow you received wasn't a very heavy one. But here I was, only three men down from the starting position. And the first half-dozen or so usually took the worst of it.

I clenched my teeth and stared straight ahead. At such times it was not good to show timidity. It could win you an extra blow or two. Then, all of a sudden, there it came! Ensign Inouye smashed his fist into my right jaw. Two seconds later, another fist plowed into the same spot. Ensign Kajima was the third officer to hit me. The men said that while he was at the Naval Engineering School he used to experiment with his punching. He would hit different men in different ways as he went down the line, to see which kind of a hit hurt the most. He must have been successful in his experiments. His punch caught me square on the mouth and nose at the same time. At once, blood started trickling in a stream over my lips and chin. I stood firm. Three gone, three to go. I meant to stand up straight for all of them. If you went down, you were often hauled to your feet and given a few extra punches for good measure, to teach you not to be such a weakling.

I did stand up through them, too, though several other men went down. When it was over we stood there, sagging a little, our shoulders slumped forward, terribly sad and ashamed. The blushes that colored our faces were nearly as red as the blood on them. Great anger burned in all of us, though we were relieved that the ordeal had ended.

The officers made us fall in and face them again. "I hope a lesson has been learned here tonight!" screamed Ensign Inouye in a high voice. "If anything like this should ever happen again, we will see that every one of you is thrown out of this base. Dismissed!"

We straggled back to our dormitory, thinking how much like common gangsters those officers had acted.

"Who said that guy was a nut?" someone asked when we were out of their hearing.

No one answered. The truth was that probably six or

seven had called him names. We had all been talking sarcastically about how foolish we had made Ensign Toyama look during the seminar. I didn't care who said what, now that it was over. Nothing would change if someone spoke up. Especially my mouth, cut badly where my teeth had been mashed into the lip by Ensign Kajima's blow. I went to the washroom, bathed my face in cold water and doused my head. That made me cool outside. Inside, I was burning.

Some of the graduates of Etajima, our national naval academy, were like Lieutenant Commander Itakura, the base commander at Otsujima, or our division officer, Ensign Miyoshi. They did not have to strike you to get things done. They simply gave orders, and you obeyed them. If you failed, they looked at you in a way that was worse than any physical punishment. They made you feel you had failed them, and you tried all the harder after that. That was the way to handle men, I thought. Harsh discipline, with beatings, only made you sulk and think of how you'd been mistreated, instead of the job you had to do. I felt contemptuous toward the six officers who had struck us. They couldn't be real officers. True officers had deep concern for their men and treated them with some respect. They didn't beat them, like dogs.

I poured more cold water over my head and returned to my room. When I got there, a wet towel pressed to my mouth and nose, Ensign Miyoshi was present. Seeing him, I burst into tears and cried out, "Oh, Sir, this is a terrible thing to have happen!"

"Ensign Toyama is my classmate," said our division officer. "Anyone can make a mistake, but one of you said something that held him up to ridicule. This is a bad thing for a subordinate to do. It cannot be allowed in the Imperial Navy. And that is why you got the beating. It must not happen again.

"All the officers insisted on beating you together," he said. "I told them the First Division was my division, and that I would take care of things. But they refused to listen to me. In fact, they said you became bold enough to act the way you did because I was too soft with you. They said all of you were too conceited, and needed a good lesson. Toyama was angry, but Inouye and Tsuboi were even angrier. I finally gave up and went to bed.

"I'm sorry that I was too ashamed to face you during

the punishment. I refused to punish you like that myself, but could do no more than that. I promise you this, however. They will never beat you again. Please forgive me for what has happened tonight. It shall never happen again. Should you require punishment, I shall do it myself, even if it breaks my hand. Good night."

Strange as it seems, his last words cheered us. The thought of our *"Seikai Nyudo"* striking us made us grin, then laugh. What a spectacle that would be! Sure, he would carry out his given word. He would strike us. And he would strike us hard, too. But we doubted that this man, who had shown in so many ways his strong affection toward all forty-eight of us, would be able to get very far down the ranks before he gave up, embarrassed. Our hearts were a little lighter as we turned into our bunks.

When we woke next morning, though, we were not grinning or laughing. All those blows we had taken were aching murderously. My own nose and lips were swollen, and dried blood made it hard for me to breathe. We began muttering about getting some kind of revenge. That would not be easy, for it would have to be something for which we could not be punished. More than one man said, *"Shigata ga nai!"* while discussing it, and after a few days we were about to give up the idea as totally impossible, when nature intervened on our behalf. Hikari, a few days later, was the scene of something rare for that part of Japan—a heavy snowfall.

Because we were so short of trained mechanics that only a dozen or so men daily could be trained in *kaiten,* most Hikari men had much time on their hands. Few of us from Tsuchiura had ridden in *kaiten,* and then rarely. The day for us usually started with morning exercise, followed by breakfast, after which came work with the technicians, or on the torpedo boats, until noon. Judo and fencing took up part of the afternoon, but after that there was little to do. Our senior officers were too occupied with the final training of men already selected for a *kaiten* mission and had little time for the rest of us. So junior instructors thus had a problem keeping our spirits up. They invented all kinds of methods of keeping us occupied. We had marathon races to Murozumi Shrine, about three miles away from the base. And rowing races. Different divisions divided up into teams and played what has been the top sport in Japan almost since the day it was introduced—American baseball.

Then that rare heavy snowfall came. It drifted down from the sky all through the night, not stopping until everything—our barracks, the maintenance buildings, athletic areas and walks was shrouded in white. When it ended, some of us thought it would be a good diversion to have a mass snowfall fight. We were starting from our quarters, intent on building giant fortresses of snow and defending them from attackers, when Ensign Tsuboi appeared and shouted an order.

"All hands, assemble on the training ground!"

We thought it might be some kind of emergency, or that some big war news was about to be announced. Maybe it was about the battle at Lingayen, in the Philippines, where the enemy had just made a landing. Perhaps our forces there had driven him into the sea. Well, we would see.

When we arrived at the athletic area, Ensign Tsuboi and Ensign Toyama were waiting for us. "At the Naval Engineering School," shouted Tsuboi, "we had very severe drills on snowy days! We used to play defense games, have snowball fights, and run horseback games. It was nothing for us to do this barefoot!"

Some Japanese naval officers were schooled at Etajima, our equivalent of Annapolis. Others took different studies, at the Naval Engineering School at Maizuru, on the Japan Sea, and then went to sea.

"Now," Ensign Tsuboi continued, "We have snow for the first time here at Hikari. So we are going to give you men a demonstration of what truly severe training can be like. We are going to have a horseback fight. It will show us how many of you have endurance!"

He looked at us with contempt. The horseback fight was often used for training in the Imperial Navy. Almost every Japanese boy has played it during rest period at school. A group of men is divided into two teams. Each team is then divided into groups of four men, and each four men make a horse-and-rider. One man simply stands straight, and two more take positions on either side of him, gripping his shoulders firmly with both hands. They act as extra "legs," to help keep the center man, the "horse," on his feet during battle. Then the "rider" mounts up, sitting on two pairs of hands and a pair of shoulders. On this steadied platform he rides out to battle, shouting orders to his horse. His objective is to avoid being unseated himself, and to unseat as many enemy riders as he can. After a given time, the side with the most riders left mounted wins the game.

It seemed to us that these two officers simply wanted to show off. They probably had far more experience at the horseback game than we did. At least, more experience at playing it in the snow, where the footing was treacherous. They would probably beat us easily, then laugh about it. Still, it was something to do. It would help pass the time. So we got ready. My First Division was made up of twelve horses, totalling forty-eight men. The Seventh Division, made up mostly of officers and men from Nara, had an equal number. Naturally, everyone wanted to be a rider, so we had to draw among ourselves to see who would be "legs." I was lucky, and laughed happily as I ordered my three assistants into position so I could mount up. All of us liked contact sports. We spent many hours practicing judo, wrestling *sumo* style, and practicing the *kendo* method of dueling with long bamboo sticks. We did little boxing, though, and here was a chance to use our fists. In horseback fighting there are no rules. The only objective is to win. Any kind of attack, or blow, fair or foul, is permitted.

I was mounted and ready, looking across the snow at the other team, when suddenly I spied Ensign Toyama. There was the "nut," right in the center of his team! Several other Tsuchiura men spied him at the same time. All remembered at once the six punches each of us had taken because that man was a liar and a poor sport. Here was the chance we never thought would come.

Petty Officer Nobumichi Sakamoto, also a rider, was beside me. Sakamoto was a particularly violent man, with a terrible temper. No one trifled with him if they could avoid it, because he held the high rank of *shodan* in judo. I don't mean to say that my friend was a bully. He was not. But he was a very tough man. He didn't make trouble, but was easily excited. He was always ready for trouble when it came his way. It was Sakamoto who, on the way back to our quarters after the beating given us by the six officers, had said, "If this weren't the Navy, I'd snap that dog's neck for him!" Several of us soothed him, calming him down. He might have actually lost his temper and gone back if we hadn't. He could have killed Toyama easily, in just a few seconds, and that would have meant death for himself not long afterward. So now, when his eyes fell on Ensign Toyama, the tough Sakamoto immediately began calling to the riders near him "Everyone gang up on the nut!"

I was nearest, and answered first. *"Yoshi kita!"* I said, "It's all right with me! You and I will work on him together, Sakamoto!"

The game was to last for eight minutes. Whichever side had the most riders up at the end of that time would be the winner. For us of Tsuchiura that meant nothing. All Sakamoto and I cared about was catching Ensign Toyama and giving him at least as much as we had got from him earlier—six solid punches! And a few kicks, too, would make it all the more pleasant.

All twenty-four horses were milling about now, ready to start the battle. Some of ours were easing off to either side, so they could rush in from an angle with a surprise attack after all others were engaged. A few more held back a little, with the intention of circling behind the enemy after the first mighty clash and attacking him from the rear. I kept my eye straight on Ensign Toyama. He was the one I wanted to attack. I talked to my six-legged horse. There would be no special tactic for us. We would not try for a surprise from the side or the rear. We would give him a surprise from the front. Perhaps he would not expect it there. He looked to be in very high spirits, from where I sat. I imagine, with all his experience, he was truly eager for the battle. He probably expected to down many of our horses.

Finally Ensign Tsuboi, who acted as a sort of time-keeper and referee, shouted, "Go!" A great battle yell went up from both sides, which were about fifty feet apart in ankle-deep snow. They charged across this white expanse at once, and I saw immediately that most of our horses were converging toward one place. Of course! That moving to one side and hanging back had been a trick. Nearly all forty-eight of us had the same idea—get the nut!

Petty Officer Suzuki was the first to close in. His men were all fast runners. But Suzuki was all will and no skill. He couldn't give the officer much of a battle. With a pull and a twist, Ensign Toyama had Suzuki flying through the air, his three helpers stumbling and slipping, unsuccessfully try-ing to regain their balance. Ensign Toyama then looked around for another opponent. He looked very powerful sitting there, ready for more battle, and had shown himself so skilled in his short engagement with Suzuki that I began to have doubts that we could defeat him.

I might not even reach him, for that matter. He was the Seventh Division's leader. He had a pair of horses flanking him, each a few steps to the front, for protection. Quite suddenly, however, while these protectors were diverted by other battlers, Sakamoto and I broke through his shield, and were upon him.

Sakamoto got there first. Instead of grappling with the Ensign, he started punching at him. Toyama, instead of seeking to establish a hold by which he could throw Sakamoto to the ground, began returning the punches. Their assistants' legs were wobbling as the two leaned far over in their attempts to get in good blows at each other.

The fight looked fairly even to me at that point. I screamed at my horse to close in, so I could help Sakamoto. Just then Petty Officer Tsuji, of the Seventh Division, saw what I planned. He came charging at me from the side, hoping to take me out of the action. He had an advantage for the moment, in that he could use two hands to my one, but I was lucky. I dodged his first grab and, while he was still leaning far over, gave him a stout *karate* chop with the side of my left palm. That was the end of Tsuji's attempt to defend his chief. He went down and out of the battle.

I looked up as Tsuji fell. Sakamoto and Ensign Toyama were still flailing away at each other mightily. Toyama appeared to be giving as many as he received, but the six legs under him weren't holding up too well. The three men who made up Sakamoto's horse were kicking and punching also, with such a fury that Toyama's supporters were so busy defending themselves that they could pay little attention to their rider's instructions.

"I'm coming, Sakamoto!" I shouted, and rocked back and forth, urging my horse to charge. We moved in fast, from the side of Toyama, slightly behind him, and began at once to kick and punch Toyama's horse. His three helpers were really getting it now, and my perch was so unsteady that I felt I was riding a runaway camel. I finally got my balance long enough to reach out and grab Toyama's neck with both hands. I shouted to my horse to get in closer, and increased my hold until I had the arrogant officer in a near-

strangle, my arms encircling his neck. This was all Sakamoto needed.

Now he really began raining blows on Toyama's face. Once
in a while one of these wild smashes would catch me on the
ear or jaw, making my head buzz. But I still hung on. Maybe
I would catch a few, but Toyama was catching ten for every
one of mine.

Still, Toyama knew the tricks of the game. His legs were
locked over the shoulders, under the arms, and around the
back of his center supporter. His strong body was still held
rigid, straight up and down. He worked his hands around
my forearms, trying for a grip to get him enough leverage
to throw me over his head. I hung on, desperate, wanting
only to hold him. So long as I kept my weight on him,
Sakamoto was free to do as he pleased. His blows kept
coming, full of fury. I wasn't sure how much longer I could
hold my grip on Toyama. A tremendous commotion was
going on below us. There was no telling when someone would
get lucky and trip someone else, and then all of us would
go down into the snow in one great heap. Or Toyama,
skilled as he was at this game, might still have a trick of
some kind to use, that would let him win. All I could do
was hold him until I was flung away. The blood spurting
from his nose and splashing on my wrist would be victory
enough for me. I remembered how much my own nose and
mouth had hurt after the officers' beating.

Then one more horse from our Tsuchiura group arrived
on the scene. It was Petty Officer Kumada, who came on so
fast that his momentum flung him right up and on top of
Toyama. He actually bowled him over like a tenpin! The
two went tumbling to the ground, my comrade who would
later die in his *kaiten* at Iwo Jima on top of the man who
would never go out on a mission. We had won! We
had beaten the gangster! I was filled with happiness, and
urged my horse off to where other men were fighting. Now
that we had toppled the leader, we would get some of his
followers!

My horse didn't obey my orders. I looked down to find
out why, and saw that my supporters, as well as Sakamoto's
three, were not yet through. They were happily kicking and
stepping on the three men who had held up Toyama. I
leaned back and caught my breath, my grin at least twice
as big as Sakamoto's. We let our supporters do all the kicking

they wanted and pulled back only when they had their
fill of it. Two of Toyama's horses rushed up to his rescue,
but the whistle blew, ending the game, just as they arrived.

I looked around and began counting. All that remained of
Toyama's side were the two horses that had been coming
to aid him. We had four horses still standing. We had won the
game. The best sight of all was Ensign Toyama. He was
standing a few yards from us, smeared with dirty snow,
blood running down from his nose. His face was beginning
to puff up. I could see he'd be nursing one black eye and
several lumps for many days. He certainly looked miserable.

We thought for a while that the Seventh Division might
challenge us to a second bout, but Ensign Tsuboi stopped
any chance of that. On seeing most of us go for Ensign
Toyama, he must also have thought of the beatings. In another bout, his friend might be a lot slower getting up off
the ground. He might not get up at all. Someone might
have to carry him off the field. What a loss of face that
would be! Ensign Tsuboi merely called out "Congratulations! You men fought very well for your first experience
in snowy footing. That will be all for today."

I jumped down from my horse and strode off with my
friends. Most of us had our arms around one another's shoulders, or were pounding one another on the back. What joy!
For more than seven minutes we had had the pleasure of
beating that miserable ensign unmercifully! And there was
not a thing he could do about it!

In our barracks that night there was much singing and
shouting. Some of us had lumps and bruises from the battle.
Others still had marks from the beating by the officers. But
none of these mattered. In every puffed eye there was a
twinkle. Every cut lip was curled in a wide, happy smile.

6 ◘ I Am Selected for a Mission

My first session in water training with a *kaiten* had been a failure. What a roasting my friends gave me at the next seminar! They continued it in the barracks, too, but in a friendly way. It wasn't anything like what Ensign Toyama had endured. Men who had ridden *kaiten* in the bay told me of problems they had with the weapon, and how to solve them if I had similar ones later. I was scheduled for more missions and did well at them because I was so determined to make up for my earlier foolishness. I successfully circled Ojima, thirteen miles from the Hikari dock, and also Minase, a smaller island nearer the shoreline, while submerged.

So my second and subsequent *kaiten* sessions were good ones. I mastered the pressure adjustment, the depth controls and trim adjustment, and eventually reached the point where I could operate the *kaiten* almost as smoothly as some people handle a motor vehicle. When I first tried submerging, I had plunged over sixty feet before recovering control, but now I could level off smoothly at whatever depth I chose. I also learned to submerge and surface without making a large splash.

The *kaiten* were being handled faster now, as the technicians became more adept at their work. We lost two men in training during January, the month in which my own training was speeded up. At Otsujima, on January 14, Lieutenant, junior grade, Kentaro Nakashima and Ensign Isshin Miyazawa died. They had been making circular navigation runs underwater around the island of Nojima. The weather turned bad that day, and a halt was called because of poor visibility. No one was ever able to learn what happened to the two men. They simply disappeared. We had to assume they crashed on the bottom of the bay or against the land while underwater. They must have died instantly, or else they would have hammered on the hull, making noises so a mother boat could locate and haul them to the surface.

We had a near tragedy when I-58 was returning from the

Kongo mission. She was steaming up Bungo Channel on the night of January 21, keeping a very sharp lookout. American submarines had been marauding right off our shores for months now. Not even Bungo Channel, the gateway through which our Combined Fleet had steamed for years, was a safe waterway. Suddenly, one of Lieutenant Commander Hashimoto's lookouts sighted a black shape in the darkness. A submarine! I-58's captain was about to attack it, then something told him not to. He kept his submarine moving up the channel, headed for home. It wasn't until morning that he learned his target was I-36, also returning from the Kongo mission. Hashimoto could have sunk her easily.

By the end of the month, all Kongo mission submarines but the ill-fated I-48 were back in port. Official estimate of the results pleased everyone. The Sixth Fleet scored the mission as having sunk ten enemy transports, one battleship, one tanker and one escort aircraft carrier of the *Casablanca* class. The Kikusui Group had been credited with three battleships and two large aircraft carriers, so the official results of the *kaiten* effort so far, in two missions, had been eighteen enemy ships sunk at the cost of two submarines, I-37 and I-48. But we had lost three other submarines since that first attack on Ulithi in November—I-46, I-365, and RO-47. Japan was suffering from a bad shortage of underseas platforms from which to launch *kaiten*.

Still, we were all eager to get into action. I kept improving with each session. The seminars helped a lot, but it was practical training that helped me the most. The days and nights passed rapidly for me. When not out in a *kaiten*, I was engaged in physical exercise, assisting on torpedo boats, or practicing identification of American warships, as well as learning how to estimate the range, course and speed of a ship accurately. When mounted in my *kaiten*, I was usually loosed at an antisubmarine vessel roughly six miles away. The idea was to "hit" this target by passing under it. The upper halves of our *kaiten* were painted white, so that crewmen on the target vessel could tell whether we passed beneath them. They also watched for our smooth wakes. If we passed under the bow of one of these small targets, our wake would appear near its stern by the indications on the surface. That was considered an excellent performance, and it was what we all aimed for. Anyone who could "hit" the bow of a small antisubmarine boat could surely hit an American ship five to ten times longer.

On January 24 a force of American battleships, cruisers and destroyers appeared out of nowhere to shell Iwo Jima, about six hundred miles south of Tokyo. We knew from this that the enemy would probably try to seize that island next. It would provide forward airfields for the fighter planes escorting the giant B-29 superfortresses striking Japan from the Marianas. Also, it would be a refuge for enemy bombers in distress, some of which had been lost in the sea. Planes based on Iwo Jima might rescue these crews, so they could fly and fight again. So our training was stepped up. It was only a short run for a submarine to Iwo Jima. The enemy fleet should be moving up and staying near it soon. *Kaiten* might do well at Iwo, for submarines would not have to cruise so far to a target. They'd be able to return quickly, take on more *kaiten* and go out once more to battle in a very short time.

I was improving rapidly during the first week of February and praying I'd be selected for a mission. Then, during the second week, it happened. On February 13, I was on my way to take my after-supper bath when Petty Officer Yoshihito Yazaki called out to me.

"Say, Yokota," he said, "Ensign Miyoshi wants to see you!"

"What for? Do you know?" I asked, starting back to get dressed.

"He didn't say," said Yazaki, "but he wants to talk to you, Kitamura and me. We can guess, can't we?"

A thrill ran through me. The three of us and Petty Officer Kikuo Shinkai had been posted for water training more than anyone else recently. Could it be we were being assigned to a mission?

"Where's Kitamura?" I asked, throwing my towel and soap on the bed and pulling on my uniform.

"I can't find him," said Yazaki. "I've looked everywhere."

I remembered that I'd often seen Kitamura walk down toward the *kaiten* shed, on the waterfront, in the evening. Yazaki and I headed that way. We found Kitamura there, admiring the weapons and staring off across the water. The three of us hastened to the instructors' quarters and knocked on the door.

"Come in." As usual, Ensign Miyoshi's voice was high and

pleasant. As we entered, he said, "It took you long enough to get here. What happened?"

The other officers in the room stared intently at us. They did not like us, and we did not like them. We just stood there, embarrassed at being so slow to report, and too loyal to a friend to say that we'd been delayed because of searching for him. Ensign Miyoshi was just teasing, though. His tone was light. When the other officers turned back to their own affairs, his voice became serious.

"Well, men," he said, "what I have called you here for is this. I have been chosen for a mission, and was told I could select three of my own petty officers to accompany me. You are the three I have selected. Are you willing to come along with me?"

The silent enmity of the other officers meant nothing to us now. "Yes, Sir!" I burst out, answering for all of us.

"Good," he said. "Besides the four of us, there will be one other officer. I haven't been given his name yet."

"When do we depart, Sir?" asked Kitamura.

"Sometime around the end of next month, they tell me," said Ensign Miyoshi. "I'm not sure of the date yet. Probably about the twentieth of March. We'll go out in I-368. That's the submarine named now, but it could change. Our mission will be to destroy American tankers bringing oil to Saipan."

Our faces fell. We hadn't minded too much when he named I-368 as the submarine to carry us into action, though she was fat and slow. But our targets seemed so insignificant. "Is that all, Sir?" I asked. I had hoped myself to sink an aircraft carrier. The others did, too. We talked about it often.

Ensign Narumi looked up and interrupted. "Don't ask for too much," he said. "It is not easy to approach enemy aircraft carriers and battleships now. They are always inside a thick ring of cruisers and destroyers."

I didn't like him, but he was right. After the Kongo mission general strategy for *kaiten* had been changed. The enemy had all the patrol planes he needed, and more, to guard his anchorages. He also had plenty of surface patrol craft and laid his anti-submarine nets well, as I-56 had found out in the Admiralties. So the Sixth Fleet command decided to hurt him in some other way. Task forces were too difficult to penetrate, so the new strategy was to hit the enemy's supply lines, the ships with little defense or none, far to the rear of his attack forces.

"Anyway," said Ensign Miyoshi, "there is no value in useless discussion. Tankers have been ordered as the target, and tankers it will be. We will concentrate heavily on target attack practice tomorrow. Be sure your charts are properly prepared. We have only a little more than a month before we go out. We will want to make the most of it. Meanwhile, we will help one another all we can in every way. None of you need worry about your personal affairs. They will all be taken care of. If there's anything you need in the next few weeks, see me about it immediately."

"Yes, Sir," we answered together. We couldn't have asked for a finer man to lead us, and I think he perceived our feeling toward him.

"Now, then," he said, "since that's over, I propose that we drink a toast to success."

He brought out cups, and a bottle of *sake*. *"Campai!"* he said, the equivalent to "Bottoms up!" and the three of us, together with all the officers, for the others had now joined us for this simple ceremony, tossed off about a half-ounce of the wine each. The three of us then returned to our quarters, where I went to sleep at once. I was a different Yutaka Yokota now from the one who reported with 100 men to Otsujima. In those days I used to think deep and long thoughts before drifting off to sleep. Now I was calm and reconciled, determined to train to a peak of skill and then force a smashing blow upon the enemy. I had been selected. Soon I would go. That was that. The next day Ensign Muneyoshi Kato was added to our group. That was good. but the rest of the day was bad. Last night I had gone to sleep very happy. Tonight I would go to sleep deep in misery. All because of a balky *kaiten*.

Our training session was to embrace underwater navigation and smooth surfacing. We were to circumnavigate Ojima. It was far out from the dock and would require a great deal of skill to reach and circle while submerged. I meant to make a success of this day's assignment. I now was a man selected for a mission. Much would be expected of me. No one would show me mercy at the seminar if I did poorly. At 1:00 P.M. I made my way to the *kaiten* shed and while walking there met Kitamura. He had been the third man to go out in the morning session, so was on his way back to our quarters.

He looked so downcast I asked him what was wrong.

"It's bad out there today, Yokota," he said, "very rough water. No one did well. Be very careful when you get out there."

I tried to forget his words as I went over *kaiten* No. 31 with the maintenance men. But I was worried. *Kaiten* No. 31 didn't help ease my worry. A few days before, Petty Officer Shinkai had struck the bottom of the bay in No. 31, and had told us its rudder and diving planes were hard to handle. I was to find this very true.

Lieutenant Hamaguchi was in command of the launch that accompanied me. We moved out quickly, and at 1:40 P.M. were at the launching point. On the signal, I shoved my starting bar. The motor roared into life, which gave me assurance. It ran smoothly, and I moved away from the launch a short distance. Then my troubles began.

When I dove, the *kaiten* kept going right down. I had to fight the controls to ease off my dive. Then, when I ascended, I had the same problem all over again. The rudder was especially bad. It tended to steer my weapon to the right. I made adjustments and tried to continue my cruise, but the *kaiten* still kept veering away to the right. Finally, I decided to hold a depth of twenty-five feet and make my run blind. If I surfaced too often, to check how far that bad rudder was throwing me off, I would get a poor performance grade from the checkers and observers on the surface above. I had to gamble this way, I decided, and did it.

Before long, I heard the boom of guns. I slowed the *kaiten* at once and brought it to the surface. My first look through the periscope showed me a great rock directly in front of me. Immediately I took advantage of the rudder's tendency, and made a sharp turn to the right and avoided this massive obstacle. Sweat broke out all over me. I dove underwater, increasing my speed, and cursed at mechanics who had not repaired this weapon's faults. How could we be expected to sink targets with *kaiten* like this one? On the way back to my starting point, I cursed everyone I could think of, by name, up to and including the chief maintenance officer.

Lieutenant Hamaguchi was full of rage when I climbed out of the *kaiten* and stood before him. "You fool!" he said, and punched my face. "You fool! You could have killed your-self! Do you know what that would mean? It would mean you had given back the enemy one ship! How can we sink enemy ships if fools like you are going to kill themselves before they ever go into action? Get out of my sight!"

I bounced back from that experience, however, thanks to Ensign Miyoshi's sympathy and understanding. And I was inspired all over again two days later by Ensign Itaru Oka-yama. He was leading us in gymnastics that morning, and when we were finished he suddenly decided to take us for a run. We had not yet had breakfast, and weren't enthusiastic about this proposition. There was some grumbling.

"Silence! Begin running!" Ensign Okayama shouted, and off we went, running three miles all told. When we got back before the barracks, he told us to form ranks once more. We were slow doing it, so he ordered: "Right face! Begin run-ning!" and ran beside us, urging on the laggards, while we covered the same route once more. No one dared fall be-hind or slow down. Ensign Okayama was quick with his fists. He took no outward pleasure in it, though. He would strike you severely, without malice, and be smiling at you a few moments later. He really commanded us. He expected instant obedience. Though he was short, he was very strong and tough. We liked him and tried to please him. His spirit was so strong we all wanted to be like him.

After breakfast, I saw that Ensign Okayama's name had been posted on the bulletin board as first man to train that day. He had known about this all the time we were running! What spirit! What endurance! Running six miles, then go-ing straight to his *kaiten* right after breakfast! There was a real man!

This was proved to us before the end of the month. Ensign Okayama went to his death in a *kaiten* attack at Iwo Jima.

The next day Tokyo was struck by carrier planes, and I made my first *kaiten* launching from a submarine. It was I-368. American carrier planes hit Tokyo on the eighteenth, also. I was glad to hear they had hit industrial targets, in the southeastern section, for my family did not live in that section of the capital.

Two things happened on the nineteenth that distressed me greatly. American marines invaded Iwo Jima, and Ensign Miyoshi struck me. I don't know which affected me most, the enemy moving onto Japan's front doorstep and camping there, or receiving a hard blow from the man we had grown to love.

The incident with the ensign came about through a minor infraction of the rules. Several of us had not folded the blankets on our beds properly. When Ensign Miyoshi demanded that the guilty ones step forward, about six men did so. I remembered that I had not folded mine properly, either, but was still thinking about it as the others moved ahead of ranks. There was a five-second interval between the time they stepped forward and the time I did. Ensign Miyoshi, who always gave orders outside the barracks in a very loud voice to cover up his true gentleness, came down the line and struck all of us once each. The others then stepped back into ranks, but Ensign Miyoshi called out to me.

"Yokota! Wait!"

He stood in front of me. "You were the last to step forward," he said, "Did you think I would favor you before the others, just because we are going out on a mission together? You should have been the first man out! I don't think I want to take you along with me now!"

He began to hit me, and continued until he knocked me down. When I got to my feet my cheeks were beginning to puff out. When he dismissed me, I was deeply ashamed. I knew why he had struck me. I had shamed him, Ensign Kato and the two other men on our mission. He asked whether I expected favors, but had already favored me by selecting me for a mission. I forgave him, mentally, at once. That evening he showed his sorrow and willingness to forget the incident by stopping by our room and leaving us some *yokan*, a sweet bean pastry he knew we all liked. There was a piece for me as well as the others, and I knew it was his way of saying I should forget the past.

The next day the Chihaya Group left on a mission. Two of the three submarines did, that is. I-368 left Otsujima carrying five *kaiten*, with three officers and two petty officers as pilots. That same day, we gave our own send-off to I-370, which departed from Hikari, also carrying five *kaiten*. Ensign Itaru Okayama, who made us run such a long distance a few days before, was in charge. Both of these submarines were lost to the enemy in the next few days. We never learned whether I-368 did the enemy any damage. She was discovered and sunk by carrier aircraft on February 27. I-370, with our Hikari men on board, was sunk by surface craft the day before, but she had already attacked the enemy. Our forces on Iwo Jima radioed that they had seen six tall columns of fire off to seaward, so it's pretty certain that the very aggressive Ensign Okayama and his comrades made some hits.

We also lost a former Tsuchiura man in I-370, when Petty Officer Masao Mori, who sailed out as a *kaiten* mechanic, went down with the ship.

I-44, the third submarine in the Chihaya Group, left Otsujima on February 23. She returned on March 9, all *kaiten* unfired. Patrols were so thick after I-368 and I-370 were sunk that they couldn't get near Iwo Jima, although many targets were there. I-44, in fact, was detected every time she tried to surface and take a look around. She could not even recharge her batteries. Enemy planes and ships kept her under the waves for forty-six and one-half hours, and the air inside her hull was slowly being poisoned. I-44's captain, Lieutenant Commander Genbei Kawaguchi, finally had to call off his operation because his crew and *kaiten* pilots were too exhausted after their ordeal to be effective. He decided to live and fight another day.

Sixth Fleet didn't agree with him. He was relieved of his command immediately after returning to port, another captain being appointed in his place. This happened at Otsujima, of course. There was no gloom at Hikari. We were elated at Ensign Okayama's success and remembered his last words at a small drinking party we had held for him the night before I-370 departed.

"I am going to *Kudan*," he said, meaning he would die in battle and be enshrined at Yasukuni. "Make sure you do things right. If you don't, I promise you that I will come back and beat you up again!" Well, we would try our best, both for his memory and the memory of his fists, which were like rocks. We wouldn't want his ghost in our midst.

The day after I-44 left Otsujima I was launched for the second time from a submarine. It was I-58, commanded by Lieutenant Commander Hashimoto. This was the submarine that would later sink the *USS Indianapolis*, the ship that carried atomic bombs to the Marianas. What a difference between this submarine and the fat, ugly I-368! I-368 had originally been built as a troop- and supply-carrying submarine. She made less than 14 knots on the surface, as compared with 20 or more for the other submarines. Her purpose was to help support island garrisons. Originally she carried two 40-foot launches, especially designed to withstand hydrostatic pressure at depths of more than 200 feet. She also carried two large rubber boats. In addition to her crew of 50 officers and men, she could carry 110 troops and 60 tons of equipment inside her hull. Another 20 tons could be lashed down on her deck, but it slowed her to the pace of a *katatsumuri*. I-368 looked like a snail, too, especially from the bow-on view. One big, fat lump!

I-58 was different. She was sleek, and looked speedy. I hoped to tour through her hull, but it was late by the time we loaded *kaiten,* and we had to get right to work. Two officers were to be launched out near Ojima Island, Ensign Miyoshi and Ensign Aizawa. Petty Officers Yazaki, Shinkai, Kitamura and myself were to be the others. I got aboard quickly, and started my gyroscope at once. This was driven by a jet of pressurized air, and took a little while to get up to operating speed. I depended on it for accurate steering, so it was the first thing I reached for whenever I had a training session. Then I put on the telephone headset and checked all controls. They appeared to be in good order. I reached for my periscope control then, and found a small piece of paper attached to it, carrying the words: "Our prayers go with you for a sure hit." On the bottom it read, "From the Maintenance Section." Those men were wonderful. They puttered over each *kaiten* as though it was a special birthday present for a favorite son, and they treated us like favorite sons too. They were the last persons to wish you well as you entered your weapon and the first to greet you with anxious eyes as you got out, and to ask how everything had gone.

After the submarine dipped down, I put up my periscope for a look around. I could see Ensign Miyoshi's *kaiten.* "This is more like real training!" I told myself, as my eye took in more of the submarine's main deck. We would soon be out on station, and be fired. There we would test the new tactic, making attacks in the open sea. This was what Lieutenant Commander Itakura had meant at Otsujima when he talked about his dream of sending "hundreds of 'seeing torpedoes' against the enemy as he passes over the sea toward our homeland."

It was, however, a very difficult type of attack to bring off. Training in the harbor, or a quiet bay, was one thing. Attacking where waves might be higher than our periscopes could reach was another. Three things had to be determined with accuracy before any such attack could be successful: the enemy's course, his speed and the angle from his bow to us. Knowing these three things, an interception course could be plotted for *kaiten*. But if judgment were off in one of them, even a little bit, a *kaiten* would have to depend strictly on his periscope. So we had a special plan, combining both methods. Just before a *kaiten* left the submarine, he would be given the final estimate of the enemy's course, speed and bow angle, so he could picture the situation. Conning tower people would give the *kaiten* pilot a course and speed he would follow for a specific time after leaving the submarine. At the end of this run he was to pop his periscope above the surface for a final sighting of his own. Theoretically he would then be about five hundred yards from his target, and off its port or starboard beam. He would determine his final course for run-in, crank down his periscope and steer straight for the target at top speed. The maximum time a *kaiten* pilot was allowed during training for this final sighting was seven seconds. Anything more, it was felt, would make too much of a "feather" with the periscope, and the enemy could sight him too easily.

I-58 was at the level of fifty-five feet. That left the *kaiten* sitting at about thirty-five feet. You had to keep remembering this, so you could hold your depth after being released. The slightest fault in maintaining proper ballast as fuel was consumed could lighten you enough to make you bob to the surface before you could get your diving planes tilted to take you down. Actually, it was best to have a slight amount of down angle on your planes when released and dip just a bit as you left the submarine, compensating a few seconds later.

I must have had too much angle on when I-58 crewmen released the last two cables that freed my *kaiten*. I dipped all the way down to 110 feet before leveling off. This was all right in the open sea, where I had maneuvering room, but it would have left me stuck fast in the mud if it had happened inside the bay.

Kaiten were fired at five-minute intervals, just as they would be in battle. I was the second one off. Shinkai had bad luck behind me. His fuel flask blew out right after he was launched, and his *kaiten* had to be recovered because it had no power after that.

I had some difficulty that day with my *kaiten*, but no more than usual, in spite of my sudden dive to 110 feet. Each *kaiten* had its own peculiarities, and even these changed from day to day, depending on how much the weapon had been used. Rust was our greatest enemy. It made valves difficult to control well. Grease was our second greatest, if maintenance men used too much of it. Sometimes, trying to help you, they greased the fittings and controls too much. When you operated these, the slippery liquid would get all over your hands. This time it was like that. I wiped my hands many times on my *fundoshi* to keep them clean. When I climbed out of the *kaiten* that day I must have had the filthiest underwear in Japan. The white cloth around my loins had turned to black by that time, but my control had been satisfactory. It had to be. I can say for the Imperial Navy that it never lowered its standards when seeking men for important jobs. An error now could still see me lose my chance to pilot a *kaiten*, in spite of all the time and effort invested in my training so far. I will not mention his name for fear of embarrassing him, but one officer I know of was immediately dismissed from the *kaiten* program when he lost a weapon in training.

We normally used antisubmarine ships for "targets" during training. But we often used passing ships, so as to save fuel of torpedo boats. Some of these ships belonged to the Army, which had its own submarine corps on the island of Oshima, in the Inland Sea. Not many foreigners know this, but the Imperial Japanese Army, dissatisfied with the Navy's desire to concentrate on building mostly fleet-type, long-range, cruising submarines, started building its own. They were large, fat, transport types.

There was no love lost between the Army and Navy. Most senior Army officers came from the peasant class in Japan, while most of our senior naval officers were the sons of *samurai*. As a result, most Navy people looked down on the Army. This gave rise to a humorous incident on March 1.

Petty Officer Yoshihito Yazaki, my very good friend and

roommate, was out in his *kaiten* when all antisubmarine boats were out hunting for an American submarine. A small, wooden Army supply boat was passing near Hikari, so Yazaki decided to get in some extra practice by making a run on it. He was about one and one-half miles from the target when he started out, and took a final look when about six hundred yards from the target ship. I was on board the observing craft, and one of the officers said, "An enemy ship would see him for sure." I answered at once, "What good would it do them? It would be too late for them to run away!" This was very brash for an enlisted man, but I had faith in my friend.

Yazaki passed directly under the target boat, as I knew he would. Then he came about and made another good pass, like the first. At that time the supply boat from Oshima hove into sight, on a course that would take it between Yazaki and us. Ensign Kozu tried to wave this craft away, but it kept right on going. Yazaki, making a run on it, was too near the surface, and crashed right into it.

The supply boat did a crazy zigzag after that, while we scanned the water for a sign of my friend. "There he is!" shouted someone as we arrived on the spot where the collision had taken place. I stripped at once to my *fundoshi*, seized a line and dove into the water. It was icy cold out there, but I managed to get the line through one of the *kaiten's* retrieving fittings. We got Yazaki aboard. He was all right, but a little stunned. We headed for the dock, put him ashore, and the observation boat returned to see if we could help the supply boat, whose crew had been dashing about frantically from the moment of the collision. Yazaki had a big lump on his forehead, but was feeling fine by the time I had taken a bath. I left him resting on his bed and went back to help the Army men. Their craft was leaking badly and had to be beached on Minase, a small islet not far from our *kaiten* dock.

By this time it was dark, and the Army officer in charge of the supply boat had been acting most arrogantly toward our executive officer, Lieutenant Miyata. "The Navy will take full responsibility," Lieutenant Miyata kept saying as we helped unload the supplies, but the Army man, although junior, kept berating him. So, when the job of unloading the boat was finished, Lieutenant Miyata said to

us, "You men might as well take along a few items as reward for your trouble."

That was all we needed to hear, for that boat was loaded
with delicacies destined for Army people on Oshima. There
were caramels, hard candy drops, sweet bean paste, hard
biscuits and many kinds of tinned foods. As *kaiten* men we
were able to get most of these things whenever we wanted
them, but the technicians who took care of our weapons
were not favored. All of us loaded ourselves down with all
we could carry and scurried toward the Hikari boats. Back
in the barracks we held a party, inviting everyone from
all over the place until the booty was all consumed. Yazaki,
and even the lump on his head, were worshipped.

All hands were still talking about the incident, smacking
their lips and sighing, *"Oishii!"* Delicious!" when an Army
delegation arrived at Hikari to protest the entire incident
and to complain particularly about the theft of rations. Of
course, none could be discovered, and the crash into the
boat was purely an accident. A formal apology was made,
but that was simply paperwork. We *kaiten* men didn't concern ourselves about it, nor did the technicians. We all felt
like the man who said, "We ought to have more such accidents around here!"

All this, of course, happened after my second launching
from a submarine. That had been I-58. My first launching,
on February 17, had been from I-368. It had not gone well.

Sometimes, in training, *kaiten* men made double runs on
a target. We came about for a second try after completing
the first one. This was in case, during combat, we missed
on the first try. We often discussed whether or not such a
tactic would work, since the enemy might have by that
time spotted our wake and opened up with deck guns or
depth charges. We also discussed the possibility of running
out of fuel in a long pursuit. Our oxygen supply would
operate the *kaiten* for an hour, and of course the mother
submarine could not possibly take a chance of recovering
us should that happen. I, however, had a special plan I
meant to follow in such an event. In combat my warhead
would not contain water, but three thousand pounds of
high-explosive. If I ever ran out of fuel, I would come to
the surface and lie there. In war, it is important to learn
all you can about the enemy. We knew the Americans were
great souvenir hunters. Also, it was very likely that they'd

try to recover my *kaiten*, so their ordnance experts could look it over. If they tried, I planned to remain perfectly still. I would let them hoist me out of the water. Then, as soon as I felt my weapon touch the deck I would throw a special switch each *kaiten* had, in case its nose detonator did not work, and take everyone on the American ship to eternity with me.

These thoughts were with me as the I-368 crew loosed my hold-down cables and released my weapon. My telephone line parted, and I was away, shut off from the world. There was to be just one run at the target ship. I made mine, dashing out first as instructed, hoisting my periscope for a last look, and then pushing ahead at full speed on a collision course.

My depth was set at thirty feet, so I could pass under the target safely. I held it well and ran a full minute more than was necessary. I wanted to clear the target so as not to be in the way of others sent out from I-368 after me. Then I surfaced, and the first sight I saw through my periscope was Gibiyama, a mountain peak north of Hikari. I was most smug. How simple, I thought! Being launched from a submarine was even easier than from a torpedo boat! They had given me good instructions, and I had followed them. No wonder Lieutenant Commander Itakura had such high hopes for the "seeing torpedo."

I headed for the pick-up boat. When I opened the hatch, Ensign Miyoshi's gentle face was peering in at me.

"How was the run?" he asked.

"Absolutely perfect! I had a good sighting, and had to adjust my course only once. A sure hit!"

"Such confidence!" he said, his eyes wide. I ignored this small thrust. At that moment, nowhere in the world was there a happier man than I. I strolled to the deckhouse, leaned against it and lit a cigarette, enjoying each puff as I watched other *kaiten* being recovered.

Lieutenant Kamiura was the scoring officer that day. He was late getting in with the target ship. We *kaiten* men washed, ate dinner, then went to the officers' quarters, our faces shining. He was there, a chart spread before him on a table. He was leaning over the chart.

I was most impolite and spoke sooner than I should have. "How did No. 2 do, Sir?" I asked.

Lieutenant Kamiura had not yet finished entering the

track of each weapon on the large paper. He should have reprimanded me, in spite of my eagerness, but instead looked up slowly. "Yokota?" he said. "Well, let me see . . . your wake was about 30 feet ahead of the target ship. Since your *kaiten* had already passed the target ship when we saw your wake, I should say that you missed by . . . about . . . 120 feet."

"What?" I was positive I had made a perfect intercept. Lieutenant Kamiura ignored my second outburst and kept on talking. He showed how all the others had made perfect intercepts. *"Banzai!"* yelled Kitamura, whose run would have taken him right into the center of a target. His wake was near the target boat's stern.

"Sir," I said, when Lieutenant Kamiura had finished congratulating everyone else, "perhaps my speed was just a little too great. My engine might not have been tuned finely. I might have indicated on my dials a slower speed than I was actually making. A thing like that would have put me ahead of the target. Sir, they'll really give me a lot of criticism at the next seminar, when they hear I was forty yards off the target. Can't you help me, please?"

Lieutenant Kamiura looked at me, half-smiling at my anxiety, and half-serious about my odd request. "Help you?" he asked. "How?"

My face grew even redder than it had been on learning of my wide miss. True, if I hit a large American ship 120 feet forward of her center I might still sink her. But I was worried. That was a pretty big margin for a man already selected to go out on a mission. With my training, I should have struck dead center, not ahead or astern.

"Couldn't you make it . . . perhaps . . . 60 feet instead, Sir?" I asked him.

His face grew stern. "Absolutely not, Yokota!" he said. "Others were watching the exercise as well as I. Would you make me a liar? Remember, exact reports are of utmost importance. Unless we make them, no one learns anything at the seminars." He started smiling then, for everyone else was laughing. "All you need, Yokota," he said, "are bigger targets. Perhaps we should save you especially for aircraft carriers. Let others take the smaller ships."

Everyone at once laughed even louder. I resigned myself to his determination and trudged back to my quarters. Actually, as the others kept assuring me, it really wasn't so bad for a first launching from a submarine. I would do better as the time went on. Calmness enveloped me. I'd go to the seminar and take my medicine. Surely I had handed out my share to others when they made errors.

It was not that way. I was not treated roughly at the seminar. Perhaps they thought it might be unfair to a man due soon for a mission, to disturb his mind with severe criticism. Aside from a few questions about my observations on surfacing for my final run-in, I was let off very lightly. The day of my first *kaiten* run from a submarine closed, in spite of everything, quite satisfactorily.

7 ▣ My Last Leave. Yazaki's Death

On March 3, I started home on leave. It was the custom to give men special leave just before sending them out on a *kaiten* mission. Mine had been set for March 1, but delayed when a staff officer from Sixth Fleet headquarters arrived for special consultations. I didn't mind too much. My leave was to be for four days, because I lived so far away, some four hundred miles from Hikari.

The night before my departure I was so excited I could hardly sleep. Comrades came to load me down with presents for my family. Hard-to-get candies, cigarettes, vitamin pills and tinned foods filled my small suitcase so I could hardly close it. When I got ready for bed I was very happy, but then I became worried. What would I tell my family when I met them? So far as they knew, I was still training as a flyer. Their mouths would be filled with questions I could not answer truthfully. The *kaiten* operation was too secret. I wouldn't even be able to tell them this would be the last time I would see them. Nor would I be allowed to tell them death was near for me. The Navy Ministry would tell them all that was necessary, later.

Lying to my family bothered me very much. I had been raised as a truthful boy. I had no knowledge of how to keep my face straight while telling a lie. My older sister, Chiyoe, would see deep into my heart at once. She would read the truth there. I knew I would fear all her glances, for she knew me better than I knew myself.

My pondering was interrupted by Ensign Iwao Kitagawa, who entered my room as I was undressing. He was chief of the maintenance section. His men looked after our weapons.

"My men have sent along some gifts for your family, Yokota," he said. He handed me candy, more cigarettes, and two bottles of whiskey. I made up my mind at once I would throw some of my own clothing out of the suitcase, if necessary, to include this last item. My father, whom I loved dearly, was fond of an occasional drink. I was sure that, with all alcoholic beverages severely rationed, he must have been foregoing this small pleasure for a long time. I would drink a toast with him out of one of the bottles. I would do my best to make my short stay at home a happy time for him. He would need some cheer. For four months now, the giant Boeing superfortresses had been attacking our homeland. Tokyo lay helpless before their might. The B-29's flew too high for most of our fighters to reach them, and Saipan was so far from our bases that only long-range *kamikaze* missions could reach it for an attack. These could not have been doing much damage. Radar, the curse of the Pacific war, would detect them while far away, allowing enemy fighters to rise up and wait in ambush for them.

Ensign Kitagawa teased me a little about not being able to sleep, then left. He knew how important this leave was to myself and other *kaiten* men, and why I was restless. When he returned a few minutes later, he had an album of phonograph records under his arm. "You once mentioned you had a record player at home, didn't you?" he said. "Take this with you."

I looked inside the album. It was Anton Dvorak's *New World Symphony*. Tears welled up in my eyes. A great many Japanese people have a deep interest in classical music. I knew what a precious gift this fine young officer was giving up. He had spun on his heel and left, though, before I could find words to express my appreciation.

March 3 opened beautifully, with a deep blue sky free of clouds. For once I did not have to think about the theory and practice of operating a *kaiten*. Nor whether I'd be selected for training. Nor selected for a mission. All that had been taken care of. I had not one military worry now. The thought of going home to visit my family gave me the same feeling I had as a child while preparing for a long excursion with my schoolmates.

Petty Officer Shinkai, Ensign Kato and I left the base together at 11:30 A.M. Our train would leave Hikari Station at noon. It was ten minutes late and had me worried. Japanese trains are most punctual. I thought our train might not come, because of the war. Perhaps it had been diverted to move troops or supplies. When it chugged into the station I was surprised to see how many empty seats there were. People didn't travel a lot, I thought to myself, because of the war.

We took seats near a window. Ensign Kato's home was in Sakuragicho, a section of Yokohama. Shinkai lived in Kobuchizawa, Yamanashi Prefecture, not far from sacred Mt. Fuji. I lived in Suginami Ward, Tokyo. Our train moved out of the station. Not long after starting its run along the shore of the highly-scenic Inland Sea it was on proper schedule.

Shinkai got off at Nagoya. He had to shift to another train line for the rest of his journey. Ensign Kato warned him, and myself at the same time, "Don't say too much while you are at home. Just smile, and try to make your families happy. The more you talk, the more likely you are to say something you shouldn't. You might reveal secret information."

We promised to remember, and Shinkai left. Ensign Kato and I chatted and dozed away the rest of the day and night. He got off the train at Yokohama, and shortly theraffter the train pulled into Tokyo Station. It was 2:30 P.M., over twenty-six hours since we left Hikari. A light rain was falling.

How good to be here, I thought! I strode through the station happily, laden down with treats, a loud song in my heart. Yet the appearance of the people I saw struck me as odd. They were scurrying back and forth, as people usually do in a big city, but they seemed busy in a different way than I remembered them. None of the young girls I saw were smiling. Nor were any of them chattering merrily, as most young girls are wont to do. Each was sober-faced. Each carried her thickly-padded cloth hood, which civilians wore during an air raid. Not a trace of femininity was to be seen, only old *kimono* and *mompei*, the baggy pants usually worn by farmers' wives or very poor working people. It was quite startling to find myself so full of happiness among people who wore sad looks or blank stares on their faces. How different from when I'd passed through Tokyo Station six months before, en route from Tsuchiura to Otsujima! Then the station had been crowded with the usual mad crush of smiling, happy people, on their way somewhere, for some purpose. Now I was among people who showed little life at all. If it was like this in Japan's capital city, what was it like elsewhere?

Back at Hikari, I had not thought much about civilians. Everything was wrapped up in my purpose for being there —to steer a *kaiten* straight into the enemy at top speed. At least, I thought, there was a purpose to my life. And I had a weapon to use in this war. These people had no purpose, except to wait and see which way the war would go. And they had no weapons. Perhaps that was why they looked so dull and lifeless.

A Lieutenant General of the Army strode by then. My smart salute brought me out of my reverie. I'd have to be back at Tokyo Station the next day, in order to catch a train that would return me to Hikari before my leave expired. No time could be wasted. I had to get home.

Before long I was among my family. Great cries of joy greeted me. *"Yuta-chan!"* shrieked my sisters. "Little younger brother! What a delightful surprise!" They embraced me, as did my father. They were full of questions. Why hadn't I told them I was coming? What was I doing in Tokyo? That's when I told my first lie. "I was sent to the big base at Yokosuka on an official errand," I said. "I can stay one night, and then I have to catch the train."

When they asked where my base was I hesitated to make an air of mystery, and said, "To the south." This threw them off, because they knew the locations of many air bases were kept very secret. They assumed I was stationed on Shokaku or Kyushu. The second is Japan's southernmost island, and the first forms the southern boundary of the Inland Sea. Many Navy pilots were flying from bases down that way to attack the enemy B-29's coming from Saipan.

More questions were asked throughout my stay, as friends stopped in to see the returning warrior. What kind of plane was I flying? Had I downed any of the enemy? Were the newer planes difficult to fly? I kept turning the talk away from military affairs, saying "I am safe and sound, as you can see. I am in good hands at my base. I enjoy my life there, and have many friends around me. So let's stop talking about me and my activities. Tell me, instead, what all of you have been doing."

Also visiting my home during my stay was an attractive young lady whom I had known before entering the Navy. I had her picture in my wallet when I first left home. If I had a sweetheart she was it, although we never talked of anything but school affairs, our families and the war. She promised to send me a neck scarf. I thanked her for this, inwardly hoping it would arrive before my departure date.

And so it went. We all talked far into the night. I did make the toast I promised myself with my father, too. I knew he'd enjoy the rest of that whiskey, hoarding it carefully to share with his oldest and closest friends. As I saw his face light up in pleasure. I gave inward thanks to Ensign Kitagawa and the kindness that prompted this gift from the maintenance men.

To myself I kept saying that the lies were really not a bad thing. Later, when my family was told how I had sunk a big American ship, they would understand. They would then have all the truth and would know why I had arrived home suddenly, without advance notice.

I had a total of twenty hours at home, only a few of which were spent in sleep. Chiyoe and Toshie, my sisters, came to the station to see me off. I watched the tears flow from the eyes of my beloved sisters, my two little mothers, as the train pulled out. I wanted to shout to them that we would soon meet again, at Yasukuni, the great shrine in Tokyo where men who died fighting for Japan are honored forever. Chiyoe and Tashie would visit there, clap their hands, bow their heads and talk with my soul, after the Navy Ministry informed them of my heroic death.

I sat down only after I could see them no more. Ashamed to let other passengers see a man in uniform weep, I held my face close to the window and let the tears run freely down my cheeks. In my hands I held *inari-zushi*, the fried bean curd delicacy my sisters had made for my train lunch. They knew how fond I had been of this in earlier days and had gone to great trouble to provide it. Later, as I ate it slowly, I wished I had not taken the leave. It had weakened my resolve about going out in a *kaiten*. I was no longer sure I had been right in volunteering. I missed my family much more than I realized, and those I had not been able to see in Tokyo, my nephews and niece, for instance. They had been evacuated to the country after the bombings had begun. Too, if I had one more day of leave, I might have been able to visit my schoolteacher. I urged the train to hurry, to bring me back to Hikari swiftly. There, among men who were determined to die, I could put such thoughts behind me.

On the day after my return to Hikari I rode double in

a *kaiten*. Ensign Kitagawa wanted to see for himself how the *kaiten* were operated. He asked permission of the base commander, received it, and selected my *kaiten* for his familiarization ride. At 9:00 A.M. he hurried to where I was standing by my *kaiten* and said, "Let's go, Yokota!" He added in a joking tone, "Please do not strike any rocks today."

We moved out into the bay and boarded the *kaiten* while it was lashed to the side of a torpedo boat. I hunched down, making myself as small as possible, so Ensign Kitagawa could squeeze in behind me. It was a good thing he was so small. I don't know how we would have managed it otherwise.

Our starting time was 9:30. From the shore I had noticed that waves were kicking up and thought what fun it would be to give an officer a rough ride. He'd have something exciting to talk about with his men later. As things turned out, we both had something exciting to talk about for we nearly lost our lives.

Upon pushing the starter bar, I set my depth for twenty-one feet. We ran along smoothly for about ten minutes, then the *kaiten* went into an unexplained dive. As the angle grew steeper, I did my best to keep from crying out in shock. I wanted to appear most competent before the chief of the men who went to so much trouble for me and the other pilots. I went about trying to establish control.

Ensign Kitagawa was calm also. "Is this normal in your experience?" he asked.

"No," I said, "but we will recover shortly." My weapon had other ideas, though. I watched the depth indicator show 50 feet, then 60 feet, then 75 feet. This wasn't so good. My chart showed bottom at 95 feet. In spite of my best efforts to recover, all happened so fast that we suddenly drove into the muddy bottom with a thump, my inclinometer showing that we were sticking up at an angle of 22 degrees. My bow was well into the mud.

I couldn't figure out what had happened, but here we were, my depth gauge showing 105 feet. "I'm sorry, Sir," I told Ensign Kitagawa, "but we appear to be stuck on the bottom of the bay."

Still, he was calm. "What time is it?" he asked me.

I told him, and he said, "Well, by using the purifier, we should have plenty of oxygen for many hours. We can't be very far from the torpedo boat, so they should have no trouble locating us. Meanwhile, we might as well relax and have a little chat."

Here I was, deeply embarrassed at putting this fine officer in this dangerous position, and all he could say was, "Let us have a little chat." True, our propeller was still turning over. If the engine kept running, oxygen bubbles from my exhaust would keep floating up to the surface. Once a search started, along the course I had taken, the torpedo boat crew should sight us easily if the waves were not too high.

An hour passed. It was now getting close to eleven o'clock. Ensign Kitagawa spoke to me urgently. "Yokota," he said, "your body is very valuable to our country. You have had much training which cannot be quickly replaced. You are worth more than I. If they do not find us, get out of here by any means posible. I don't think this accident is your fault. It could be mine. Perhaps the inspection conducted by my men overlooked some defect."

He was blaming himself for our predicament. I knew his thoughts. He had lost face, or would if an examination of this *kaiten* upon recovery showed something mechanically wrong. I tried to cheer him up.

"Please don't talk that way, Sir," I said. "I'll get out the emergency rations. And we could have a drink of whiskey to help us against the cold."

Under the pilot's seat in every *kaiten* was a small box of emergency food. It included a canteen holding less than a pint of whiskey. I brought this out, and we took drinks alternately. The small sips warmed us, and we began to feel better.

Some time passed. Finally Ensign Kitagawa said, "The waves must be higher than when we started, and giving them trouble in the search for us. It's a shame, too, because our dear friends, the Americans, are being spared one ship if no one saves you for your mission, Yokota."

I was about to answer, playing down his high opinion of me, when we both heard a gun report overhead. They found us, just 100 minutes after we had left the torpedo boat. About 20 minutes later a diver was walking around on top of my *kaiten* and hammering the signal, "Are you all right inside?" I rapped out an answer that all was well, and pretty soon we felt the weapon being hoisted up from the bottom of the bay. Heaven had seen fit to spare both of us.

That incident gave me plenty to talk about for a while, and a letter from the young lady in Tokyo gave me much to think about. I wrote her at once, asking if she could send the neck scarf in time for it to reach me before the twentieth. That was a hard letter to write, for fear of giving out information I should not, so I hinted that I might be transferred and my neck scarf would not catch up with me unless it came quickly.

Then good news captured my attention. On March 13, Lieutenant, junior grade, Miyoshi, who had been promoted while I was on leave, informed us that I-47 would carry us out into battle. What a relief! We had been fearing that I-368 would do the job, not knowing that she had been sunk off Iwo Jima.

I-47 had carried Lieutenant Nishina and others of the Kikusui Group to the first *kaiten* attack, on Ulithi. She had also fired *kaiten* into Humboldt Bay, Hollandia, New Guinea. Officially, she was credited with eight enemy ships from *kaiten* attacks. Her captain, Lieutenant Commander Zenji Orita, was one of our finest submarine commanders. He had operated off the American coast and in the Solomon Islands. He had a top crew, also, who were very proud of I-47. "Our submarine is the 'no death ship,'" they boasted, a motto they derived from the ship's hull number.

Kanji, the ideographs with which the Japanese language is written, can be "read" in different ways. I-47 crewmen did this with their ship's hull number. On the conning tower it bore "47-I," meaning "submarine, hull number 47." The Kanji characters were "shi" (four), "nana" (seven), "i" (I). When run together, they can also make "shinanai," which means "don't die" or "never die" or any similar interpretation meaning "immortal" that one may wish to give it. The crew's record of sinkings and safe escapes from enemy detection had made them believe that, truly, their submarine possessed a charmed life. Their spirit was known to be among the highest in the Imperial Navy. We were pleased to be sailing with them, and hoped to keep their *kaiten* record perfect.

"The name of your group will be Tatara," Lieutenant Miyata told us. "You will depart on March 27, to attack enemy shipping in the vicinity of Okinawa." I-47 could carry six *kaiten*, so Ensign Kishie Kirizawa was added to our group. We set about final training with a strong will, being launched next day from I-47 for practice. That day, March 14, we set an all-time high for *kaiten* men. Every one of the six of us—Lieutenant Miyoshi, Ensigns Kato and Kirizawa and we three petty officers—passed directly under the target ship. Every run was perfect. Had it been combat, the Americans would have lost six fine ships and many hundreds, perhaps thousands, of men.

Less than a week after the night I spent with my family in Tokyo, a great fleet of American B-29's had raced in at low level and showered the city with fire bombs. Stripped of nearly all armament so they could make greater speed and carry large bomb loads, these monsters swept in and scattered destruction, taking the capital by complete surprise. By the morning of March 11, Tokyo was one vast field of fire. Just as in the Great Kanto Earthquake of September 1, 1923, high winds generated by the fire itself scorched the earth. This horrifying news had me watching the mails closely, and I relaxed only after learning that the red sweep of death had been centered mainly in the downtown section of Tokyo. Out in Suginami Ward, my family should be safe, although over 125,000 Japanese were killed and 1,000,000 left homeless. Then more tragedy came, with the death of my closest friend, Petty Officer Yoshihito Yazaki.

It happened on the last day of our submarine training, March 16. We were to get in one last practice. I-47 would then depart for the giant shipyard at Kure for last-minute outfitting. She would later return to pick up us six *kaiten* men and our weapons before steaming out through Bungo Strait into the Pacific. With each of us, of course, would be one leading seaman or petty officer, acting as personal maintenance man to each weapon.

We would be part of the fifth *kaiten* group to go out on a sortie. The first had been Kikusui, meaning "floating chrysanthemum," after the flower-and-water crest of Masashige Kusunoki's family. The second was Kongo, named after the mountain near which Kusunoki's retainers trained. The third was the Chihaya, named for the mighty castle south of Nara, our country's ancient capital. That had been Kusunoki's castle. Ensign Okayama, who'd made us take such a long run before breakfast, died with the Chihaya

Group. Fourth was the Shimbu Group, which did not accomplish anything, being called back due to change in
operational policies at Sixth Fleet headquarters. I-58 and
I-36 had gone out, the latter returning March 9, and Lieutenant Commander Hashimoto's submarine on the 16th, the
day of Yazaki's death. "Shimbu," translated freely, means
"God's Warriors," and such a glorious name must have
seemed a bitter irony to Lieutenant, junior grade, Minoru
Kakizaki, Lieutenant, junior grade, Hajime Maeda, Petty
Officer Shichiro Furukawa and Petty Officer Shigeo Yamaguchi, of whom I will tell much more later. They had gone
out as a unit before, with the Kongo Group in I-56, and
had been turned back by antisubmarine nets in the Admiralties. Now they were back again, without seeing action.

The morning of the day I-58 returned to Kikari from
the recalled sortie, March 16, was cloudy. Winds were high,
and made the bay waters very choppy. Yazaki, Kitamura
and I noticed this at once as we went to the *kaiten* shed,
but it didn't bother us at all. "Rough water like that will
make it more nearly like actual combat in the open sea,"
we agreed as we got ready to board the submarine. This
was not the same sentiment expressed by others when,
after breakfast, we had gone to the officers' quarters. Captain Orita and some of his officers were there, as well as
Lieutenant Keisuke Miyata, our base executive officer.

"It doesn't look very good out there today," said Miyata,
"and it will probably get a lot worse. Perhaps it would be
best to cancel today's operation."

"That would be silly!" said Lieutenant Miyoshi, ignoring
the rank of the other officers present. "The submarine returns to Kure tonight. It is our last opportunity to practice
being launched from a submarine. Surely we cannot cancel
it just because of a few small waves!'

The rest of us, standing behind our leader, could have
no voice in this discussion, of course. But we all nodded
our heads vigorously in agreement. Miyoshi was right. What
was Miyata thinking of, anyway! Anything that would
make us more capable of performing our duty could not be
passed up. And anyway, how did he expect us to sink great
ships in the open sea if we were going to let a little rough
water in a bay hold us back?

"Well, Sir, what do you think?" asked Miyata, turning
to Captain Orita.

"True," said Orita, "it is rough out there. Perhaps even too rough for good vision through the short periscopes of the *kaiten*." He sounded as though he was ready to agree to the cancellation. I cannot be sure, though, for at that moment his executive officer, Lieutenant Obori, spoke up.

"Since the *kaiten* men themselves seem so anxious to get on with it, Sir," Obori said, "let us do it. We can't very well refuse them training they desire, can we?"

That closed the argument. The scheduled training would take place.

None of us had to help load *kaiten* on that occasion, so we were taken on a tour of the submarine. I was fascinated by what a precise instrument of warfare I-47 was. No area seemed bigger than six feet square. Yet important equipment had been installed where it should be located, with every inch of space employed effectively.

We were shown through the officers' wardroom, where a small shrine had been mounted on one wall. A small piece of white cardboard, about three inches by five inches, hung from it, bearing the word: "My offering . . . one large aircraft carrier." It was signed by Sekio Nishina, first *kaiten* man to make a kill. There were also mementos from the other seven *kaiten* men who had set forth from I-47 on their one-way rides to death. The sight was deeply inspiring to all of us. We knew that, in a few weeks, six more such cards would be added and that they would bring courage and inspiration to the *kaiten* men who came after us.

The officers, who had been most friendly all this time, offered the six of us some chestnuts. We were still munching on them when word came that all *kaiten* had been loaded, so we went on deck for a final look. I-47 had been redesigned to carry six *kaiten* instead of four, and all had access tubes running to them from the submarine's hull so that they could be manned without having to surface the ship.

Before long we were out in the bay, ready to start on our final submarine practice. Yazaki, during a chat with me in the submarine's toilet, warned me to be careful. "Those high waves can throw you off, Yokota," he said. "They can flip you up and into the target ship easily, or throw your controls off the other way, sending you right to the bottom. Be very careful."

"Shimpai nai!" I told him, "Don't worry!" Yazaki had always shown his friendship for me in many ways, sharing his tobacco when I had none and telling me in detail every little thing he learned in his own *kaiten* training. I had a deep affection for him, he was so helpful to everyone and of such cheerful disposition at all times. You could count on him to boost your spirits when they were low, to say some humorous thing that would make you laugh and come up out of a sad spell.

It was really rough that day outside the bay, rougher than one could realize from the shore. I had a most difficult time sighting my target for the final run-in. I did it, though, and was sure I'd done well as I swung around to return to the waiting pick-up boat. I was the last *kaiten* of the six to be fired, and I assumed the others would be waiting for me when I climbed out onto the deck. All were, except Yazaki. My face grew as worried as the other four when there still was no sign of him after another half an hour.

"He'll be all right," Miyoshi kept saying. "All launches will search for him. It's not likely he got stuck on the bottom. It's too deep out here for that." But Miyoshi's face was as pale as ours. He was even more worried than we, and trying to hide it.

Better if we had been inside the bay, I thought. Then Yazaki could hammer on the side of his *kaiten,* as Ensign Kitagawa and I had done when we heard a rescue vessel overhead. But if my friend had gone down in the open sea, no one would ever find him. No diver could reach him. He would die alone, unaided.

Just then one of the torpedo boat crewmen, looking through binoculars, shouted, "One of our boats has the *kaiten* in tow! They are heading this way!"

We gave a great shout of exultation. "I'll wait here for him," said Miyoshi. "The rest of you go on ahead and fill out your reports while I try to find out what kind of trouble Yazaki had."

Ensign Kato led the rest of us to the officers' quarters, where Lieutenant Miyata recorded our charts and our statements. We told him the other two had been delayed, but would be along in a few minutes. When thirty minutes passed without their appearing, we began to grow impatient. Ensign Kato told Kitamura to see what was keeping them. The rest of us then turned back to our discussion of the training session. We were still talking when Miyoshi and Kitamura entered the room.

"Sir . . ." they began, addressing Lieutenant Miyata, "Yazaki . . ." Lieutenant Miyata did not wait to hear more. Their tone was enough for him. He rushed from the room, all of us following him to the waterfront. Maintenance men were lifting Yazaki from his *kaiten* and placing him on a litter. I rushed up to them.

"Yazaki! Yazaki!" I shouted, taking my friend by the shoulders and shaking him. Though his arms dangled limply from the litter, he showed no signs of injury. His face had plenty of color, too, the cheeks rosier than ever. "Come on!" I shouted to everyone, and we rushed with the litter to the infirmary. There artificial respiration was applied at once and kept up for more than two hours. The medical officer finally made us stop. It was no use, he said. Yazaki was dead.

Thus did my friend pass from life, only ten days before we were to set out on our mission. The doctor said he had suffocated, dying when carbon dioxide leaked from the exhaust into the operator's chamber of his *kaiten*. I started to curse the maintenance men, then stopped. Those mechanics had always shown such concern for us *kaiten* pilots, working far into the night to make sure our weapons were in the very best condition. I could not blame them for my friend's death, even if it had been due to someone's small mistake.

For the rest of that day and night, I was a pot full of mixed feelings. My final thought was that, like Lieutenant Sekio Nishina, I would see that my friend realized his ambition, in spite of everything. Petty Officer Yoshihito Yazaki would ride a *kaiten* into the enemy still. I would carry his ashes in my compartment on the final run.

8 ☐ Another Tragedy, and Mission Reorganization

Petty Officer Kikuo Shinkai was chosen to replace my lost Yazaki. His ability in handling a *kaiten* was well-known. Shinkai was held in high esteem by observer officers, instructors and the rest of us for his skill. In fact, on February 13, when I had been selected by Miyoshi for a mission, I had wondered a little why Shinkai had not been asked to sortie with the Tatara Group instead of one of us. It seemed there was no particular reason. Miyoshi had been allowed to select his own companions. He had chosen Yazaki, Kitamura and myself.

So, since Yazaki had to be replaced, I was pleased that Shinkai was the man chosen. He had been a friend of mine since my early days at Tsuchiura. When I had been chosen to go with the Tatara people, he did not complain or make bitter comments. All he had said was, "Good fortune, Yokota. I will not be long behind you. Wait for me outside Yasukuni Shrine. We will enter together, like true comrades." There had been frequent mention of Yasukuni among us *kaiten* men. We used to tease sometimes, saying, "I will arrive at Yasukuni before you do, and will therefore be senior." We'd talk then about all the awful things we planned to do to the later arrivals.

I-47 had moved on to Kure for refitting and reprovisioning, but we still had nine days of training ahead of us before departure. We worked with all our might. At first I did harbor dark thoughts about deliberately crashing my *kaiten* into a rock in the bay, so as to join my dear friend in death. In my *kaiten* I spoke aloud to him, though, and turned back to my resolve to carry his remains with me against the enemy. The sharp pain of loss was eased somewhat a few days later, when the promised gift from the young lady in Tokyo arrived.

It was a crimson neck scarf, a muffler, made of knitted material. Pilots of Japanese aircraft wore white silk mufflers, and I thought this would be one. I was glad of the red color, though. It would be different.

Many Japanese men who went to war had sweethearts, about whom they talked sometimes, and to whom they wrote daily. I, of course, had none. I was only nineteen years old at the time and had been nearly two years in the Navy. This girl had given me her picture a long time before, dressed in the sailor-suit type uniform Japanese schoolgirls wore. At Tsuchiura I had been reprimanded for having it, because it might distract me from my duty of training to fly airplanes. I still had it, but never showed it to anyone. When one is banded together with men who have pledged to give their lives for their country, such ties to life are dangerous. In truth, I did not really have a sweetheart, just a friend. But, I told myself, if I did have one, perhaps it would be this young lady. I began to think romantic thoughts, and that night I wore the red muffler to bed. I would keep it with me at all times, I promised myself, right to the last moment of my life.

That was on March 19. On March 20, four days after Yazaki died from exhaust fumes, tragedy pierced my heart again. Lieutenant Mamoru Miyoshi died in his *kaiten*.

The day was a rainy one, but weather had no part in the accident. Perhaps Miyoshi made some kind of mistake in maintaining proper depth, or perhaps one of his instruments was out of adjustment. In any case, as he passed beneath the target ship, he was running too shallow. His periscope struck on the underside of the target ship's hull. At a speed of thirty knots, my division officer and *kaiten* group leader was thrown against the periscope eyepiece and knocked unconscious. It had to be that way. He drowned in the water that leaked into his *kaiten* when the periscope's top was sheared off. If he were conscious, he might have been able to open the top hatch and swim away.

I later learned that he had no chance whatever. The *kaiten* was recovered, and the top hatch could not be opened. His body had to be removed through the bottom one, a great mass of water pouring out when it was opened. When I saw his body, I could not say a word. Two tragedies in five days was too much. I followed the litter bearers as they carried Miyoshi's body to the infirmary. Everyone there became very excited and tried to help. Artificial respiration was applied, on the slim chance life might be revived. I was so upset I lost my senses; I found myself rubbing his naked body with a rough towel, trying to restore blood circulation. When the doctor finally announced that Miyoshi was beyond all help, I broke down completely. Weeping, I ran from the room.

I recalled a conversation I'd had with Miyoshi just one day before Yazaki's death. Though we enlisted men associated closely with officers during training and spent a great deal of time with them, we never really were close personally, so far as discussing our families, and so forth, was concerned. But on that day Lieutenant Miyoshi surprised me. He began talking about his home life.

"I was born in Ogikubo, Yokota," he told me. I was surprised. Ogikubo was on the western outskirts of Tokyo. I was born in Koenji, not far from there. He had gone to Tokyo Prefectural Sixth Middle School. What a coincidence! To get there he would have had to take the Chuo Line, which I had so often ridden. I had met many students from his school on that train. Perhaps we had once spoken to each other! How strange life was, that two men who were born not far apart, and led widely different lives, should be joined together in something like the *kaiten* training program.

In Japan boys are raised to show great devotion to their parents, but Miyoshi was a model for all of us to follow. He wrote home daily to his mother and talked often of her to others. His filial piety was complete, and a beautiful thing to observe. So I knew how sad he must have felt as he told me how, during his leave, he had not found his mother home when he arrived there. Food was not easily come by at that stage in the war. Rationing was severe; all diets cut nearly in half. People had to add to it as they could, so Miyoshi's mother had gone all the way across Tokyo, to Chiba, east of the capital, to obtain some vegetables at the farm of her maid's parents, who lived on the long peninsula that forms the eastern boundary of Tokyo Bay. When Miyoshi heard this, he told me, he simply collapsed on a couch in his house, overcome by grief.

He showed me a picture of his mother, who was most beautiful. He told me he had no sweetheart but her, which made me very envious. My own mother had died when I was five years old. I had two wonderful sisters who did their best to take her place, but Miyoshi's adoring glance at his mother's photograph showed me in one instant how much I had missed in the years I was growing up.

Like myself, Miyoshi had only one day at home. At the last minute, fortunately, his mother arrived. They had but twenty minutes together at the station before he started back to Hikari. How grief-stricken the woman would be when she learned of her son's death. She might never learn how brave and wonderful he was, and how we, his men, adored him. The Navy Ministry would probably disclose no details, just say, that he had "died in action." She would not know how, or where and, since the rest of us would also die, might never learn.

I was thinking about this as, still weeping, I bumped into Lieutenant Miyata. Our executive officer had heard the news. He was no doubt sad, too, but was abrupt and sharp with me. It was perhaps the best way to deal with me at the time.

"Your tears will not please the spirit of your leader, Yokota," said Lieutenant Miyata, "nor will they help you." His voice grew deep and angry as I continued weeping. "Your country needs you more than ever now, with two trained *kaiten* men lost. A military man must keep going forward, as you've been told many times, even if he has to advance over the bodies of his beloved comrades."

I tried to establish some composure, and did steady myself. Then, to prove that bad luck comes in threes, Ensign Kato fell sick and was dropped from the mission. He had earlier spent some time in the hospital, after crashing into a submerged submarine with his *kaiten*. Never a robust person, the hard training of the past three weeks had put its mark on him. All of us had urged him many times to see the medical officer, but he would not hear of it. In spite of his poor physical condition, he kept training as diligently as the rest of us. "All I need do," he said, "is hang on until we are safely out to sea. After that, it will not matter whether I am ill or not, so long as I can steer my *kaiten*." He would give a little laugh then, and add, "After all, one does not have to be in the best of health for dying, does one?"

Two shocks in such a short time caused the final undoing of Ensign Kato. Miyoshi had been loved by all, and Yazaki was Kato's particular favorite. Kato collapsed the day Miyoshi died and was taken to the hospital. His condition was diagnosed as extreme weakness, his health having been completely run down. Later he trained again, after much rest, but finally ended the war training other *kaiten* men, on shore. Physical and mental strain prevented his operating a weapon at a degree of skill high enough for him to be assigned a later mission.

Kato's collapse left Kitamura, Shinkai and myself in quite a quandary. Half our original group of six pilots had been eliminated. This was a bad thing. *Kaiten* groups were made up of men who had very nearly equal training in the weapon. There was no one at Hikari who could be brought up to our level of training in the few days remaining. At our barracks we worried ourselves much about this. Then, on March 23, a sailor came and said Lieutenant Miyata wanted to see Shinkai and me at once.

We went to the executive officer's quarters. Lieutenant Mitani, one of the maintenance officers, was there with him.

"Your group has been dissolved," said Lieutenant Miyata, "but I-47 will still go out as scheduled, after a short delay." He gazed intently at us, perhaps to see if we had lost our spirit after the triple tragedy. We returned his look calmly, to show we were still ready.

"At Otsujima right now," he said, "are four men who had to return from the Kongo mission without being fired. They are still training there, but will depart from this base. Chief of the group is Lieutenant, junior grade, Minoru Kakizaki. You two will join his group. Do you understand?"

"Yes, Sir," we said. We were surprised at this turn of events. A few moments before we had been concerned that no one at Hikari had as much experience as we did. Now we were assigned to fight beside true veterans, who had been out to the war and back.

The other three men who had gone to Manus, in the Admiralties, and had to turn back when antisubmarine nets blocked their approach to the enemy anchorge, were Maeda, Furukawa and Yamaguchi. Lieutenant Hajime Maeda was what we called in Japan a "typical Kyushu boy." On that southern island lived the mighty Satsuma clan, which had always produced our nation's hardiest seafarers. Most of our senior naval officers were from Kyushu, and it was a great achievement for a boy from any other part of Japan to win appointment to the naval academy.

Kyushu was, you might say, all-Navy, and boys in that part of Japan usually grew up with a strong love for the sea.

Shichiro Furukawa was the typical Imperial Navy chief petty officer, smart and tough. He was older than the rest of us and had been in the Navy seven years. He was truly an expert on torpedoes. They were his life. But he had not hesitated when volunteers for *kaiten* training were sought. Furukawa was an honor graduate of torpedo school and was held in great respect by all the officers. It was a privilege to be associated with him.

Petty Officer Shigeo Yamaguchi had also come from torpedo school. He was serious, too, but only on duty. When off-duty he relaxed completely, and he had a great capacity for *sake*. He could drink nearly two quarts of it and hardly show any effects at all. Shinkai and I really felt like young amateurs alongside these men.

It was too bad Kitamura had been left out, Shinkai and I thought. We felt sorry for him, but Shinkai was optimistic. "One man had to be left behind," he told me, "and we were lucky. Kitamura won't have to wait very long. As good as he is, he will be getting his chance soon enough."

Later, in the bathhouse, soaking in the big tub, I thought once again of Yazaki and Miyoshi. How sad they must have felt, on dying before they intended. Well, wherever they were, I would be joining them soon. It would be good to look upon them. And upon my dear mother, whom I did not recall very well because of being so young when she died. Then I realized again that neither Yazaki's nor Miyoshi's mothers knew how their sons had died. It made me sad.

I was still in this mood as I got out of the *ofura* and started to dry myself. Shinkai came in at that moment and spoke to me softly. "After you're dressed, Yokota, we'll have a small celebration. I have a bottle of whiskey Ensign Anzai gave to me. And a little food, too."

"What if we are caught drinking?" I asked. Selection or not, we could still be dismissed from the *kaiten* group for disciplinary reasons. It's odd, now that I think back on it, but it was actually possible at Hikari and Otsujima for men who had volunteered for death to be sent away from the base if they did not obey every regulation.

"We won't be caught," said Shinkai. "We'll be quiet."

I joined him and Petty Officer Teruyoshi Ishibashi, another *kaiten* pilot, a few minutes later. My hot bath had left me feeling a little weak in the knees, and the alcohol took effect almost at once. Before long I was totally drunk, for the first time in my life. Shinkai and I woke up the next morning flat on our backs on his bed, where Ishibashi had thoughtfully dumped us when we passed out on the floor. We both had terrible headaches when we were introduced to Lieutenant Kakizaki.

"I am pleased to meet you men," he said. "They tell me you two are the best *kaiten* men here at Hikari. That is good. We will have a training session this afternoon, and I will take great pleasure in observing your performance from the target boat."

Shinkai and I looked at one another. Our heads felt so big that we should have been carrying them in baskets. And now this officer was going to check us over! What a catastrophe this could be. And what a mistake it had been getting drunk! True, we had reason for it. The deaths of two friends and the illness of a third had thrown down our spirits, and the alcohol had made us happy and able to forget for a while. Now we would pay for those carefree hours. I was so nervous that all I could do was answer, "Yes, Sir," and leave. I completely forgot to make the special request of Kakizaki I had planned. I meant to ask him if he would carry Miyoshi's ashes with him in his *kaiten* while I was carrying Yazaki's.

Walking out, I was despondent. If I didn't make a good showing Kakizaki might regret my being assigned to his group. I wanted him to have faith in me. Also, together with Shinkai, I had the responsibility of upholding the Tsuchiura tradition and the honor of the First Division and of my dead comrades, who had helped me train to the point where men from Otsujima had been told fine things about us.

Meeting Furukawa and Yamaguchi didn't help. They looked so efficient and competent that Shinkai and I grew more worried than ever. We kept making excuses to slip away, soaking our heads secretly in cold water at the bathhouse. At 5:00 P.M. we went out for a run. By that time I was feeling a lot better. Once I stepped into my *kaiten*, my head mysteriously cleared completely. I was where I belonged now, all my confidence back. I was certain I would do a good job.

The target ship, a small wooden one, was moving at a good speed. Waves were not high, though, and that helped a lot. This practice was supposed to be a double run, each *kaiten* making a second strike at the target after passing beneath it once. This, as I have said earlier, was in case we missed in combat and had to try again.

After launching, I ran for a while, then surfaced for a look. The target was in good position, 50 degrees to my left, about 700 yards distant. From this position, I decided, I had an excellent chance. I dipped down, swung to an intercept course and pushed my *kaiten* to 40 knots. I stayed down for a full three minutes, and came up for a new look, before making my second run. The target was then to my right. I came about, pointed my bow at her, established her course and speed again, made quick notations on my chart, picked a new intercept course and made for her underwater, a second time. Lieutenant Kakizaki gave me the results of my runs a little while later.

"You splashed too much when you made your sightings, Yokota," he said. "You'll have to be more careful than that." He meant that my periscope was up for more than the maximum seven seconds allowed us, causing me to make a spray with it. Usually I was able to make the necessary sighting in five seconds or less, my many trips in the *kaiten* making me proficient in this skill. But on that day I must have been distracted, perhaps by fear of making a poor showing, for he had seen my periscope twice.

"On your first run," he said, "you passed fifteen feet astern of the target. On your second, you were forty-five feet ahead." This wasn't so bad. If it had been a large American ship, I would have hurt it seriously, quite probably enough to sink it. I would have caught it in the bow or stern.

Shinkai's runs were similar to mine. When Lieutenant Kakizaki said we had done well, we smiled. We were very relieved. I knew there'd be no more private drinking parties for us in the future.

"Now, then," said Kakizaki, "I want all of us to dine together this evening. Your meals will be brought to my room. All four of you petty officers will come there at dinnertime."

At once I caught the old feeling we had enjoyed at Otsujima, where these men had been training. Here was a

Naval Academy man who did not stand on ceremony with his men. He and Maeda acted at dinner like old friends, not officers who had to associate with enlisted men for duty. They were informal and made the rest of us feel in every way at ease. I mean myself and Shinkai, actually. Their bond with Yamaguchi and Furukawa was one of long standing, since they had been together for more than three months. But they gladly extended it to include Shinkai and myself. A strong feeling of friendship grew quickly between us and these men who had already once gone to the brink of death.

At both Otsujima and Hikari, there were those who felt that *kaiten* men selected for a mission should have their last few days free to consummate any desires they might have. They should be given complete freedom of action, some persons used to say. After all, they were about to sail off to certain death. None of the Tatara Group, I'm proud to say, ever uttered thoughts like these. They were as composed and dignified a group of men as one could imagine. They paid no attention when those of different leanings proposed that departing *kaiten* men be furnished whatever alcohol, food or women they liked. My associates were polite, but did not join in such conversations. They were friendly to everyone, as well as to one another. None wore sad looks, nor overly proud ones, as you really could expect of people who were the best-trained of any *kaiten* men up to that moment. In addition to all these things, they laughed a lot and said many humorous things to make other people laugh.

This made me wonder about myself. Outwardly I tried to act like them, to look composed and to be light-hearted, but inside I was full of tension, counting the days to our departure. I was curious about what the other five were thinking. Had Maeda really given up all thought of living? Did Kakizaki think often of his family? And Furukawa, who had been cited twice for bravery since the war's beginning. He was supposed to have a sweetheart. Did he long for her? And what about Yamaguchi? Could he put from his mind all that he would leave behind? How could he and the others be so nonchalant in these last remaining hours?

I tried to get some answers to these questions one evening from Furukawa. We were in our room, having just taken a bath. The four petty officers all lived together.

"Furukawa," I asked him, "have you written your will?" Japanese soldiers and sailors, about to face the enemy and possible death, often wrote memorials so those they loved would have something of those last few hours to treasure. Unlike the Occidental idea of a will, it didn't always bequeath something. Instead, it was a parting message, composed in the hope it would live on long after its author. There are many famous such wills in Japanese song and literature.

"Why do you ask?" said Furukawa, smiling.

"Well . . . not for any special reason. . . ." I stammered. "It's just that you have gone out once already and know what things are usually done by *kaiten* men at this time."

"Wills are all nonsense!" said Furukawa. "I'm not going to write any will. I did write one, when we were out before. Then, when I-56 couldn't get us close enough to the enemy, and we had to turn back, I read that will. It was so pompous and presumptuous that I actually blushed when I read it. So I tore it up and threw it away. Men like us don't need to write a memorial of ourselves. If we were truly great men, with lots of people wanting to know our last thoughts, that would be a different matter. But when one is not himself a great man, it is silly for him to try to write great things.

"Last night, for example, one of the mechanics came to me. He asked me to write on a strip of white cloth for him. He wanted a message, he said, for a keepsake. I told him over and over that I had nothing to say, but he insisted. So I wrote down what I had to say: *MU*—nothing—in great sweeping strokes!"

He laughed loudly as he recalled the incident, and the look on that mechanic's face.

I laughed, too, and agreed it was a good joke. "But," I said, getting serious again, "don't you think we at least ought to write something for the members of our families?"

"It's not necessary," said Furukawa. "My family knows me. I am a Navy man. They know how I think. They know how I feel. All I care is that someone tells them that I died like a Navy man, gallantly, and in battle. When I first joined this Navy I told my family that I would meet death bravely if the time came. They are aware of my feeling.

Now the time has come, that's all. No need to scribble about it. Besides, it's just too much trouble."

Petty Officer Yamaguchi was just sitting there, listening to all of this and smiling. Every once in a while he would nod agreement with Furukawa's words. "*So da!*" he would say, "That's right!" The conversation turned to other things after Furukawa finished, but I kept thinking what wonderful men this pair were. The mission was everything to them. Everything else was, as Furukawa had written, nothing.

The thought of a will still lingered in me, however. After the others were asleep, I sat up, thinking. Finally I took my suitcase down from the shelf, found some note paper and sat on my bunk, using the suitcase for a writing desk. My will would be written, whether the others' were or not.

My Dear Father, Elder Brother, and Sisters,

Please forgive me, I could not say it in Tokyo before, but now I speak my last goodbye to you. The truth is that I have not been piloting planes for many months. I have been training instead in a new weapon, a guided torpedo which I shall ride alone. We are going out for an attack very soon. That is why I had special leave, so I could come and see you. I am proud to be going out. What would become of God's favored country, Japan, and her history of three thousand years, if we refused to make sacrifices of ourselves for the Empire?

I will die the moment my torpedo hits an enemy ship. My death will be full of purpose. We have been educated here to forget all small things, and to think only of the one big thing. I lied to you when I said I was flying fighter planes. Please forgive me. When you hear that I have died after sinking an enemy ship, I hope you will have kind words to say about my gallant death.

I have no regrets, nor anything more to say. All of you have always been very kind to me, and I have done nothing in return for this kindness. But please remember always that I thank you from the bottom of my heart.

Masakuzu and Shinji, my nephews, and Setsuko, my niece, I hope that the three of you will grow into great personages, and always honor your parents. I shall be looking down on you always after my death. If you want to meet your uncle, come and visit Kudan. I will be waiting there to greet you, with many smiles.

I signed it and began reading it over. Could this be my last memorial? Did these sentences convey what I really had in my heart? I should have had many more things to write about than this—my happy childhood, for instance. My will read like it was written only to impress someone with what a wonderful person I was. And didn't it have a little boasting in it? That part, for instance, where I invited my nephews and niece to visit their great hero uncle at the Yasukuni Shrine. What did I truly want to say? How could I be fully honest?

Perhaps it is true that I do not fear facing death in my *kaiten*. But is it my own will to go out? Or am I swept along by the military emphasis on *Yamato damashii*? Am I just caught up in a hurricane of national spirit? In one corner of my mind do I still desire to live, while I am yet propelled into dying because by doing so I will achieve a great reputation?

Why try to write anything? I could not possibly uncover and set down the real truth. Why could I not have an open and honest mind, as did Yamaguchi and Furukawa? I will tear up the sheets containing these foolish thoughts I have written. I will imitate Furukawa, and write "nothing" instead, on one sheet!

I did pull many sheets from the note pad. As I tore them up I thought of the motion picture, *Unfinished Symphony*. In the final scene, Schubert ripped up his carefully-composed scores. On a blank piece of musical score paper, he wrote: "My composition will never be finished, just as my love will never end." I had seen that picture several times and had always been deeply moved by the final scene.

Like Schubert, I decided, I am also finished. There is just one more thing to do: sink an enemy ship. I have nothing to write, nothing to leave behind. That decision swept all other thoughts from my mind. I turned and looked at Furukawa and Yamaguchi, sleeping peacefully. All tension left my body. At last I felt I was one with them.

The following night, after a quiet day which did not require us to train in the water, Shinkai and I took a little "unofficial leave." We went over the base fence and got a ride in a truck to the home of Mr. and Mrs. Harada in Hikari. They kept a sort of continual open house for submarine and *kaiten* men of Hikari base. Mr. Harada was a naval officer. Two of the Harada sons were naval aviators, the eldest having died at Rabaul during the Solomon Islands campaign. Mrs. Harada and the one daughter always made us welcome.

It surprised Mrs. Harada to see us, for it was not our usual holiday. "*Sumi masen*, Mrs. Harada," I said. "Please forgive us. We just want to relax in the happy atmosphere of your delightful home. Don't go to any trouble for us. You know what we are training for, and that we cannot talk of the training, but this may be the last time we will see you."

The lady of the house kept a smile on her face, as always. She was used to seeing young Navy men going away from her house, never to return. We didn't expect to have a meal with the Haradas, just to enjoy their company. But Mrs. Harada insisted. We gave in to her wishes, feeling it was our last time there. During the meal, her daughter excused herself. When she returned she was laden down with phonograph records.

This touched me deeply. The young lady had often heard me comment on classical music and my love for it. So she had gone around to friends and neighbors, borrowing records, so we could have a musical evening. We listened to music, and readily assented when Mrs. Harada asked permission to summon a photographer so a souvenir picture could be taken. On returning to the base, we lightly turned aside Furukawa's angry protest at not being taken along. So far as Shinkai and I were concerned, this had been the happiest night of our lives.

9 ◻ Our Tatara Group Goes Out on a Mission

I-47 returned to Hikari in the last week of March. I watched her enter port as I stood on the deck of a torpedo boat, observing Lieutenant Kakizaki making *kaiten* runs. The submarine had a new coat of anti-radar paint. On her hull she carried in large white ideographs the crest of the Kusunoki family, *kiku sui*. I waved my cap to I-47's crew as Kakizaki made the second of two perfect passes beneath my vessel. We finished our practice and got back to the pier just after a launch from I-47 carried Captain Orita ashore. We six *kaiten* men went at once to the officers' quarters.

"*Ah, Kakizaki-Chui! Shibaraku, dana?*" Captain Orita greeted our group leader effusively, uttering the Japanese equivalent of "Long time no see." His wide smile then turned to a sober frown. "Quite a change has been made in this *kaiten* group, hasn't it? I was sorry to hear of Petty Officer Yazaki's death, but when news of Lieutenant Miyoshi's death followed it almost immediately I fell into complete shock. When word was brought to me I sank back into my chair, completely paralyzed. I was actually unable to move for some time afterward."

"It is our intention, Sir," said Kakizaki, holding himself very stiff and erect, "to make up for the loss of Yazaki and Lieutenant Miyoshi!"

"That is the correct feeling to have," said Captain Orita. "I think you will do it, too. After all, you six are the most experienced *kaiten* men we have at this moment."

"Thank you, Sir," said Kakizaki. "May I now please introduce the other members of our group?" He turned to us, and we each made a respectful bow. During that meeting, the origin of our group's name, Tatara, was discussed. Back in the fifteenth century there was a great warrior of Japan named Tokimune Hojo. He was charged with defending the homeland against a great armada of Mongol ships attempting to invade and conquer us. Aided by a typhoon which wrecked most of the enemy fleet, he defeated them in battle off Tatara Beach, in northern Kyushu. The typhoon was one of two "divine winds" so often written about in our history. The *Kamikaze* Corps of one-way pilots was named for it. Our group was given this name because we, too, would attack an invading force, the Americans, who were then getting ready to take Okinawa, in the Ryukyus portion of our island chain.

Flagship of the Tatara Group would be our submarine, I-47, carrying Kakizaki, Maeda, Shinkai, Yamaguchi, Furukawa and myself. There would also be three other submarines. I-44 would sortie under a new commanding officer, Lieutenant Commander Kiyoshi Masuzawa. She would have *kaiten* pilots Lieutenant Hideo Doi, Ensign Yasuhiko Ikaku, Ensign Takaharu Tatewaki and Petty Officer Hikogo Sugahara on board. These men had already endured a severe trial, having gone out earlier in I-44 with the Chihaya Group. They never got a chance to go into action, being detected and kept underwater by American ships and planes for nearly two full days. It had been their submarine captain who had been relieved at once on returning to port, though no *kaiten* man ever had a low opinion of him.

I-56 was commanded by Lieutenant Commander Keiji Shoda. This boat had also been refitted to handle six *kaiten*. They would be manned by Lieutenant, junior grade, Seiji Fukushima, a graduate of the Naval Academy, Ensign Hiroshi Yagi and four petty officers. It would be the first time out for all six.

The fourth submarine would be Lieutenant Commander Mochitsura Hashimoto's I-58. Lieutenant, junior grade, Nobuo Ikebuchi would lead three others, Ensign Ichiro Sonoda, Petty Officer Hidemasa Yanagiya and Petty Officer Raita Irie. These men had already gone out once also, in the same submarine, I-58, as part of the Shimbu Group, which had been recalled. Thus there would be a total of twenty human torpedoes going against enemy ships gathering off Okinawa.

I was surprised to learn that our prime objective would be enemy warships, probably at anchor off the island our forces held. We had believed that tactic had been dropped permanently. It was true, though. We would not attack

other ships unless we overtook them in large numbers, thus
making the expenditure of *kaiten* worthwhile. Only a convoy was to divert us from our main targets—carriers and
battleships. This change, I guess, was due to the situation
lately having become so desperate.

By now the number of Japan's fleet-type cruising submarines had shrunk to almost nothing. Besides the four
of the Tatara Group, there were only a few others left. They
had to be employed against the best targets, which is why
warships were to be our prime objective.

Kaiten were to be mounted on I-47 the day after her
arrival at Hikari. She would take us out to sea a ways
so they could be pressure-tested in deep water. If all
checked out satisfactorily, we would depart for an attack
on the twenty-ninth.

On the day of his arrival, Captain Orita took the six
of us on a launch to his ship, after we had lunch. Lieutenant
Obori, his executive officer, summoned all hands to general
assembly as soon as we stepped aboard. In a few moments
I realized why I-47 had such a wonderful combat reputation. Men came from everywhere at top speed and fell
into precise ranks. This was how they must act at sea, in
combat, I told myself. If so, no wonder this submarine
fought so well.

"I want to introduce our *kaiten* pilots to you," said
Orita. Beginning with Kakizaki, he called out our ranks and
names. Each of us nodded in turn to the crewmen, who
smiled whenever their eyes met ours. I felt very comfortable, standing there before them, seeing the welcome in their
eyes.

When the gathering was dismissed, Leading Petty Officer
Fujisaki of I-47 approached us. He was the submarine's top
enlisted man, equal to the American "Chief of the Boat."

"I am very glad to have you on board," he said. "Our crew
usually presents an amateur show when we are getting ready
for a departure. We have a lot of talent in this crew, and
the officers join, too. If you are free this evening, I hope
you can attend. Perhaps you, too, may have some talent
to offer."

Lieutenant Kakizaki spoke for all of us, accepting the
invitation. Then we took a look at our individual *kaiten*.
Near the bow of mine were the four ideographs for "sure,"
"enemy," instantly" and "sunk." My heart went out to

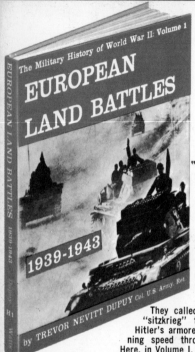

Petty Officer Yutaka Yokota, taken on March 10, 1945, not long before he sortied with the Tatara Group.

A *kaiten.* This is the Number Three Model, never used in combat. Note the white paint on top, making it more easily visible for observers on "target ship" during practice.

At left is co-inventor of the kaiten, Lt. (jg) Sekio Nishina, who hit U. S. tanker *Missinewa* at Ulithi. With him is Lt. Yoshinori Kamibeppu, also of Kikusui Group, who died in I-37.

Kaiten pilots who sailed with I-37 of the Kikusui Group, first sortie of kaiten. Left to right are: Ens. Kazuhiko Kondo, Lt. (jg) Katsumi Murakami, Lt. Yoshinori Kamibeppu, and Ens. Shuichi Utsunomiya. None of these men got into action. They perished when I-37 was sunk enroute to Kossol Passage by U. S. destroyer *Nicholas*. All hands were lost.

The 12 men who hold short swords in their hands are the 12 who went out with the first kaiten sortie, the Kikusui Group. This is the souvenir photo taken of them before they departed. Sixth from the left (first row) is Vice Admiral Shigeyoshi Miwa, Commander Sixth Fleet (submarines).

Six kaiten men of the Tembu Group, bearing branches of *sakura* (cherry blossom) in full bloom. Left to right are: Petty Officer Yutaka Yokota; Petty Officer Shichiro Furukawa; Lt. (jg) Minoru Kakizaki; Lt. (jg) Hajime Maeda; Petty Officer Shigeo Yamaguchi; and Petty Officer Kikuo Shinkai.

Wake of a kaiten, taken while Yokota was piloting it in training.

Lt. (jg) Minoru Kakizaki leads Petty Officer Yutaka Yokota's group through two files of comrades to board I-47 and sortie with the Tatara Group in March 1945.

Lt. (jg) Nobu Ikebuchi, kaiten pilot (died in action).

The Todoroki Group, ready to depart for a sortie. Left to right: Petty Officer Eizo Nomura; Petty Officer Yutaka Yokota; Ens. Ichiro Sonoda; Lt. (jg) Nobo Ikebuchi; Ens. Minoru Kuge; Petty Officer Hidemasa Yanagiya. The three men at right died on this mission, the other three coming home alive only because of trouble firing their kaiten.

Yutaka Yokota,
taken in 1961.

Harrington interviewing in 1959 M. Hashimoto, I-58 skipper who
sank the *Indianapolis* (see Chapter 17).

All photos courtesy Yutaka Yokota
printed in U.S.A.

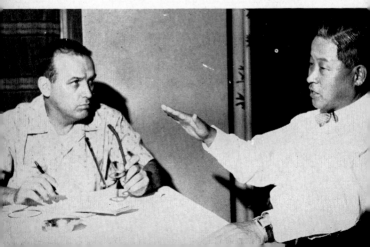

the maintenance men who must have painted them there. The characters brought good luck that day, too. Every test came out perfect. But, when we came back into the bay, we found we could not accept Fujisaki's invitation to the amateur show. A semaphore signal from the base ordered all six *kaiten* men to come ashore.

The next day, the twenty-seventh, was a quiet one. All *kaiten* were ashore, mounted in their cradles, and we checked them over and over again, getting the mechanics to make final adjustments so they would be combat-ready. Since nothing was said all day about dinner together, I assumed there would be no send-off party, as there usually was for departing *kaiten* men. But the word was passed, shortly before supper, that there would be one. About seventy persons, all told, gathered in the officers' mess a little while later, to honor us six men.

When we were all seated, Rear Admiral Mitsuru Nagai, who now had command of the Sixth Fleet, entered. All hands stood while he and members of his staff proceeded to their seats. Lieutenant Commander Koreeda, the Hikari base commander, opened the ceremonies after we all sat down again. "We are honored tonight by the presence of Admiral Nagai," he said, "as we gather to honor and pray for the success of Lieutenant Kakizaki and his five comrades. Please enjoy yourselves and have a very happy time, so that we can send these men away with many pleasant memories."

Admiral Nagai stood up and spoke. "I want to wish you men of the Tatara Group every success," he said. "I hope each of you will strike our enemy. At that moment your souls will fly to Yasukuni, there to watch forever over God's country, Japan. Please be assured that the rest of us in Sixth Fleet will do everything possible to comfort and assist those you leave behind. Your families will be well taken care of."

Our executive officer, Lieutenant Miyata, came quickly to his feet then. "Men," he shouted, "pour *sake!*"

Large bottles of *sake* had been placed here and there on the tables, so everyone could fill his cup as often as he liked. Admiral Nagai personally poured the first six cups for us *kaiten* pilots. Lieutenant Commander Koreeda then raised his cup high.

"I offer a toast to the gallant ones soon to depart," he called out. "Will all please join me!"

I had rarely drunk wine before coming to Hikari, but I considered this a special occasion, and so drained my cup in one swift gulp. There was a period of serious silence after this opening toast, broken when Lieutenant, junior grade, Hiroshi Hashiguchi, an intense young man who would later commit suicide, rose and suggested that all hands join in singing "The Warrior's Song." I and the other *kaiten* men sat stiffly at attention during this homage to us.

> "At sea we may sink beneath the waves,
> On land we may lie beneath green grasses,
> But we have nothing to regret
> So long as we die fighting for our Emperor."

The song echoed through the large room. I closed my eyes, listening to the words, and thinking of Nishina, Yazaki, Miyoshi and the many others who had gone on ahead to die. At that moment, all doubts left me. I was committed. No more would I need to ponder the pros and cons of dying or question myself as to why I was going out. In two days I was going, and that was that! I would not pledge to do anything great, as I'd heard others do at these parties. I would simply go, without great promises, and do my best to destroy the enemy.

With that thought I thrust my cup toward Lieutenant Mitani, who was sitting near us. He filled it. I tossed it off. Then another. And another. The room began to swim before my eyes. I remembered seeing Lieutenant Kakizaki, Lieutenant Maeda and Petty Officer Furukawa somewhere across the room, singing. Struggling to my feet, I staggered across the room toward them and leaned against one, while I joined them in song.

Lieutenant Hamaguchi, whom I had long since forgiven for hitting me the day he'd scolded me about a poor *kaiten* showing, joined us as the party reached its height. *Sake* was plentiful. Every voice got louder and louder, mine included.

"Don't forget!" someone shouted. "We expect you to do your best!"

"We will soon be following you in an attack of our own!" cried someone else.

"Six American aircraft carriers! Get them!" shouted a third voice.

More songs burst out, including the "Navy March" and other songs popular with Japanese sailors. More than five dozen of us were still singing at the top of our lungs when the party came to a halt at 10:30 P.M. with three *banzai* cheers for the Hikari *kaiten* men. Though there would be a busy day ahead of us in the morning, I could hardly stand. Shinkai was in no better shape. Lieutenant Kakizaki and Lieutenant Maeda had been carried off to the officers' quarters. I couldn't see Furukawa and Yamaguchi around, either, but I had a good idea that they might be hiding away somewhere, and still drinking. Yamaguchi, especially, was a big drinker. "I am a man from Kyushu," he would say after drinking a quart or so of *sake*, "with strength for drinking and more strength for women." I didn't know how much truth was in his latter statement, but I had good reason to believe his first one. He could drink more than any man I have ever seen, without showing any effect, and be ready for duty, clear-eyed and eager, the next morning. During his drinking he would often say that his only regret about being a *kaiten* man was that "there will be no *sake* in the world of the dead."

The evening ended for Shinkai and myself when Lieutenant Kozu escorted us to our room, holding one of us up with each arm. We tumbled into bed with our clothing still on.

Next morning I felt that my head weighed as much as the Great Buddha at Kamakura. What a hangover! I remembered the other time Shinkai and I had gotten drunk, and how I had vowed not to do it again. The send-off party had to be an exception, of course, but this hangover would truly be my last one. It was 8:30 A.M. when I awoke, and the first thing I did was to lurch across the room to where we had a small kettle, used for making tea. Tilting my head back until I feared it would fall off and roll down my back, I drained every drop in the kettle. It made me feel a little better, but it was the first of many drinks of water I would be taking that morning, to quench my terrible thirst.

"I'm going to have a hard time today," I told myself. I had to be at the submarine when the *kaiten* were loaded. I also had to straighten out this room and wrap up most of my belongings. Not much would be required on board the submarine, and what I left here would be shipped to my family after I had made my attack. I wanted to send some postcards to a few friends, too. Besides that, I'd have to draw some rations from the canteen so as not to impose on the submarine men. Perhaps I might even pick up a few treats for them.

The other petty officers were still sleeping, and snoring. I hated to wake them up. But I had to. They had as many things to do as I did. Then I washed my face, took several more drinks of water, and went to the officers' quarters to see if Lieutenant Kakizaki and Lieutenant Maeda were awake yet.

As I entered their room, I burst out laughing. The two of them, unshaven, were asleep in one bed, their arms around one another like a married couple. They had taken off none of their clothes but their jackets. Lieutenant Kakizaki's hair was all ruffled. Lieutenant Maeda was cradling his chief's head in his arms. Both were snoring loudly. It made me wish I had a camera with me.

"Lieutenant Kakizaki, Sir!" I called out. I called it out again. He opened his eyes. They were glazed, though, and I was sure he could not see me standing there before him. He blinked several times and finally recognized me. He grinned and heaved himself out of bed and began to shake Maeda. The two of them were putting on their jackets as I left for my own room, satisfied everyone was awake and doing what they had to do. I used the next two hours packing things for shipment home and generally tidying up.

Kaiten were loaded on I-47 at 11:30 A.M. They had been inspected carefully by our maintenance people and ordnance men had replaced the warheads. Now each *kaiten* had 3,000 pounds of deadly explosive in its nose, as a floating crane towed them out to midstream where I-47 lay.

My *kaiten* was No. 3, mounted near the stern. I patted its side as one might pet a favorite animal. "Do a good job!" I said to it, just as countless naval officers had said to me during the past eight months. Then I climbed inside for a check of all meters and gauges. Everything was perfect. I was well satisfied as I climbed out again and reported this fact to our chief and Captain Orita. All checks were finished and we were back at the barracks by 4:30 P.M.

Shinkai, Yamaguchi, Furukawa and I had something

waiting for us there. On our beds lay four brand-new uniforms, including shirts and white gloves. They were the reason the supply officer had asked for our measurements a few days before. "So this is my clothing for death!" I thought. It seemed such a waste of needed goods. Especially the shoes. They would probably be worn less than a week, Okinawa being such a short distance away. I felt it would be better if these items were given to someone who could get more use out of them. But if this was the way it was to be, *shikata ga nai*. I could do nothing. No use getting upset over what was, after all, a trifle.

Now I had to hurry, to make my final preparations. I had already sent letters to my family, hinting vaguely that this was the last time they would hear from me. I still had two more letters to write. Both were to men who had been my friends since childhood. I could spare little time now for grand and glorious thoughts, especially since I had promised myself not to think any more about the reasons for my leaving on a *kaiten* mission. And I had determined to leave no will. So I made my postcard letters nearly identical, writing them without very much thought.

Dear Kazuo,

I must apologize to you for not having written in such a long time. I am well, and I hope that you are, too. The war is getting harder every day, according to what we hear. I often wonder how you people who are not in the military are getting along. We here are not downcast about the war. We are doing our best, and I hope you are doing the same. You must apply yourself earnestly to your studies, so you will be useful to our country in the future days. Take care of your health, too. That is very important. As I close, I want to thank you for the many kindnesses you have shown me throughout our lives.

Y. YOKOTA
No. 1, U-455,
% Postmaster, Kure

It was not much of a letter, nor was the other. But I was not going off to my death without sending a message to two boyhood friends. I asked one of the other men in the barracks to mail them for me once I-47 was at sea and felt good when he promised to do so. Every loose end was now tied up. I was ready to go.

Next morning, March 29, 1945, I awoke full of eagerness. I bounded from bed, grabbed my towel and headed for the washroom. I was scrubbing merrily, humming a little song, when a voice behind me said, "Good morning, Yokota." It was Ensign Kishie Kirizawa. He too was a *kaiten* pilot, and shortest of all the men at Hikari.

I stopped washing, and turned around. "Good morning, Sir," I said brightly, wondering what it could be he wanted.

Ensign Kirizawa had one hand behind his back. "I went to your room," he said, "to wish you good luck on your mission, but did not find you there."

"Thank you for your good wishes, Sir," I said. "We will try to take the places of Lieutenant Miyoshi and Petty Officer Yazaki."

"Good!" he said, and then drew his hand from behind his back. In it he held a small and very beautiful doll. "I wonder if you would take this along with you," he said, holding it out to me.

"Utsukushii desu!" I exclaimed. "It is beautiful! It must be handmade! Why do you want me to take it with me?"

"Please don't ask me any questions, Yokota," he said, stepping back a little. "Just take it with you on your mission. I will be most grateful if you do."

I decided not to press the inquiry further, having noticed a troubled look in Kirizawa's eyes. "I will take it with me, Sir," I said. "I will hang it right under my periscope."

"Thank you, Yokota, very much."

He left, and I continued washing, puzzled. What was his reason for giving me this doll? Was it a gift, just for me? Or was he using me to get rid of it because he did not have the heart to throw it away? Perhaps it had been given him by a former sweetheart, whom he now wanted to forget by sending this gift into oblivion. Or perhaps his family had made it for carrying into battle as a good luck charm. With so few submarines remaining, it was certain some *kaiten* men would never be selected for a mission. Maybe he despaired of ever going out. I shrugged, thinking one man cannot fathom the thoughts of another. Slipping the doll into a pocket, I finished washing. I was in a hurry. I needed to squeeze in enough time to get around and say goodbye to Hikari officers who had treated me well.

I met Lieutenant Miyata at the door of the officers' quarters. "Good luck, Yokota," he said, and I answered with a smile and a salute. Then I walked the length of the corridor and, starting with the room furthest from the entrance, knocked at several doors, thanking various officers for their treatment of me during my time at Hikari. It had been, I felt, not so bad after all. Not like Otsujima, of course, but not bad. Maybe we Tsuchiura men really had been spoiled at the other base.

As I proceeded from one door to another, bowing and shaking hands, a thought I had read somewhere popped into my head. "What is a man's happiness? It is to live forever beautifully in the minds of those who know him best." In a few more days I would no longer exist. I did not know exactly how I would die, of course. I might not even get to make an attack. I might die, with all hands, on the bottom of the Pacific Ocean, as some other *kaiten* men died, killed by the enemy when the submarine carrying them was prematurely discovered. I wanted to be remembered a little, to live on in the minds of my associates here at Hikari. This knocking at doors would be probably my last attempt at happiness, in my lifetime.

When I got back to my room, Shinkai, Furukawa and Yamaguchi were already dressed in their new uniforms.

"Where have you been?" asked Shinkai. "It's getting late."

"Visiting the base officers," I said.

"You would!" he teased me.

"Well, I thought it was the polite thing. . . ." I started to say, but realized there was no point in discussing my inner feelings. Shinkai had his own, and he probably didn't feel like discussing them. So why should I? I reached for my new uniform and lightened the conversation by saying, "Now turn your backs and don't look at me. I'm putting on a clean *fu*."

I danced around, naked, putting on a new *fundoshi*, while Shinkai cried out, "*Hazukashii, masume-san.*" Calling me a bashful young girl was just the right thing to do at that moment, for other men in the barracks had gathered around and had started to put on sad faces at the solemn occasion of our dressing. By the time I'd gotten into my new clothes some sailors who worked in the officers' mess arrived. They had a gift for us from the officers, a large *tai*, salted and broiled. In Japan it is customary on happy occasions to send a complete sea bream like this. *Tai* is given by friends to a family when they celebrate someone's homecoming after a long absence, or when someone is leaving to take an important job, or appointment, or for school. It is given at the birth of a new baby, and on New Year's Day. That's the day when Japanese really "clean house." New paper is put in the *shoji* doors and the windows. All debts are paid. Everyone's home is spruced up, with new *tatami* replacing old on the floor. The ladies of the family usually put the head of the household immediately back into debt with their purchases of beautiful *kimono*, in which they then stroll about much as Americans do in new finery on Easter Sunday. I felt as though it was New Year's Day for me. Everything had been cleared away, and even my mind was clean. I was ready for my new, though short, life.

We thanked the sailors for this fine fish and invited other men to join in as we ate our fill of it. We had hardly finished stuffing ourselves when the loudspeaker called for all *kaiten* men to gather in the assembly hall. "*Iko!*" shouted Furukawa. "Let's go!" He was on his feet and running in an instant, the three of us close behind him, wiping our mouths as we ran and anxiously scanning our uniforms to make sure they had no food spots on them. Our rooms had been tidied. All personal belongings were placed neatly on our beds. Everything to be done had been done.

Special ceremonies were conducted at the assembly hall, during which short swords were presented to each of us. We six stood rigid in a row. Behind us were ranged Petty Officers Yoshio Hagita and Teruaki Mizuno. With them were Leading Seamen Mitsuo Kobayashi, Taketoshi Tsukumi, Eishun Oshiro, and Shoji Nao. These six men would board I-47 with us. Each of them was responsible for maintaining one *kaiten*. He would make all last-minute checks and assist his pilot into the weapon when the attack call was sounded.

All hands on the base had been summoned to this special ceremony. Some had to work hard to hide envious glances. They were happy for us, but still a little sad that their turns had not come. A shortage of *kaiten* had slowed the beginning of the program at Otsujima. Then, when *kaiten* started rolling off assembly lines in number, and Hikara opened, there was a shortage of technicians. That had been partly overcome by *kaiten* trainees helping the mechanics and other men being trained during the actual conditioning of weapons for each training session. Now it was a shortage of carriers, the submarines for transporting us into battle. Only a few *kaiten* could go out at a time, in spite of all the efforts made. I felt sorry for those who had to stay behind.

Each of us stood forth in turn as his name was called, taking off his cap and bowing. A white cloth was spread upon a large table, in back of which stood Lieutenant Commander Koreeda, the base commander. The swords, plus six *hachimaki*, lay on the white cloth.

I was the last to be called. Lieutenant Hamaguchi, division officer for the maintenance section, who was calling out the names, took up the sixth *hachimaki* and tied it around my head. Written on it in graceful brush strokes were the characters for *"Shichi sho hokoku,"* signifying Masashige Kusunoki's loyalty to his Emperor centuries before. My *hachimaki* carried the slogan, "Reborn seven times to serve the nation."

Each of us was then given a shallow cup of plain water, and drank it. This was the death toast, and a most solemn moment. A Japanese warrior facing death traditionally drank water, not *sake*, to signify his purity of soul. Not a sound could be heard from the hundreds present as we slowly sipped this drink. Then we stood before the base commander and he handed each of us a short sword. "These are the special gifts," he said, "of Admiral Soemu Toyoda, Commander-in-Chief of the Combined Fleet." We all raised our swords together, holding them straight out at a level with the tops of our heads so we could see beneath them. Thus did a *samurai* formally address his opponent in Japan's feudal days. Thus did we now throw down our challenge to the American fleet.

We marched outside then, so pictures could be taken. The others formed two lines when this was over, and we marched between these files to the pier, holding our swords at the forward salute. The eyes of everyone were glittering, and some had tears in them, bravely held back so as not to dismay the departing warriors. I spoke cheerfully to friends along the way, wishing them good fortune in all future endeavors. Yazaki's ashes were contained in an urn and box I carried in my left hand, my short sword was in my right, and a smile still wreathed my face as I reached the pier.

The motor launch ride to I-47 was as inspiring as everything else had been. From the floating cranes, torpedo boats and small craft were streamed large banners, each with a special phrase of encouragement written upon it. We waved our caps over our heads to the people remaining on the pier, and they waved theirs to us. Others, alongside the pier on the shore, gave cheer after cheer, until the sound was like a thousand thunders. The special prayer I had said to the Grand Shrine at Ise, near Nagoya, to which all Japan, including the Emperor, makes obeisance, passed through my mind during this short trip. "I pray," I had said, "that the sacrifice I make of my life will help one hundred million people of my country have peace in their lives."

We were soon alongside the submarine and stepped aboard. Admiral Nagai was there waiting for us. He shook hands with each of us. "Goodbye, and good luck!" he said to me, the tears flowing freely down his cheeks. Admiral Nagai truly loved the young *kaiten* men. It grieved him to see each one leave, in spite of what that man might do to the enemy. I tried to appear nonchalant, remembering my promise to myself not to have any regretful feelings or show emotion, but it was a difficult promise to keep with my hand in the hard grip of the Admiral's. I remember that my hand ached a long time after he let it go.

Admiral Nagai then made a short, final speech, while I-47's crew stood at attention along both sides of the main deck and we *kaiten* men stood at attention atop our weapons. He boarded his launch then, moving toward the shore, and a bugle sounded to order the crew to stations for getting the submarine underway. "Swords up!" called out Lieutenant Kakizaki, as I-47 began to move seaward. Motor launches and torpedo boats cruised on both sides of the submarine, escorting us from the harbor. I spotted Torpedo Boat #220, from which I had set forth for my first *kaiten* cruise, so many weeks before. People aboard it were waving and shouting. I could recognize Petty Officer Yuasa. He had served on board the giant battleship *Yamato* at one time, and was a very literate, argumentative man. I liked him. He had always assisted me when training in *kaiten* and had taken best care of my weapon.

"Make it good, Yokota!" he was shouting.

"I will!" I shouted back, waving my sword in circles about my head. "You will get big news soon! In a week, at the most!"

The torpedo boats started to lag behind. They could not use up too much precious high-octane gasoline, even on this important occasion. They hove to before long, shutting down their engines. The other craft did, too, after a while, but they waved and shouted until we were so far away we could hardly see them. Finally, when they were no longer distinguishable, I got down from my *kaiten*, the faces of Anzai, Nagato, Ishibashi, Ozawa, Tsuda and others who had called out a final farewell still sharp in my mind. I-47 had turned her bow and was heading for Bungo Strait. Once through that narrow passage, we could meet the enemy at any time.

10 ▣ Disappointment, and Return

I was still on deck when I-47 passed Iwai Jima, about twelve miles south of Hikari. Ushi Jima was now astern, and Oshima also. The island-dotted Inland Sea, as always, looked beautiful on that spring day. What a lovely land, this one for which we were giving our lives. I was proud to be fighting and dying for this country, which seemed all the more appealing in my final view of it. Then Lieutenant Kakizaki broke into my reverie.

"Say, Yokota," he called to me, "what are you day-dreaming about?" His pleasant voice came from a rough farm boy's face and never failed to impress me with its soft, polite tone. I knew he didn't mean his question in ridicule. He had simply noticed that I had been gazing off to the northward.

"Oh, nothing, Sir," I said, not wanting him to think me overly sentimental.

"Come here," he said softly, and summoned the other *kaiten* men to his side at the same time. "I want to remind all of you to take the best of care of yourselves from this moment on. Rest every chance you get. We may be called upon to go at any time, day or night. We could be off Okinawa in two days, or we might get into action sooner, if we run into a large convoy of enemy ships. Understand?"

"Yes, Sir," we said.

"Good! Now let us all make our last farewell to our families."

I blushed as we all faced outward along the starboard side, each looking along a line he estimated was the correct direction to his home city. It shamed me to think that all the excitement of the departure, the cheers and the well-wishes, had blanked my mind. I bowed deeply toward Tokyo, and uttered prayers for my deceased mother, my father, my sisters, my brother, my former teachers and my boyhood friends. "I grew up a very pampered child," I said to them across the waters, "and I have been trouble and work for all of you. But please forgive everything when you hear how I have died. My life has been a short one but, because of your kindness, full of happiness." Then I opened my eyes and watched the submarine's exhaust as it blew out through an opening right near my feet.

By 1:30 P.M. we were at the north end of Bungo Strait. When the Imperial Navy had dominated the seas across one-third of the world, this had been the gateway through which our mighty task forces sortied to victory. Since the severe defeat at Midway Island, however, Japan's naval forces had been pushed back steadily and whittled down almost to nothing. Little was left for stopping the American advance but our *kamikaze* aircraft and the *kaiten*. Only a handful of submarines passed through Bungo Strait en route to attack the Americans. Nearly all of them were small, coastal types, with limited range and fire power. To Okinawa and back, with a half-dozen torpedoes to fire, was the best they could do. Even then the American destroyers and aircraft sighted and sank them with terrible regularity.

Now I could see the green mountains of Kyushu on my right as I-47 swung straight southward. How often had people along these shores felt their hearts swell with pride as the Combined Fleet steamed majestically by, lumbering to and from its main anchorage at Hashirajima in the Inland Sea. I had only seen the Combined Fleet once, in Tokyo Bay, as a very small boy. But it had made enough of an impression so that from that time on all I wanted was to be a Navy man. How sad must Kyushu people be now, as ships straggled in and out through Bungo Strait in small groups, or one at a time, the returning ones often listing heavily from battle damage.

What will the future hold? I wondered? Would the Rising Sun flag someday again be flown throughout the Pacific? We six would die, but what would the world be like for those who would live on? Tokyo was being attacked regularly now, by the giant B-29's, as were other major Japanese cities. My fellow citizens were suffering badly and would suffer still more after life had ended for me. Well, we first six *kaiten* men of Tatara Group were on our way, and the others would follow soon, but into what a situation! While the mountains of home were still in view, we would be in hostile waters. It had become a saying in Japan in 1945: "Once out of Bungo Strait, you are among the enemy."

The word was passed throughout I-47 for all hands to shift

to full readiness condition. This is the last stage before manning actual battle stations. While cruising the Inland Sea, at least, we could relax a little. Radio would warn us of approaching enemy planes in plenty of time for us to submerge. But now, although still in the Japanese waters of Bungo Strait, we were getting ready to build up speed and follow a zigzag course. American submarines now prowled right off our shores. We could not let a sharp Yankee eye calculate our course and speed through his periscope, then loose a deadly spread of torpedoes at us. Zigzagging would confuse him.

The main deck was ordered cleared. I had to go below. Only a few officers and the lookouts on watch remained topside. I stepped to a hatch, took a last, long look at my homeland, and climbed down the ladder. Inside the submarine's hull I really felt compressed, after the broad, grand view I had been enjoying. We four petty officers were quartered near the bow, with the submarine's crew. Leading Petty Officer Fujisaki had made sure we were given those berths closest to the officers' wardroom, in which Kakizaki and Maeda were billeted.

I found myself with nothing to do for the moment. My few belongings were put away. They were not much more than a stop watch and some chart paper. Not even spare *fundoshi* had been brought along. I could not bathe, and did not expect to be on board more than three or four days. By that time we would have sighted an enemy and been launched. I didn't feel like writing anything, and I was still too ill-at-ease to strike up any acquaintances with crewmen. I thought I'd get a book from I-47's small library and was on my way to do so when a voice over the loudspeaker introduced the captain.

Orita's voice was calm and full of confidence. I could see the faith his men had in his leadership as I looked from face to face during his address. "We have now cleared Bungo Strait," he said, "and expect to run on the surface until dawn tomorrow. It will require the best efforts of every man in this submarine to get these six *kaiten* men of the Tatara Group close enough so they can strike at the heart of the enemy. You have done this twice before. I know you can do it again."

He broke off speaking. I stood there, not knowing what to do. Off-watch submarine crewmen lay around, talking, reading books or sleeping. I felt a little uncomfortable among them. They looked at the four of us with kindly faces, but perhaps they felt they should not try to become intimate with men whose death stood only hours or days away. And it was especially difficult for them, because we were the first enlisted *kaiten* men to travel in I-47. Before us they had carried only officers, who did not live among the crew. I could feel a mood of depression and doubt start to creep over me. I could not let that happen, so I suggested to the other three that we find Lieutenant Kakizaki and Lieutenant Maeda. We did, and were beginning to relax, when the general alarm sounded through the submarine.

It came without warning, late in the afternoon. The emergency bell was still ringing when we heard a shout: "Take the ship down!" We were too stunned to decide whether this was a drill, or whether we were about to experience our first taste of real war, but at least we knew enough to stand aside while crewmen rushed to diving stations.

"We are hardly out of Bungo Strait!" said Lieutenant Kakizaki as the rush of air down from the open bridge stopped, along with the ship's engine. A change in pressure pushed at my ears as I-47 tilted downward through the waves. Everything grew quiet.

After a while, I could hear noises. They came from outside the submarine. "What can that be?" I asked.

"Enemy planes, probably," said Lieutenant Kakizaki.

The submarine's navigator entered the wardroom right after that. "Our lookouts spotted a formation of aircraft," he said, "and we naturally thought they were a flight from Miyazaki." He said he couldn't understand how they might be anything else, while the mountains of Kyushu still loomed up in binoculars. They had to be aircraft from the big airbase near Kagoshima. "They weren't, though," he said. "They were Grummans. Those sounds you have been hearing are some of their bombs. Fighter pilots are not skilled enough for attacking submarines, unless they can arrive overhead without being discovered. We got below the surface rapidly, and they missed us by a wide margin."

He waved one hand before him. "If it's like this so close to home," he said, "we can expect plenty of trouble ahead." He spoke matter-of-factly, his words not seeming to affect his manner. They affected me, though. I was miserable. Not only was the enemy at Japan's gateway, he was pounding with a steel fist at the gate itself. Enemy carriers were just a short distance from our shores! And enemy planes were flying over those same green mountains I had so recently been admiring.

We surfaced about an hour later, Captain Orita having decided all was clear. The compressed air rushing into I-47's ballast tanks made a delightful sound. It was then about 5:30 P.M. The ship's great batteries transferred the task of propelling I-47 back to its diesel engines.

Supper was served. I was impressed to find I-47's crew undisturbed by the bombing. The food was good—stew, fried eggs, pickled vegetables and white rice. Not many Japanese were getting white rice in those days. All hands, including the officers, ate the same food, which made me feel ever more warmly toward men of the submarine service. Everyone was treated the same, for everyone was equally important. All had affection for one another, too. It didn't always show, but it was there.

The crewmen laughed when we made a polite comment about the high quality of food I-47 served. "Just wait!" they said, as they urged us to fill up. "After a week on a submarine, you lose your appetite completely. Cruising beneath the surface throws your stomach off. By the time fresh food is gone, no one feels like eating the tinned stuff. Almost everyone comes home thinner than when he went out."

We *kaiten* men looked at one another. I knew all four were thinking the same thing. What did it matter about food? We and our appetites would be gone before long.

I-47 ran on the surface the rest of that night. I played cards with Shinkai and the two officers until 10 P.M. Shinkai was very good at card playing. He had been a schoolteacher before entering the Navy, and possessed quite an agile mind. With him, in I-47, he had a small packet of letters written to him by his former students. He intended to carry them along on his last ride, just as I would carry Yazaki's ashes.

At ten o'clock Kakizaki said, "We'd better retire, men. Sleep while you can. Starting at dawn, we'll have to stand especially alert. We can meet the enemy at any time now." I returned to the crew's compartment, took off my jacket and turned in. Shinkai was asleep almost at once, but I tossed and turned for hours. The bunk was much narrower than what I had been used to. Only the night before, I had slept in a bed nearly twice as wide as that berth. I could not even sit up. If I did, my head would bump the berth above me.

I looked around at I-47 crewmen, sleeping peacefully. It was awful for them, I thought. They slept in three shifts. If a man didn't rest during his rest period, he became very tired during his working hours and the times when he stood watches.

The atmosphere in the compartment itself was not bad. We were still running on the surface in the darkness, at good speed, and blowers sucked down cool night air to us. But I was used to sleeping on my side, and one had to sleep on his back or stomach in a submarine berth. Otherwise you kept scraping your shoulders on the berth above and waking up. That's what kept happening to me every time I dozed off. One movement, and I was awake again. I tried to settle down and adjust to this situation, telling myself it wouldn't be for long. Once the enemy was sighted, and my *kaiten* fired, I would be gone from this most uncomfortable place.

I was still awake, though drowsy, when the general alarm sound again. I-47 started downward almost at once. I could feel her plunging. The string that suspended my flashlight from the berth above me, so I could reach the light quickly, moved out of the perpendicular about fifteen or twenty degrees. Something in the compartment fell to the floor with a loud thump. I got out of my berth, as did everyone else. We were milling around, grabbing at clothing, when I-47 began to level off.

"Do shitanda?" people were asking. "What happened?" Then three sailors who had been on lookout watch came into the compartment, their rubber coats dripping water from the salt spray that swept over them on the open bridge. "We've sighted two big enemy ships!" they said. "Maybe cruisers!"

The loudspeaker then blared out. "All hands to battle stations, submerged!" In seconds the compartment was empty except for Shinkai, Yamaguchi, Furukawa and myself. I looked at my watch. It was 2:50 A.M., still the middle of the night. Would Captain Orita want to employ *kaiten* in the pitch blackness? I didn't think so, but wanted to be ready in case he did. I got my flashlight and chart, my heart beating rapidly as the loudspeaker spoke again.

"Prepare for torpedo attack!"

We moved forward, nearer the conning tower. We stayed out of everyone's way, but were close enough to hear the captain's order if he decided *kaiten* should be manned. It would give us a few more seconds' start than if we waited to hear it over the speaker. We could hear all the bustling activity in the control room and sound operator's room.

"Ship, left, forty degrees. Sound intensity three," reported the sound room.

"Listen carefully!" urged Captain Orita. "Try to determine whether it is a single ship, or more than one." Then he ordered, "Take the ship up to 55 feet." His calm tones impressed me, nothing in his voice indicating how favorable or unfavorable the situation might be. We rose to periscope depth. The captain wanted a look around, and at 55 feet he could raise the periscope above the surface for this purpose. But the next second he was calling out: "Take her down to 200 feet! All hands stand by for depth charge attack!"

How strange! One moment we were preparing to kill off an enemy, and now we were fleeing for our lives! I moved toward the officers' wardroom.

"Sir, what do you think it is?" I asked Lieutenant Kakizaki.

"The lookouts made an error, I think," he answered, his voice gentle as ever. "Those could be American destroyers up there. I just hope they don't find us."

We could still hear reports from the sound room as they were called to the conning tower. "Ships on both sides of us now," a sound operator said in a dry, mechanical voice. "Propeller sounds have high count. May be destroyers."

All we could do now was try to get away. An hour passed, during which the sound room made continual reports, but no depth charges came crashing down. I learned during that time what had happened. When Captain Orita put up his periscope, he expected to find a fat target waiting for him, because he had maneuvered while underwater to get into correct position. Instead, he saw a destroyer, very near and bearing down on him! So he ordered I-47 to go deep and try to hide.

Everything not necessary for maneuvering the submarine at this depth was shut off. Crewmen moved about quietly, making sure no tools or other hardware struck against anything and gave off a sound. I-47 steered this way and that, making very little speed, trying to creep away from the hunters. The sound room continually reported enemy ships nearby, their propellers churning loudly in his phones.

"What do you suppose is going on above?" I asked Lieutenant Kakizaki. "Why hasn't the enemy launched depth charges at us?"

"They are still trying to locate us, I think," he said. "When they do, each will take sound bearings on us. Where the bearings cross is where we are. Or perhaps only one ship will find us. When that is done, they will then come after us with depth charges."

"Oh!" The exclamation of fear leaped from my throat before I could choke it back. But Lieutenant Kakizaki was reassuring. *"Shimpai nai!"* he said. "Don't worry! Captain Orita has much experience at this sort of thing. He will get us out of this safely, even if they do find us. He will use the noise of their own depth charges to deceive them. When they explode he will have something to cover the sound of our engines for bursts of speed. What I'm really concerned about is how much damage those depth charges might do to our *kaiten*. They don't have thick hulls like this big submarine does, you know."

His face showed some worry as he said those final words. And my fear for I-47 also changed to fear for the *kaiten*. They could not be used against these enemies. Of the four cables holding each weapon in place, two had to be released from on deck while we were surfaced. The others could be let go from inside the hull. So all we *kaiten* men could do right now was wait and fret. The submarine's crew was highly trained and battle experienced. Each had his own special tasks to perform. We were just spectators. We could not help the ship at all.

All cooling systems had been turned off, even the small electric fans in each compartment. The temperature where we were kept rising. It didn't help my apprehension any.

"A ship is left of the stern, fifty degrees," called out the sound operator. "Sound intensity increasing . . . now three . . . now four . . . now five!" At that moment I could hear the propeller sounds myself.

"He is going to pass quite near us," said Lieutenant Kakizaki, his voice still cool.

"Full right rudder!" called out the captain. He wanted our stern to those depth charges, and us running away from them as they came down. The propeller noises became louder and louder, then began to diminish. That destroyer was simply making a final run to establish our position with complete accuracy. He could do this quite safely, too. At a depth of 200 feet there was nothing we could do to harm him.

A few minutes later the sound room reported, "Ship right,

ten degrees . . . sound intensity four . . . now five!" A second ship, or perhaps the first one again, was about to pass near us. Again I could hear the propellers myself. Captain Orita ordered a left turn this time and increased speed a little.

"He's directly overhead!" shouted the captain at last. "Stand by for the depth charges! Here they come!"

We'll be hit, I thought. What a horrible way to die! Helpless! This is how men in I-37 and I-44 must have felt when the Americans trapped and sank them.

About ten seconds later there came a series of monstrous explosions. They reminded me of the great summer thunderstorms in Tokyo, but were many times louder. The deck lurched beneath my feet, and I nearly fell down. The entire length of I-47 groaned and shrieked, and the lights kept blinking on and off. Would this be our end? Would my next sight be that of green sea water rushing in to engulf me?

The propeller sounds faded with the last depth charge explosion. "All stations report damage!" ordered the captain. Each area passed the word to him in turn, making me marvel again at the close teamwork necessary for operating a submarine. No heavy damage was reported, and I breathed a long sigh. It surprised me to learn how tough a submarine could be. Those depth charges had sounded very close.

A few minutes later another run was made on us. Depth charges came raining down again, more than a dozen. I-47 was thrust heavily to one side, though the explosions to me did not seem as close as before.

"Now, that is more nearly like their usual marksmanship!" said Lieutenant, junior grade, Tajitsu, with a smile. He was I-47's radar officer, and he was trying to ease me out of my obviously nervous state.

Furukawa spoke up. "I thought that first group would be the end of us," he said, and turned to Tajitsu. "Do you think our *kaiten* are all right? I hope they haven't sprung leaks."

Tajitsu had no comment.

By this time it was 7:00 A.M. We had been under for more than four hours. Our course was northwest.

"How many depth charges have they dropped so far?" I asked Tajitsu.

"Oh, about twenty, more or less," he answered. "But they are not doing a good job. The fact we're still alive is proof of that. Once a submarine is trapped by two destroyers, they should be able to kill it."

"Their second barrage was quite far off," I said. "Do you think they still know where we are? Could we be leaking oil, or something?"

"It's hard to say," answered Tajitsu. "We may have a few rivets loosened, but we can't say for sure how much other damage has been done until we can surface for a good look at ourselves. I'm afraid we'll find it serious, though. Those two runs didn't hurt the ship internally, but they were close enough to do plenty of damage on deck. To the *kaiten*, for instance."

He was so cool as he said this that I know a look of admiration spread over my face. He made me forget my own predicament and start thinking of the precious *kaiten*. With them damaged, I would not get into action.

A long time passed before we could put ourselves at ease, although no more attacks came. Then we heard another report from the sound room.

"Ship, right, ninety degrees. Sound intensity three . . . now four . . . now five."

The destroyer passed directly over our bow. But, strangely, no depth charges came down. Perhaps something had gone wrong with his detection equipment.

Two more hours passed. Our sound room kept picking up propeller noises, but only at an intensity of two or three. That meant the enemy was not closing in on us. No depth charges were dropped, and I said to the others in the wardroom with me that perhaps the enemy had exhausted his supply of them. I was not sure how many a destroyer carried.

"Oh, no!" said Tajitsu. "He has plenty more. Dozens more! He's saving them. He knows we can't stay down here forever. He also knows that we can't run away from him very rapidly underwater. All he is waiting for now is for us to come to the surface to charge our batteries. Then he will pick us up on his radar and move in for the kill."

His light tone didn't help my condition. I was sweating freely now—the temperature inside I-47 had risen to ninety-seven degrees. Though I drank much water, it seemed to gush through my skin as quickly as it flowed down my throat. And through every bone in my body was creeping a slow exhaustion. I was finding it difficult to breathe the stale air and began thinking of all the submarine men of every nation who had perished in the watery depths. This was what it must have been like for them. Sweating, gradual loss of strength, followed by death, either rapidly from more depth charges, or slowly through suffocation.

"Ease down to 250 feet," said Captain Orita. "All hands rest as you can at your stations." Men lay about here and there, moving as little as possible. I slumped to the deck, and made no motions except to wipe myself now and then with a towel that was getting dirtier and dirtier. I felt as though I were in a steam bath, with every impurity being forced through my pores by this heat.

"Sounds are receding," the sound room reported. "Degree of intensity has dropped off to one." Voices of the sound watch now held a pleasant tone. They assumed that the enemy was moving further and further away. It looked as though we might escape after all.

At 1:00 P.M., now down for more than ten hours, we ate lunch where we lay, men moving slowly and quietly to bring it to us. No more reports of enemy ships came from the sound room after that. We were safe!

"They tried hard," said the navigator as he joined the six of us in the wardroom, "but now we are too near Tanegashima for them to follow." Tanegashima was an island not far south of Kagoshima. Should enemy destroyers dare come this close, our land-based aircraft at Miyazaki would sink them for sure. Still, Captain Orita was taking no chances. He kept I-47 down, cruising slowly, until 4:00 P.M. Then he ordered, "Surface! Blow the main tanks!"

How long we had waited for that order! The sibilant sound of air blowing water from the tanks was only a little less welcome than the first cool blast of air that came into the wardroom as the submarine surfaced. I jumped to my feet and breathed in that sweet breeze. I could actually taste it on my tongue, and it was more delicious than any dish I have ever eaten, before or since. I stretched and breathed deeply again, feeling my blood move more rapidly and strength return to my tired body.

Lieutenant Obori, I-47's executive officer, told us that the captain meant to put in at Tanegashima. "We'll be able to take a good look at the *kaiten* there," he said, "and learn how much they might have been damaged."

That was welcome news, and we began looking forward to

arrival at Tanegashima. But in less than a half-hour we dove the submarine again. A flight of small aircraft had been sighted. Captain Orita didn't wait around to see whether they were friendly. He kept us under the surface until after 8:00 P.M. It was dark when we returned to the surface, and the engines were just reaching cruising speed when once more the general alarm sounded.

"More planes!" said the lookouts as they dropped, one by one, through the hatch. Either bombs or depth charges came right down upon their heels. I ducked my head as the explosions went off. They seemed to be right over my head. Damn the enemy! First his planes make us dive, then his destroyers pin us down more than half a day, and now his planes were after us again! And practically on the beaches of Japan!

Leading Petty Officer Fujisaki tried to strike a cheerful note. "Those bombs were too close not to have hurt us some," he said. "It looks like your Tatara Group is *tatarareta*." He laughed loudly at this joke, because in Japanese *tatarareta* means to have a day filled with bad luck. No one else laughed.

Early next morning we entered a small bay of Tanegashima. Our radar antenna was kept turning all the time, and a full lookout watch posted, just in case the enemy appeared again. We four *kaiten* petty officers had finally gone to sleep in the early hours, so it was late morning when Lieutenant Maeda shook me. His handsome face was drawn into harsh, haggard lines. "Get up, Yokota!" he said sharply. "Lieutenant Kakizaki wants to talk to everyone!"

Barely dressed, and still rubbing sleep from our eyes, we made our way to the wardroom. "Sit down," said Lieutenant Kakizaki. "They tell me that those airplanes last night did enough damage to cause a large oil leak in this submarine. The captain says he cannot take the ship to sea in such a condition. It would make us very easy to detect. We would never get near enough to the enemy to attack him."

Furukawa was horrified. "We are going back?"

"Where is the captain?" I asked.

"On deck," said Lieutenant Kakizaki. "He is checking the *kaiten*."

Lieutenant Obori's voice broke in from the door. "Captain Orita wants you *kaiten* men on deck."

As I climbed through the hatch, I could smell the thick,

heavy odor of fuel oil. "It's a big leak, all right," said Yamaguchi, who was on the ladder ahead of me.

"Ooooh!" I exclaimed when my feet were on deck. Our
six *kaiten* looked just like celluloid toys do when they are
accidentally dropped into very hot water. They were full of
dents, as though a giant hand had closed around each and
tried to crumple it. I shouldn't have been surprised at this,
for the greater part of their outside shell was only one-fourth
of an inch thick. The hull of I-47 was scratched and dented,
too, and much anti-radar paint had been peeled from the
conning tower.

"*Naka naka taihen desu!*" exclaimed Shinkai. "It is most
terrible!"

To complete the picture, even the sea looked terrible.
Instead of the beautiful blue I had admired on the way out
from Hikari, it was now a muddy brown, thanks to fuel
oil spreading from I-47.

Captain Orita walked over to where we stood. "With this
damage, we cannot proceed any further," he said to Kakizaki. "I'm sorry, Lieutenant, but you will have to try again.
I know you detest the idea of returning to base. But we
cannot repair this kind of damage here. If I continue toward
Okinawa this ship would leave one continuous trail behind
it. All of us, including my crew, would most certainly die
for nothing. We would never reach Okinawa. I think you
understand my feelings, but I will also remind you of your
own training. Remember how often you have been told that
it is pointless to dash toward the enemy unless there is a
good chance for success? Well, at this moment we have no
chance of success. Absolutely none!

"Resign yourselves to what has happened," he added.
"I'm going below now and have the wireless room tell Sixth
Fleet we are returning."

None of us answered. Though we should have understood
and accepted the situation, we could not. Even the evidence
of our own eyes was not enough to convince us.

"Can't you do something, Sir?" pleaded Furukawa. "We
cannot return to the base. We understand your feelings,
but please try to understand ours. This will not be the first
return for four of us! Nor the second. It will be the third!"

We were amazed at Furukawa's speaking to the commanding officer of a Japanese warship like this. It was un-
heard of conduct. "*Chotto matte!*" said Lieutenant Kakizaki

to him, in the roughest voice he could manage. "Just a moment!" He was about to say more when Captain Orita interrupted. "That's enough, Furukawa!" he said, his face showing that this enlisted man was going too far with such talk. In a moment he would lose his temper, and then there really would be trouble.

Kakizaki stepped between them, apologizing for his man. The incident closed with Captain Orita's decision. No one could do anything more. Our four veteran comrades showed their grief in their faces, though. Fourteen pilots in the Kongo Group had died for their country, but these men returned. And they had been called back from the Shimbu operation, too. It must have been awful for them, but they had to obey.

For Shinkai and myself, it was a little different. True, we had to go back, but we had never been out before. We could just shrug and treat it as a quirk of fate. But the others had waited so long for this chance, and now it was gone. Lieutenant Kakizaki tried to console them after we went below.

"Look," he said, "Captain Orita says it will take only three or four days at Kure shipyard to repair this damage. Then we will be coming out again. Let us cooperate with him by not showing any resentment. He and the I-47 men have done their best for us. Didn't they save us from those two destroyers? And the airplanes? Be grateful! If it were not for their skill, we might all be dead this minute. But we are alive, and with still a chance to strike the enemy."

No one spoke. All were finally resigned to what had happened. The next day, April 2, we were back at Hikari, a long streak of oil part of our wake. I was the only one, I think, who was not deeply despondent. In spite of my fierce promises and my intense self-examination, I was glad to have a few more days of life to enjoy before giving it up forever.

11 □ Another Change in Tactics. Out with the Tembu Group

While I-47 lay at Tanegashima on April 1, examining her wounds, the Americans had stormed ashore at Okinawa. More than 1200 enemy ships, with nearly 200,000 troops, had steamed right into the heart of the Japanese Empire for an all-out thrust. American destroyers alone numbered nearly 150, more than Japan possessed at any moment during the war. So it is not surprising that two of these wide-roaming craft had spotted and attacked I-47 just as she cleared home waters.

The return of I-47 was an omen of what was to come. The Tatara Group was a complete failure, although the finest of our remaining submarines had been included in it. I-56 left Otsujima on March 31. On board as *kaiten* pilots were Lieutenant Seiji Fukushima, my very dear friend, and Ensign Hiroshi Yagi. Four Tsuchiura petty officers, Yoshikatsu Kawanami, Shingoro Ishinao, Kazuo Miyazaki and Kiyoshi Yashiro, made up the rest of the group. Yashiro had been very popular at Otsujima while I was there. He was a natural mimic. He made everyone laugh uproariously with his comical imitations of famous persons during the amateur shows we used to put on for our own amusement. I was most grieved to learn of his fate. The ever-laughing Yashiro never got into battle. I-56 was not heard from after leaving port. Postwar records showed she had been sunk on April 18 by carrier aircraft and destroyers, near Okinawa. All hands were lost.

The day after I-47 returned to Hikari, I-44 left Otsujima for an attack. Eleven days after I-56 was sunk, American carrier aircraft found and sank I-44, also near Okinawa.

I-58, however, was again lucky, although she did not get into battle. She approached Okinawa from the westward, alternately surfacing and diving as enemy planes and ships were sighted, and enduring very bad weather, which also

154

protected her from the enemy. Lieutenant Commander Hashimoto, as he did on his earlier run to Iwo Jima, successfully brought his submarine near to the enemy fleet, but had to dive and run when sighted once more by aircraft. Then he received orders to rendezvous with the mighty battleship *Yamato*, which was making a last-ditch dash for Okinawa in company with the light cruiser *Yahagi* and eight destroyers. The overall strategic plan sent about seven-hundred *kamikaze* aircraft against the Americans off Okinawa. The *Yamato* force was to follow these in and smash the enemy's amphibious forces off the beachhead. At that time, our troops on Okinawa were to fight down from their cave fortifications and push the remaining enemy into the sea. *Yamato* and the ships in company with her had pumped part of their precious fuel supplies ashore before leaving the Inland Sea, so it could be used by other warships. They also left much food behind. If they smashed through to victory, they could refuel and provision at Okinawa. If not, well, there'd be no need for either.

But before Hashimoto could meet with this small task force, *Yamato* had been attacked and sunk by more than three-hundred American airplanes. *Yahagi* and four destroyers went down with her. Conflicting orders then poured into I-58's wireless room. "Rush in and fight to the death!" Hashimoto was told. He obeyed, and was running toward Okinawa at top speed when sighted by American Navy patrol bombers. He was harassed day and night by these, but kept trying to burst through and make an attack. On April 14, after a week of trying, he was suddenly ordered to stand out past Okinawa, into the Pacific. So effective was the American dragnet of destroyers and aircraft, however, that I-58 had to steam far southward, between Okinawa and the Chinese mainland, all the way past Formosa, before she could safely swing eastward. The submarine had more than fifty general alarms and emergency dives while running northward for another try at shipping east of Okinawa. Hashimoto was still trying to work his way in for another attack when he was suddenly ordered back to Japan. Lieutenant Nobuo Ikebuchi, Ensign Ichiro Sonoda, and Petty Officers Hidemasa Yanagiya and Raita Irie were thus forced to return to port a second time, their *kaiten* unfired.

April was a bad month for Japan's submarine force. Besides I-44 and I-56, six other submarines were lost. RO-41 went down on April 5, RO-46 on April 9 and RO-56 on April 17. On April 15, two more submarines were lost right in Japanese home waters, when RO-64 and RO-67 fell victim to American-laid mines. RO-109 went down April 25 under an attack so severe that at one point she radioed Sixth Fleet that she had survived more than three-hundred depth charges! No other word was ever received from her. The enemy must have found her again.

Now two of four *kaiten* submarines had been lost out of the Tatara Group, and two of three *kaiten* carriers sent against Iwo Jima earlier. This resulted in a very hot argument at high levels. The Naval General Staff, in Tokyo, still insisted that *kaiten* submarines could operate effectively against anchorages, bases and amphibious forces. Commander Tennosuke Torisu, of the Sixth Fleet staff, fought fiercely against this kind of thinking. He claimed that *kaiten* should now be sent well out to sea, far behind enemy main forces. There they should be used, he said, for attacking the vital supply ships and tankers that brought up what American advance forces could not do without—ammunition and fuel. Without these, they would have to retreat. At the very least, their advance would be slowed somewhat, giving Japan time to prepare for an overpowering, all-out assault.

Still, there was some merit in the Naval General Staff's position. "How can such a small craft as a *kaiten*," they said, "operate effectively in the open sea, where waves are so high? It is impossible!" They also claimed that *kaiten* men could better prepare themselves if they were assigned a specific mission and date. It would be too hard, they claimed, for a man to keep his spirits up unendingly, waiting for an opportunity to strike at random.

Their main contention was that, if properly operated, submarines could still slip close to the enemy without detection and loose *kaiten* at ships at anchor or near shore, in reasonably calm water. Actually it was not so simple as the Tokyo planners thought, a fact which Sixth Fleet staff people pointed out again and again. Our submarines could run and hide beneath the surface all day, but at night they had to surface and recharge the batteries which operated the ship's engines while under the sea. And darkness was no longer a safe cover. Enemy ships and planes had excellent radar. Nothing was getting past them now, as the sinking of eight submarines in the month of April would show. Forcing one's way through their scouting lines was simply impossible. And even in the remote chance that a submarine did get through, counterattack was certain to be swift and accurate. Since that first successful surprise accomplished at Ulithi Atoll, the situation had changed a great deal. The United States fleet now had extensive patrols out, on the surface and in the air, very far from their main body. These patrols sank our submarines quickly, or called for help that did.

Attacking rear echelon ships would be a different matter. They would be lightly escorted, or not at all. We could punch through, Sixth Fleet claimed, and get them. Our submarines could escape and return for more *kaiten*. And, of course, they would be free to use regular torpedoes as well. A compromise was finally reached, when neither faction would give in. The High Command agreed to let just two submarines make attacks on enemy supply lines. Their performance would be judged, and a final decision on policy would be made.

Imagine my joy at learning that I-47 would be one of these two ships! I-36 would be the other. Her captain was Lieutenant Commander Tetsuaki Sugamasa, youngest submarine skipper in the Imperial Navy. The six of us were to get the quick return chance that Lieutenant Kakizaki had prophesied.

It was hard, waiting for I-47 to come and get us. We had been told at Tanegashima that it would be just a couple of days before Lieutenant Commander Orita's submarine would be ready for sea again. But on arrival at Hikari we learned the period would be two weeks. This was most disheartening, because we had nothing to do but wait. Instead of bringing veterans to a peak of performance, as had been the practice before, emphasis was now being placed on getting the untrained men trained. Kakizaki and the rest of us were considered "graduates." Not once during the layover did we get a chance to ride in a *kaiten*. We were veterans now. I never tired of telling eager listeners what it was like to undergo a depth charge attack. I had actually been in battle at last and was looked up to by my comrades, even though I had not yet struck a blow at the enemy.

There were, of course, not enough submarines available for taking out all the men who were now being trained in *kaiten*. So most of them were scheduled to be employed in a new tactic called "base *kaiten* attack." A plan had been drawn up whereby a large number of pilots, having qualified in *kaiten*, would be transferred with their weapons to various points along Japan's shoreline. These points were near where an amphibious attack could most likely be expected. *Kaiten* men were expected to secrete their weapons at these points, and do nothing. Then, when the enemy was just offshore, they would receive a signal from the High Command. While the enemy was immobile, sending his troops in, the base *kaiten* would rush out and sink as many transports as they could. The long-time Japanese naval strategy had not changed—give the Americans a blood bath they could not tolerate, in one massive pitched battle. It was the strategy used at Midway, the Marianas, the Philippines and in the *Yamato* thrust at Okinawa. So far it had not worked to our advantage, but as the enemy's distance from Japan decreased, hope for this plan built up.

We passed some of the intervening time practicing on a homemade training aid in our barracks. On a table in our room we placed an American ship model. About thirty feet away we had a wooden partition, on which a spare *kaiten* periscope was mounted. It took three people to operate this crude device, one to change the ship models, one to rock the periscope by hand so as to simulate motion in a *kaiten*, and one "student." Whoever acted as student would kneel behind the partition until a model was put on the table. Then he would peer through the periscope and call out the type of ship, as well as the angle from its bow. We often continued this far into the evening, until we were absolutely sure of our ability in this regard.

On April 15, when I had grown weary of being weary and bored with standing about, a wireless came from Kure. "Repairs on I-47 completed," it said. "Ready for sea. Underway for Hikari tomorrow morning."

Lieutenant Commander Koreeda summoned the six of us to a conference when I-47 arrived at Hikari. "This new mission is named the Tembu Group," he said, the words meaning "heavenly knighthood." There would be just two ships, I-47 and I-36. "The plan is for both submarines to take stations on a line between Ulithi Atoll and Okinawa," he said. "The Americans have made Ulithi their major base. You will attack the supply ships they are sending to their advance forces."

We looked at one another. At last the *kaiten* was going out to do what Lieutenant Commander Mitsuma Itakura, Otsujima's first commanding officer, had said it would do. We were serious-faced as we discussed this new tactic. Everything was now up to us.

On April 20, the day of departure for the Tembu Group, the six of us were like new men, all filled with confidence. As each held a *sakura* branch in his hands and posed for our souvenir photo, I looked at my bit of cherry blossom tree with the blooms still on it and said to myself, "How fortunate, Yutaka Yokota, that you were born a boy! A woman could have no adventure such as this!" We were bubbling with eagerness. Shinkai and I swore to each other we would sink the largest ships we could find. I thought of my age, nineteen, and of the saying, "To die while people still lament your death; to die while you are pure and fresh; this is truly the *bushi do*." Yes, I was following the way of the *samurai*. My eyes were shining as I stepped on board I-47 once more. I remembered with pleasure Ensign Nobuo Anzai's quoting from a poem and telling me I would "fall as purely as the cherry blossom" I now held.

More *banzai* cheers sent us on our way. My mind was full of what Lieutenant Sadao Fujimura, one of the Tsuchiura instructors, had said so many times to me. "Never shirk facing death. If in doubt whether to live or die, it is always better to die. But never let death come until you have downed the enemy!"

We stood atop our *kaiten* again, waving swords until the trailing, well-wishing boats turned back. Then I climbed down inside the *kaiten* and placed the ashes of Yazaki and the *sakura* branch near the seat. Maintenance men again had put a slip of paper near my periscope, I saw. It bore the words "a sure hit on the enemy!" and was signed by those who had fitted my weapon for this mission.

By 11:00 A.M. the clouds that covered our departure had dissipated, another good omen. With the bright sun shining, it was a fine day to be at sea. I enjoyed once more a last look at the green mountains of Japan, but they raised no intense emotion in me this time. I was able to look on them calmly, though with tenderness.

En route to Bungo Strait we loosened the main tie-downs on our *kaiten*. If the enemy was waiting for us outside the passage this time we would give him a big surprise. It would take only minutes to fire 18,000 pounds of high explosives into him if he detected I-47. The hunter would become the hunted.

Captain Orita gave each of the weapons a rigid, personal inspection. Lookout watches were carefully posted even while we were still in the Strait, and after we cleared it we swung slightly south of east and ran on the surface, making a speed of twenty knots.

I ran into another good omen as soon as I entered the crew's compartment. No longer was I a stranger. This time several men greeted me with shouts and smiles, asking how I had been for the past three weeks. They teased me about how I was probably loafing around while they worked so hard getting this ship ready. I was struck with the odd thought that there was nothing like a good depth charge attack to break down the reserve that sometimes exists among men.

I woke many times that first night, though all was quiet. I was having a hard time obeying Kakizaki's instructions to get as much sleep as I could. And the morning brought gloom along with the usual restrictions on use of water. It was strictly rationed aboard submarines, and at once I missed Hikari, where a man could brush his teeth or take a bath as often as he liked. But I reminded myself that this would not continue for long, and that I still had it better than the crew. They'd been putting up with this for weeks at a time, and would do so again, after I was gone.

I got up, finally, and went to the officers' wardroom. Kakizaki was asleep, but Maeda was awake, reading a book. I admired Maeda very much for his intelligence. He was twenty-three years old, and the only reserve officer among those of the Tembu Group. Maeda had entered the Navy with a commission while attending Kokura Normal School. College students who could pass naval tests were given commissions and classified as student officers, and he was one of these. A quiet man who never talked about his family, Maeda usually had his nose in a book. He was a great student of men's minds, and even brought books on philosophy into the submarine with him. I guess he wanted to keep studying and exploring right up until the moment of his death.

He had amazed me some time earlier by telling me how he expected Japan would be defeated.

I couldn't believe my ears, an officer talking like this! "What was that you said, Sir?" I asked.

"Japan will be defeated, Yokota," he told me.

I was shocked. I didn't know what else to say at the moment, for I had never heard anyone in the military discuss this possibility before, so I came back with, "Then why do you volunteer to die?"

"A man must do what he can for his country," was his simple answer. His death meant nothing, he added. "Japan will be defeated, of that I am sure. But she will be born again, and become a greater nation than ever before." Maeda went on to claim that a nation had to suffer and be purified every few generations, so that it could become stronger by having its impurities removed. Our land was now being bathed in fire, he said, and she would emerge all the better because of it. He was right about the fire bath, at least. Tokyo had been burned out and other cities in our country were also becoming familiar with the silhouette of the dreaded B-29, the plane that couldn't be stopped.

"Did you sleep well?" asked Maeda, when I got to the wardroom.

"No, Sir, I didn't. It's very uncomfortable in our quarters."

"Well, you'll get used to it," he said, closing his book. "After all, you must rest."

"It will be difficult, Sir," I said. "I'm just hoping that I'll get so tired during the day that I'll not notice the discomfort at night."

"It must be nearly daylight," he said, looking at his watch. "Let's go up and have a cigarette before we submerge." Smoking was not allowed in I-47 while she was cruising beneath the surface. We went up to the conning tower and stood beneath the hatch to the open bridge, enjoying the fresh air blowing in on us. This was the only chance for a cigarette we would get all day. We stayed there, talking and smoking one cigarette after another, savoring each puff. After a while Lieutenant Kakizaki came in, followed by Yamaguchi. With them was Petty Officer Tanaka of the I-47 crew.

Tanaka spoke first. "I noticed you were not in your bed, Yokota," he said to me. "Do you still find our berths too narrow, like the last time?"

"You are right," I answered. "Last night made me appreciate more what you submarine men have to endure."

"Time has changed many things," he said. "When the war started, I went out to Hawaii. My submarine was in the great screen around Oahu. We were to torpedo any American ships that tried to escape from Pearl Harbor. The war was very far from Japan in those days. Now it is at our door, after only three years."

"What is so different?" I asked. "The hardships are the same, aren't they? Tinned food, no fresh air, and all the rest of it?"

"Ah, but the hardships are much different," Tanaka said. "In 1942, I operated in the Indian Ocean. It was a long cruise, but it was very enjoyable. We were even dirtier than we are now, and always smeared with grease. But we had a lot of fun."

"Enjoyable? Fun?" Yamaguchi was puzzled. "How can war be fun?"

"War was different then, that's why," said Tanaka. "Not this running and hiding kind of thing we do now. In 1942, we were calm and composed. We were winning the war then. We were full of fight. We openly sought out the enemy and clashed with him. We had no radar, but that did not stop us. We sighted our enemy, fought him and sank him.

"Today we are lucky if we find him at all. Usually he finds us instead. Three years ago a sighting almost always meant a sure sinking. When one of the lookouts called out 'Enemy ship!' everyone cheered. We ran to our battle stations laughing and shouting. Sometimes singing, too. Even before the order was given to man our battle stations.

"Down would come the order 'Ready Torpedoes!', and the gunners would begin, right away, arguing. Gunners kept insisting that torpedoes were too expensive a method of sinking an enemy, because they cost thirty-thousand *yen* each. They would ask the captain to surface the submarine and let them sink the enemy by gunfire instead.

"If he gave permission, up we would go. The gunners

would jump out on deck and run to the gun. The rest of us would watch. It was just like a sports show. When the gunners made a hit we would all give a big cheer. The enemy freighters were slow, too. They could not run away. We could chase and overtake them easily.

"We loved our power, especially when we saw an enemy ship list and roll under the waves. Sometimes I would feel a little sorry for the men on such a ship, but our younger men would be very happy about the whole thing. Today, the situation is just the other way. Today it is the American submarine sailors who do all the cheering and shouting and laughing and singing. Our opportunities have all been used up. We will never get chances like those we used to get three years ago."

Tanaka's tale was fascinating. We found ourselves leaning forward, craning to hear every word he said.

"When I tell my stories to the young men of this submarine," Tanaka said, "they wish for the old days, too. There aren't many of us left from the 1942 submarine fleet."

He was so right, I realized, as he left the conning tower to begin his day's duties. Some sixty of Japan's submarines had been sunk since the attack on Pearl Harbor, more than a dozen of them by enemy submarines!

We *kaiten* men went to breakfast after Tanaka left. After eating we gathered in the wardroom, a big chart spread before us, trying to estimate where we were. Lieutenant Kawamoto, who relieved Lieutenant Obori as I-47's executive officer just before we left Hikari, called us to the conning tower. The captain was there, together with the navigator.

"Well, how do you feel?" Captain Orita asked us. Without waiting for a reply, he continued speaking. "We evaded the enemy off Bungo Strait this time. When we get further to the south, however, there will be plenty of American ships everywhere. If we encounter any large ones, I intend to launch *kaiten*.

"We will be underwater all through each day. I will frequently conduct *kaiten* drill, in order to speed up your time in getting into them. We will time you with a stop watch from the moment I give the order until the moment you report from your weapon by telephone. In each drill I want you men to do it faster than before."

That was a novel idea, and I liked it. It would relieve the boredom and take my mind off the discomfort of life in a submarine. We returned to the wardroom, which by this time had become our usual gathering place, and stood by for a call. When a half-hour passed without any word, Lieutenant Kakizaki said, "There's no use just standing here idle. Let us have some ship-spotting practice."

Lieutenant, junior grade, Tajitsu, the radar officer who had been so unruffled when we were depth-charged, helped us. He put a small ship model on a table about fifteen feet way. We would take quick looks at it and estimate the angle from its bow to us. It surprised Tajitsu to discover how accurate we were. During one of my turns I thought the angle from the model's bow was more than thirty degrees, but not quite forty degrees. So I called out, "Right! Thirty-seven!" This so amused Tajitsu that he would not let anyone move the model until he could obtain a protractor and measure the exact angle. He was dumbfounded when he found it was thirty-seven degrees, just as I had called out. "You must have practiced this very much," he said. "If you are that accurate in battle, I don't see how you can miss!"

Time passed rapidly, and the messmen had started bringing in lunch when, suddenly, came the order, "Man *kaiten*!"

We scrambled out of there fast. I was the slowest, because I had started laughing at Shinkai. He was in the toilet when the order came. He was a ridiculous sight, running and trying to adjust his clothing at the same time.

The six *kaiten* were mounted on I-47's main deck as follows. Four were in a sort of a diamond, aft of the conning tower. Point of the diamond was No. 1, Lieutenant Kakizaki's weapon. Furukawa's No. 2 and Yamaguchi's No. 4 were a little behind him, side by side. My No. 3 was nearest to the stern. Shinkai's No. 5 and Maeda's No. 6 were almost side by side, forward of the conning tower.

Lieutenant Kakizaki's *kaiten* was not nearest to the wardroom, but he got a head start. He was into his access tube by the time the rest of us had reached ours. I scrambled through mine and could hear submarine crewmen closing the hull hatch behind me. The access tube was about twenty-four inches in diameter. Turning on my flashlight, and being careful not to smash my stop watch against the side of the steel tube, I crawled through the lower hatch of my *kaiten*. I scrambled up into the weapon, closed the hatch tightly behind me and got into my seat.

"Number 3 is on board!" I shouted into my telephone.

"Can you hear me clearly?" asked a voice from the conning tower.

"Very clearly!" I answered.

"Good! All *kaiten* pilots are now in their weapons. Elapsed time was two minutes and five seconds."

I had been the last. Later I learned that Lieutenant Maeda had gotten into his *kaiten*, the nearest of all, in fifty-five seconds, and was on the telephone, calling to report. Captain Orita seemed pleased with the drill. At least, there was no unfavorable comment about it.

At 6:00 P.M., we surfaced. Normally we were not allowed on the open bridge at such times, but I wanted to see the rolling ocean, which we could feel from I-47's side-to-side motion. Shinkai wanted to go, too. It might be our final chance to look broadly upon the ocean before seeing a last, tiny patch of it through our periscopes. We asked Captain Orita for permission. He seemed about to refuse us when Shinkai said, "Please, Sir. Even thirty seconds would be plenty."

"All right," said Orita, "but if we have to dive fast we may leave you up there." He was smiling when he said it, but I didn't know whether he was joking or not.

Lieutenant Kawamoto was on the open bridge, a pair of binoculars hanging from his neck by a strap. He raised them often for a sweep of the sea. With him up there were six lookouts. None of those men moved at all, except as was necessary to keep scanning the surface, horizon and sky with their glasses.

My eyes took in the majesty of the sea. Up to now, any great water I had seen was either surrounded by land, as the Inland Sea, or had a shoreline at its edge. But here everywhere was water, reaching out endlessly. There were clouds above the western horizon, looking like great birds flying to the north. Their bottoms were red, reflecting the setting sun. My tomb would be somewhere in these waters. How small was man in comparison to this great work of nature!

After a short time Shinkai said, "We'd better go back down." I agreed, knowing we'd be in the way if Lieutenant

Kawamoto had to sound the diving alarm. But I was slow climbing down the ladder, reluctant to give up that beauteous sight. In the control room I asked the navigator just where we were at the moment.

"On about a line with Tanegashima," he said, "but far to the east of it."

That made me curious. We could have been much further south in the time we had been sailing, so I asked why we were not.

"We do not simply race toward the enemy at top speed, Yokota," he said. "In the daytime we do not want to get too close to the enemy while we are on the surface. So we go slow by day, or we sometimes reverse course, so as to be in good position for a long night run. Tonight we will probably cover two-hundred miles or more, during darkness. When we submerge, we will proceed slowly, so as to conserve our batteries against emergency. Then, to-morrow night, we will make another long surface run if the captain orders it. But for our first day on the surface, we wanted to stay close to Japan, so we could summon help if attacked. We also wanted to stay out of range of the enemy's air patrols, if possible."

From now on we would keep moving out past Okinawa, running east on the surface by night, and underwater by day, until we were well clear of it.

I ate my dinner and turned in early. Captain Orita would probably not want to use *kaiten* during darkness. But when dawn came, anything could happen. I wanted to be fully rested so I could stay alert the next day.

12 ▢ I-36 Draws First Blood

A week passed without action, while we cruised well to the east and south of Okinawa, looking for targets. Hell was raging at Okinawa itself, where a massive attempt to drive the Americans off was taking place. Nearly two-thousand *kamikaze* attacks were made by our aircraft on the great armada, plus an equal number of conventional attacks by torpedo and dive bombers. Over forty American ships were hit, but the major power of our air strikes was blunted. Early warning of many attacks was given by destroyers, equipped with excellent radar, that the Americans had strung out on a sentry line.

Even when our aircraft concentrated on these floating radar stations, which kept the invasion fleet from being surprised, it did not help. As fast as one was sunk or damaged, another moved in to take its place. The Americans could produce a second ship faster than we could produce a replacement aircraft for the *kamikaze* that had struck their first vessel.

Our planes hit carriers, cruisers, battleships and destroyers without making any change in the enemy's effectiveness. Losses on both sides staggered imagination. Historians would later call the Okinawa struggle the bloodiest campaign in world history. The Americans were at their best, and our side was at its most desperate. Everything was tried, including ferrying human bombs out over the American fleet. These were attached to the undersides of our bombers and loosed for a final dive into the American ships. They didn't help much. An attempt at base *kaiten* attack was a failure. Eight *kaiten* pilots and nine mechanics, sent to Okinawa on a transport ship so they could shove off from shore into the enemy, were lost with their weapons when the ship was attacked and sunk on the way.

Meanwhile, the B-29's from the Marianas were doing everything they could to accomplish two things: destroy Japan's ability to make war, and destroy the will of the

Japanese people to fight. They were gaining success with their first aim, but not very much with the second. The West then had no real idea of Japanese feeling toward our Emperor. Perhaps it does not now. In any case, my country-men were still carrying on the struggle. In spite of severe rationing, which caused the growth of a black market, the people kept working hard. When food was short in the cities they journeyed into the country and obtained extra vegetables from friends and relatives who had farms. The rice crop was a big one, actually greater than that of 1944, though bombings slowed down its delivery to market. Our fishing fleets, in spite of American submarines, kept going out in search of the second chief staple of Japan's diet. Our aircraft production had slowed down. Replacements were not rapidly made for the losses over Okinawa. Hundreds of aircraft were being deliberately held back, not even sent up to defend against the hated B-29's. They were being saved for the final defense of the homeland. A great plan was being devised, of which I'll tell more later, for one massive attempt to smash the Americans, should they ever reach our shores. To build spirit for this, signs were already beginning to appear on streets and in railroad stations, saying: "One hundred million people die in honor!" People in villages were being told to make themselves spears out of bamboo, so they could help the military defend their country.

So it can be seen that, despite the worsening of the situation everywhere, people were still bearing up. All our outposts had been cut off from reinforcement. Many of them were ringed by Allied positions and subjected to daily harassment or bombing attack, like Rota and Saipan, in the Marianas Islands. There our few surviving men served as targets for American ships leaving Guam for the for-ward forces. These ships conducted gunnery practice as they passed our isolated groups. And B-29's, aborting from missions against the Japanese homeland, would jettison their bombloads on these people rather than into the ocean.

My countrymen are often described by Occidentals as being fatalists, which may or may not be true. It can never be denied, however, that they loved their country so much that they were willing to endure all kinds of hardship for it. In that darkest moment, when our troops were starving or dying of disease in New Guinea, being slaughtered in the

Philippines, and holding out against odds on Okinawa, while at the same time troops were being shifted from China to Korea and Manchuria to meet the growing Russian threat in those places, they held fast. They worked harder, for longer hours, on less food, with fewer necessities, than at any time in their lives. With such spirit supporting us, I-47, her crew and her *kaiten* pilots, had to help in the fight. We had to find some targets soon.

Each morning we would have *kaiten* drill. I increased my speed in this exercise, bit by bit. I had memorized the route to my access tube until I could have raced to it in pitch blackness. I knew where every projection, every locker, every bit of machinery was, and the shortest trail past or around it. I knew where men would be standing watches, and which way they would move to get out of my way. When the word "Man *kaiten*!" was passed, I'd be out of the wardroom in a flash, dashing through the control room, radar room and engine room to my tube. Crewmen would give me a quick and mighty boost so I would not even have to use a ladder. Then I'd crawl rapidly through the access tunnel and slide like a snake up into my seat as though I were oiled. By these means I brought down my time from that first two minutes and five seconds to just thirty seconds.

During this time I-47 had moved out behind the enemy forces around Okinawa. When she had the Kikusui and Kongo groups on board, the ship had conducted dramatic send-off ceremonies on the night before each of the two attacks. Things were different now. We had no scheduled date of attack. We had to sink what we could find. At any hour we might encounter the enemy, so there was no point in having special ceremonies that might be interrupted right in the middle. Or for something that might never come off at all. No enemy had been sighted yet. We would feel pretty foolish if we conducted elaborate send-off rites, then had to return to port again, I thought. So we steamed on without incident, sometimes patient, sometimes tense, but always ready. At one time we sighted a flight of enemy planes, but submerged at once without being attacked. Perhaps they had not sighted us.

The six of us filled our idle hours with playing cards, having chess games, playing the Japanese *go,* and keeping our eyes sharp with ship-angle training practice. Maeda joined in often, but spent most of his time reading books. This continued to amaze me, how that man could search for philosophical truths when his life might come to an end in the next fifteen minutes. He was not a talkative man, but an excellent listener. He seemed to want to preserve himself from the harsh military way of approaching things. While at Hikari, he had been generous to us enlisted men. Whenever we needed pocket money for a trip into town, he supplied it. He did not leave the base often, and there was a lot of romantic speculation about him, that he had left a very beautiful sweetheart back in Kokura and could not bear to look upon another woman. I never dared to ask him about this, but it could have been true, for he was certainly a man who showed himself constant to the things that were important to him.

Then, one evening, we did have a sort of send-off party. It wasn't much, being a very humble thing, as Captain Orita explained, but it was the best that could be managed under existing conditions. "It would be better on shore," said the submarine's navigator when he gathered us in the wardroom, "but tomorrow we will be along the supply line between Ulithi and Okinawa. Anything can happen after that. This is all the time we can spare for a ceremony, and this is the best we can afford to give you."

It warmed our hearts to see I-47 men lay the last of their fresh provisions before us, together with the choicest of their tinned foods. We even had some beer, after which Lieutenant Commander Orita spoke to us.

"My dear *kaiten* pilots," he said, "we may be in an attack at any time after tomorrow's dawn. Unlike the Kongo and Kikusui attacks, this mission will come upon us so quickly that I will probably not have time to shake your hands. In fact, I may not even be able to look upon you one last time, because I will be hurrying to my own battle station. This, therefore, will be my farewell to you. I wish you every success, and trust that all of you will score direct hits. Now then, let us drink a final toast."

"Dom'arigato gozaimashita!" we told everyone. "Thank you very much for what you have done!" We drank our glasses of beer. As with everything else I had experienced during that month of April, I thought this would be another last, the last time I would taste beer. It tasted especially good, for I-47's interior grew stuffier and less com-

fortable daily. I would have enjoyed much more beer than one glass, but it was out of the question under combat conditions. I settled for a first quick glass, a second slowly-sipped one, and stopped.

The small party, held at dinnertime, lasted until about 8:00 P.M. I-47 was then running on the surface. I hurried to the conning tower for one last cigarette before turning in. I wanted to be filled with vitality for the next day. But, as usual, I could not sleep. Odd fragments of memory kept my mind too active to let me drift off into the rest that was so important at this point. I thought of my nephews and niece, who had treated me as their favorite relative almost from the day they were born. And of the hundreds of hours I had lazily spent lying about in the home of my sister Chiyoe, listening to phonograph records of classical music. And of life in the dormitory of First Higher School in Tokyo, where my schoolmates and I had seemed to spend so much of our time in the singing of songs. I thought, too, of a friend who was supposed to be studying the operation of manufacturing machines at a school in Yonezawa, and wondered how he was faring at this troubled time. This brought me once more to pondering whether or not I should leave behind a memorial, writing down my final thoughts about all these things and people. After a few moments, though, I thrust the idea aside, and finally fell into angry sleep, disturbed at myself for wasting time in reminiscences.

The next day, April 28, was a quiet one for us. All day long we four enlisted *kaiten* pilots fidgeted. We wandered back and forth between the crew's compartment and the wardroom, our chartboards, flashlights and stop watches dangling from our necks. We were very restless, and didn't know what to do about it. We were ready in every respect to go, and kept muttering, "Where is the damned enemy? If we do not sight the enemy, we have no target! Why doesn't he appear?" Fretting did no good. All that happened was that we became more and more nervous. The I-47 crewmen tried to understand our feelings. They looked at us pleasantly, but did not speak until spoken to, for fear of upsetting us still further.

In the evening, when I-47 surfaced to recharge her batteries, the four of us went to the conning tower for a smoke. "Well, there goes another day of nothing!" said Shinkai.

"Here we are, fully ready, and no enemy comes into view."

"Cheer up!" said Yamaguchi. "Perhaps they will give us another send-off party. I could certainly enjoy some more of that fine beer."

I think Yamaguchi would have drank all the beer on the submarine if they had let him. He loved alcohol. I had seen him take a bottle of *sake* holding almost half a gallon, and drink every drop of it without showing any outward effects except that his very red face became a little redder. The morning after the big send-off party at Hikari for our earlier mission with the Tatara Group he had been very clear-headed, although I was positive he had taken more *sake* than any two men at the celebration. Only a week before this mission, however, we had found out that drink did effect him, though it did not show outwardly very much. But that time there was an outward sign, a cigarette. After putting away great amounts of *sake*, he absently put the lit end of a cigarette into his mouth and kept it there on his lip for a number of seconds before realizing he was being burned. "Now, Yamaguchi," we had teased him while he nursed a very sore mouth, "you will have to give up either drinking or smoking. Obviously you are no longer able to do both."

He gave the same answer others of us had given to questions during the last days of training. "What does it matter?" he said. "Before long I will have given up all my bad habits completely!"

Captain Orita came down from the open bridge while we were in the conning tower. Furukawa, the bold one, spoke to him. "I thought we were supposed to meet the enemy today, Sir," he said to him.

The captain was taken aback a little by this question, I am sure. But his answer was cheerful, as though he understood our feelings exactly. "There will be other days, Petty Officer Furukawa," he replied. "I have said there will be lots of enemy ships along this route. You can rest assured that we will find them. Just relax. Our chance will come." He continued toward his cabin.

Relax? How? All we did was get angrier at the enemy. He had thousands of warcraft in the great Pacific now. Where were they all hiding?

The next day was April 29, the birthday of our Emperor. At noon, having been given the proper bearing by the navigator, all hands stopped work for a moment and bowed toward Tokyo, to show reverence for our ruler. Japanese people bow often, in greeting, saying goodbye, and showing respect to one another. That is a small bow, however. The "deep bow," in which one bends very far over, is reserved for ceremonial occasions. That was the kind we made, facing along a line of bearing that ran through the Imperial Palace. Navy crews in the Inland Sea did the same thing whenever due south of Tokyo or due south of Ise, where the shrine to Amaterasu, the sun-goddess ancestor of the imperial line, is located.

After lunch I tried to relax in the wardroom by playing cards with Lieutenant Tamaru, the ship's engineering officer. I played for more than two hours, then suddenly decided to stop.

"That's enough for me, Sir," I said, "You're too easy a victim."

He laughed. "You certainly played well this time, Yokota," he said. "It must be because you are tensed up and alert. One's faculties are much more sensitive at such times, they say. You are all alert for a fight, so it makes you more alert for playing cards."

Perhaps it was true that I had played exceptionally well. But I didn't think so. I suspected Lieutenant Tamaru of letting me win because it might be the last game of cards I ever played, and because he wanted to keep my spirits up. I liked Tamaru a lot. Though he was not much older than myself, he was a man of much knowledge, far more than might ordinarily be expected in a man his age. He had a fine flair for journalism, too. Besides his regular duties, he was editor of I-47's ship's paper, the *Underwater News*. This was published now and then, and contained stories by various crewmen and himself. I had often seen Tamaru alone in a corner of the wardroom, writing for the newspaper. In a special Emperor's birthday edition, published the day before for the benefit of *kaiten* men who might not be alive to see April 29, he had written a special poem, dedicated to us of the Tembu Group. I had cut this poem out, and it was now in the same pocket in which I carried the picture of my dead mother.

In the evening of the Emperor's birthday, after I-47 had surfaced, I went to the conning tower for my usual cigarette, then to the crew's quarters, where I quickly got into bed, seeking a full night of sleep. But I was still awake an hour later when Captain Orita put his head in the door. This startled me. It was a rare occasion, for ship commanders did not often visit the crew's quarters, except to make an inspection.

"All *kaiten* men come to the wardroom at once!" he said, his voice loud enough to wake those who were sleeping. His face was bright, and he looked very happy. We leaped out of bed and were on his heels, fumbling with our clothing, as he reached the wardroom. There he took in his breath, looked all around, and said "I-36 has made a successful attack! It was two days ago. She encountered a convoy of thirty ships. Two *kaiten* had trouble, and could not be sent off, but she fired the other four. They sank four large ships, estimated to be transports or cargo ships. We just received this information in the wireless room!"

Everyone cheered this news. The Sixth Fleet's contention was proven! A *kaiten*-carrying submarine, operating in the open sea, had struck down four of the enemy and escaped! She still had two more *kaiten*, and plenty of torpedoes. She could strike down more ships!

When the cheering stopped, and I had time to think, I began feeling glum. I-36 had not left port until two days after us, and she had already made a successful attack. Two days ago! She had only been one week at sea. The six of us looked at one another and wished we had that kind of luck.

I-47 crewmen reacted just as we *kaiten* men had. They were happy about the news at first, but then envious. Their ship and I-36 were friendly rivals. Both were new submarines, completed after the war had started. I-36 had been Kure-based and I-47 Yokosuka-based before they were assigned *kaiten*-carrying duty. They were of similar classes, and competed even in training exercises, I was told.

In the Kikusui operation, I-47 was credited with four ships. I-36 was only credited with one. Three of her *kaiten* failed to operate in that first attack. In the Kongo operation, each was officially credited with four ships. That made them eight-to-five when they had started out on this mission to prove the value of *kaiten* in open-sea operations. Now I-36 had a nine-to-eight lead because of those four sinkings made two days before. We six *kaiten* men, as well as the crew of I-47, made up our minds to exceed that new accomplishment. I-36 *kaiten* pilots sank four of the enemy, so we would sink six! And why not? We were sure we could do it. Of I-36's pilots, only Ensign Kuge had been out on a mission before. All six of us had been out, Shinkai and I once, and the others twice. We considered ourselves far more expert than the men in I-36. We assured I-47 crewmen that we would match and beat I-36's score for them, putting them back in the lead.

There was no action on the thirtieth. We grew nervous. We snapped at unimportant things. The temperature inside I-47 didn't help our dispositions any. The captain was shutting off all cooling systems frequently, so that their sounds would not interfere with the use of our detection equipment. Orita was growing as impatient as we were. We could tell by his frequent visits to the sound operators' room. We could also tell by the tone he took with us as we stood near the conning tower hatch, enjoying our nightly cigarette.

"You men must relax!" he said. "Otherwise, you will be too tired to fight when the time comes. Stay in your berths more!" Then he told us, "Tonight I am going to pull back at least one-hundred miles. We will then surface and give every *kaiten* a complete check. When I'm sure they are all in perfect condition we will return to this area. Somehow, I have the feeling that we will encounter some of the enemy then."

I was at once relieved when I heard this. The captain's words stilled my impatience. I believed in him, and that what he said would prove true. The long, tension-filled waiting would be at an end. I went over in my mind the routine I would follow when the enemy was sighted. At the general alarm bell, I would check my flashlight, stop watch and chartboard. Then I'd position myself as near to my access tube as I could get without being in anyone's way. When Orita called out "Man *kaiten*!" I'd be into that tube in an instant. In half a minute I'd be seated in my weapon, the hatch below me closed and sealed. I'd check all instruments, and report "*Kaiten* No. 3 ready!" Then would come the long dragging wait after all *kaiten* reported ready for action. Lieutenant Kakizaki, as our leader, would have the honor of being fired first. Then, perhaps, Lieutenant Maeda. After that it could be any of us. Meanwhile, I would sit in my *kaiten*, charting reports as they came to me from the conning tower and plotting an intercept course.

I would be helped in this by the navigator and torpedo officer. They would be plotting one, too. The conning tower might tell me, "Move off to the right, 40 degrees. Run at 30 knots for 2 minutes, 15 seconds. When you surface, the enemy will be 500 yards away!"

Then would come, "*Kaiten* Number three, ready?"

"*Kaiten* Number three, ready!"

I would feel my weapon lift just a tiny bit as the hold-down cables were slacked off from inside the submarine. Then I would reach back with my right hand for the starting lever.

"Go!"

I would hit the starting lever at that moment, just as the last cable was released. At the same time, with the thumb of my left hand, I would start my stop watch. The great engine behind me would roar into life. I would be on my way!

Then would come the hardest part of all. I'd be at about thirty-five feet when launched. I would have to go into a right turn of forty degrees immediately, and at the same time make a smooth ascent until I was fifteen feet below the surface. As I straightened out on my intercept course, I'd have to adjust the oxygen feed smoothly until I was making thirty knots. At the same time I'd have to start taking on sea water to compensate for the oxygen I used up. This would keep my weapon stabilized. My eyes would be darting here and there, from compass to fuel gauge to depth meter, while my hands would move rapidly from rudder control to diving plane control to fuel valve and ballast controls. Perhaps, during all of this, one hand might lightly caress the small box containing Yazaki's ashes, if there were time.

I would read my stop watch frequently. Then, fifteen seconds before my required run was over, I would ease up my periscope. The target would be, or should be, dead ahead, crossing my bow. I'd take a quick look and, if she were where she should be, I would make perhaps one small adjustment to my rudder, crank down my periscope and push my *kaiten* to its top speed. Not very many seconds after that I'd be blasted into eternity, taking a ship and hundreds of the enemy with me.

Yes, that was just how it would be. I could picture every detail in my mind as clearly as though all those things were actually happening right at that moment. Now I would rest, making sure to get a good night's sleep. Tomorrow I would be bursting with strength. No enemy would be able to stop me.

For once, I was able to go right to sleep. Even the uncomfortable berth had no effect on me. The next day found me full of vigor.

No enemy was sighted. We spent most of that day well off the supply route of the enemy, checking over our *kaiten*. All appeared to be in good condition, and late that night we reversed course and steamed for a point where we might intercept enemy ships. We dove at dawn and stayed down all day. Then, after dark, when I-47 had been running on the surface for about twenty minutes, a lookout sighted something.

"Ships! About twelve miles away!" he called out.

This was a remarkable sighting, but not too unusual for Japanese sailors. Our lookouts were selected carefully and equipped with far more powerful binoculars than those of any other navy. In the early days of the war, before radar was developed to full efficiency, this special training of lookouts had enabled our forces to achieve surprise even against radar-equipped ships. It had been done in the First Battle of the Eastern Solomons, which Americans call the Battle of Savo Island, and on other occasions.

I-47 stayed on the surface after this sighting. Lieutenant Commander Orita rushed to the radar room. He wanted to see for himself what the enemy looked like, before he made his final approach. Once we went under the waves he would have only his night periscope to see through. Its field was very small. I followed him to the radar room, curious to see for myself what the enemy looked like on radar.

It was a wondrous sight. Between 180 and 190 degrees on the round scope there was a small, bright green line, not much bigger than a fat dot. Beyond it, further from the center of the glass, there were other such small lines.

"Good!" said Orita, satisfied that his lookout had seen the enemy. He estimated the convoy at more than a dozen ships. None of them had turned toward us, so he knew their radar had so far not detected our presence. Perhaps they had no escort. Or perhaps their escort had grown careless, supposing there were no Japanese submarines left to fight.

Captain Orita went into the conning tower. "All hands to battle stations!" he ordered. "Prepare to fire torpedoes!" After that he ordered full speed made toward the enemy convoy.

Below, torpedomen heaved and hauled on torpedoes, ramming them into tubes. I-47 had eight torpedo tubes and carried twenty torpedoes. She was the only survivor of her powerful class of submarines, the other seven having been sunk in the war. We dashed ahead on the surface for a while, cutting the range in half. Then Orita, fearing the enemy might sight us, ordered the ship down to periscope depth. We *kaiten* men gathered with our equipment in the wardroom, below and just forward of the conning tower. There we would hear everything that went on, and yet be poised for a dash to our weapons should the captain order it.

"Tubes loaded!" the torpedo officer reported.

"Stand by tubes Numbers One, Two, Three, and Four!" Orita ordered. We were then running at our best speed, straight for the enemy.

"Sound is right, five degrees. Degree of sensitivity is two," said an operator from the sound detection room. "Multiple sounds. It must be a convoy."

If it were only daytime now, our *kaiten* would have an excellent opportunity. We were within five miles now, and the sea was relatively calm. From this range we could hardly miss. If this sighting had only come a few hours in the future, we could easily have surpassed I-36's record. But now it was late at night. And there was no moon, the navigator said. The six of us sat down, knowing we could not possibly be sent off.

But disappointment didn't stay with us long. The feeling was washed away by the excitement of watching and listening to the I-47 crew go about the work they knew so well. This would be our first real combat. It would make fine revenge for the battering given us by those two American destroyers a month before.

Forty minutes had passed since our lookout had first sighted the convoy. "Range closing!" reported the sound room. "Intensity three!" At a fifty-five-foot depth we raced in, enemy propeller noises growing louder in the ears of our sound men. Captain Orita and Lieutenant Kawamoto were taking turns at the night periscope. At last Kawamoto sighted the enemy.

"He's right, ninety degrees!" we heard him shout. "Range, two miles!"

We had slowed down, and were almost dead in the water as Captain Orita swung our bow toward the leading ships. Now he gave his final orders. At intervals of two seconds he called out, "Fire One! Fire Two! Fire Three! Fire Four!"

My eardrums popped a little as each Model 95 torpedo went off. As the first one moved away, I pressed the button on my stop watch. Lieutenant Kawamoto had called out the running time as two minutes, forty seconds.

The seconds ticked slowly past. I was rigid with expectation when the two minutes, thirty seconds mark was reached. Only ten more seconds to go! They ticked off, one by one, but no sound came. Had we missed? Five more seconds passed. Were we to be disappointed again? First we had been depth-charged and damaged so much we were forced back to port. Now an easy prize was slipping through our hands. What had gone wrong? My stop watch had ticked off two minutes and fifty seconds when I heard a distant, metallic click, then a big explosion.

"We did it!" I yelled, and slammed my fist, stop watch and all, into Shinkai's back.

Seconds later there was a second explosion. Leading Petty Officer Fujisaki shouted down, "A direct hit!" All through I-47 people were cheering. Even Tanaka must feel good, I thought. This is what the old days in 1942 must have been like for him.

A third explosion followed close behind the second one, and the captain spoke over the loudspeaker. "Three of our four torpedoes have made hits," he said. "One ship is already starting to go down, and we can see a column of fire rising from a second one." All of us began singing then. Of four torpedoes fired, only one had missed. Two had hit the target, and a third, running further, had struck a second ship.

"Take the ship down to 250 feet!" shouted Orita. Then he called to the sound room, "Keep a close watch! Listen for destroyer propellers!" He was sure that enemy escorts had put their helms hard over and were heading our way.

I-47 started downward. Before long we were leveled off

far beneath the surface. On board everything was quiet. The sound room kept reporting no trace of high-speed propellers moving toward us. "Only breaking-up sounds detected. All other propeller sounds are receding."

This made us feel good. The other ships of the convoy were running away. Were any of them staying to help those we had hit? Maybe not. Maybe they had received news of I-36's successful attack of four days before, and were taking no chances. At any rate, we would have no chance for a second attack. The enemy was now alerted. He would call for patrol planes or bombers from an aircraft carrier. Messages received in our wireless room indicated many American carriers east of Okinawa.

Captain Orita kept I-47 down in the depths. A victory had been won. Now we had to hide for a while. We began to move as far away as we could. About 4:00 A.M. the submarine rose to the surface and cruised until dawn, recharging her batteries. Before us lay a day never to be forgotten.

13 ◻ "Kaiten, Away!"

That morning was May 2, 1945. We submerged at dawn, our batteries charged for an all-day run under water. *Kaiten* pilots had rested well. We were ready in every respect for action. All we needed was the captain's summons to battle, though we in fact held little hope of it for that day. Either the enemy would be nowhere in sight, or he would be present in overwhelming numbers, sweeping the seas for us with many destroyers and airplanes.

Most of the morning dragged past. With nothing else to do, the *kaiten* men gathered in the wardroom. Equipment dangling on strings from our necks, we engaged in our customary pastime of practicing the estimation of angles. We became so intent on judging the various angles from the ship model that we didn't notice how much the noise level in our submarine had been dropping off. Nor did we hear the report that must have been passed from the sound room to the conning tower. At 9:30 A.M. my five comrades and I were jolted from our concentration by the general alarm bell. Its clanging was still going on when Captain Orita called out, "All hands to battle stations! Move up to periscope depth!"

I-47 rose to see in the periscope what her sound detection equipment had noticed. That order spun us *kaiten* men into action. The six of us began making final checks to see we had all our equipment at hand. I pressed my stop watch button, let the hand run a few seconds, stopped it, and reset it to zero. All I needed now was the order to go into my *kaiten.*

"This looks like it at last, Sir," Petty Officer Shinkai said to Kakizaki.

"I think you are right," said the lieutenant. "Now let us do a good job for these brave men who carried us out here from home." He was smiling, and so was Lieutenant Maeda. When I saw Maeda tying his *hachimaki* around his head, I

181

got out my own and put it on, giving the knot a hard tug so it would stay tight.

Then the captain called out, "Stand by for *kaiten* attack!"

A minute or so later he shouted, "*Kaiten* men, board your weapons!"

"Let's go, Shinkai!" I yelled, nudging my friend. He headed forward while I dashed aft toward the stern, nimbly avoiding objects I had noted the position of during earlier drills. Men at their battle stations watched me race by, and cried, "*Yareyo, Yokota-san!* Good luck!" as I passed.

My access tube was near the after end of I-47's engine room. As I climbed toward it I called to everyone, "*Sayonara!* And thank you for everything!" A split-second later I disappeared from their sight.

Two maintenance men were crawling through the tube behind me. I climbed into the weapon, picked up my telephone and called, "Petty Officer Yokota, in *kaiten* No. 3!" Then I looked down. Two faces were looking up at me in the dim light of a single bulb that illuminated the interior of the pilot's compartment. "We will close this hatch for you now," they said, their faces glimmering with tears.

"Very well," I said. "And thank you very much for everything." Perhaps I might have used that moment to shout some last triumphant slogan, but it just did not occur to me. I was too occupied with getting ready to be fired. In a moment the hatch clanged shut. I turned the handle below me to secure it tightly.

"Number Three? Number Three?" A voice was coming through my receiver.

"Number Three is on board!" I called back in a firm, clear voice. I had reacted just as I did during the manning drills. But this was no drill. I reached into my pocket, took out my dead mother's picture, and placed it beside my compass. That dear woman, whom I had never really known, would be the last sight my living eyes would see before my soul joined hers in death.

I could hear sea water gushing into my access tube now. It was filled in a few seconds. I was all ready, only two things necessary to fire me away—releasing two tie-down cables, and starting my engine.

Every motion, every action, every requirement of concentration came to me automatically. It was just like one of the perfect drills I had experienced back at Hikari. "Come on! Come on!" I silently urged the voice at the other end of my telephone line. I had only been inside my *kaiten* about seven or eight seconds, but I was already impatient to go.

"Control! Number Three is ready to go!" I called into the telephone, hoping I might prompt the conning tower to send me off at once.

The voice answering me was condescending. He sounded as though he had been expecting me to say something like that. "All *kaiten* are ready to go, Yokota," he said, speaking as to a small child. I realized his opinion of me might be lowered if I appeared too anxious. After all, Kakizaki was supposed to go first. I would be considered a very rude person if I asked to precede him. So I took several deep breaths, sucking strength into my stomach, and tried to calm down. I checked my instruments and stop watch again and fussed with my *hachimaki,* setting it more firmly down on my forehead. My hands kept moving automatically over the controls. I readjusted my depth gauge, setting pressure so I would not suddenly leap out of the water when fired off. Soon all was ready. I needed only to push my starting lever to get going.

Then, in much slower tones, to assure the conning tower that I knew my place, I asked, "What is the enemy?"

"There are two ships. One is a large-sized transport. The other is a destroyer."

"Only two?" This information upset me. I had hoped and prayed we would catch another large convoy, so that all six of us could go off in one general volley, dying together in a single, six-pronged onslaught.

The voice in my phone gave me further information. "Angle is right, 60 degrees. Range, 2 miles. Enemy speed is 14 knots. Enemy course, 270 degrees."

I repeated this back, according to our procedure, to show I had it correct, and noted it on my chart. My compass had been aligned with the submarine's fore-and-aft axis. That line would be my reference point when launched.

A new voice came through the telephone. It had cut into the general circuit, addressing all six of us together.

"Number One and Number Four will be fired. All others, remain ready."

That meant Lieutenant Kakizaki and Petty Officer Yamaguchi would go. What would happen to me?

"Is Number Three going?" I asked, forgetting how calm I had intended to remain.

"Wait!" said the conning tower voice abruptly. "There are only two enemy ships right now!"

I was ashamed of myself for being so presumptuous. Naturally Yamaguchi, very senior to myself in service, should go ahead of me. I sat still, holding my breath until it nearly choked me.

"Number One, get ready!" No voice was on the general circuit now. What I heard was another voice in the conning tower, coming dimly through the mouthpiece of the man who was in touch with me. I could not hear Kakizaki's voice. I bent forward and peered through my periscope. The water was a lovely blue, and at this level there was light enough for me to make out the stern of Kakizaki's *kaiten*, about thirty-five feet ahead of me on I-47's after deck. He had started his engine, and the noise was smooth, assuring me everything was going well for him. The image before my eyes jolted suddenly. Kakizaki's fourth tie-down had been released.

I had not heard the order "Go!," but it had been given. In a second or two, Kakizaki started moving away. I spoke his name softly as a great mass of white bubbles floated back over around my weapon. These were from the high pressure air used to turn his torpedo's engine over for its first few revolutions. When they dissipated, and I could again see clearly, he was gone, his *kaiten* rack empty.

A short time later I heard the drumming, humming sound of a second engine. Yamaguchi was going, his bubbles also obscuring his departure. Two persons, two friends who had laughed and joked with me on the deck of a torpedo boat at Hikari, who had shared their cigarettes so often with me, were gone. I closed my eyes, conjuring up their faces for a final look at them.

A long wait came after that, followed by an explosion that rocked I-47 and those *kaiten* still on her deck. "A hit!" I shouted, not caring whether it went over my telephone line or not. Shortly after that I yelled, "Another hit!" as a second explosion jarred me in my seat.

My two friends were now dead. Their lives were over. At that moment their souls were flying, side by side, to the great shrine at Yasukuni, there to be eternally revered like gods. I ached to join them, my voice shaking with sobs as

I called the conning tower and asked, "Are there any more targets?"

"Lieutenant Kakizaki and Petty Officer Yamaguchi have both scored direct hits," was the answer I received.

This enraged me. I lost all control. "I didn't ask you that, stupid!" I screamed into the transmitter. "Don't you think I have ears? I asked you whether there were any more enemy ships out there. Answer me!"

The conning tower must have been bedlam by then. I could hear shouting sounds on my line. Furukawa, Shinkai and Maeda were also calling into their transmitters and being answered. The conning tower watch let us shout all we wanted for a little while, then interrupted with, "No more echoes have been detected by our sound operators. All *kaiten* are to stand by."

That soothed me a little, as it must have soothed the others. The line became quiet, and my hopes rose. When selected for this mission, we had spoken often of how we would all die together, like true comrades. We had shared pleasure, hardship, discipline, danger and disappointment. Surely fate would not separate us now! Even destroyers would suit me for targets, though I knew sinking one would not damage the enemy much. They had hundreds of them. Four might not even be missed, for all I knew. Still, Furukawa, Shinkai, Maeda and I needed four more ships if we were to join Kakizaki and Yamaguchi this day at Yasukuni. If there had been some way to summon the enemy to us, to tell him where we were, I would have done it. So would the others, I am sure.

Some more time passed, and then I could hear another dim voice in my receiver. "Number Two," it asked, "are you ready?"

Furukawa had been alerted!

"Angle is left, seventy degrees. Target is a destroyer. Range, three miles."

I wanted to call out a protest again, but Furukawa was getting final instructions. If I began shouting, it might confuse him. I kept silent. Furukawa was my senior. I had to show him full respect.

Furukawa's telephone talker must have moved close to mine. His voice suddenly came through my receiver, loud and clear.

"The angle is not too good, but you can still be successful.

Run at full speed for ten minutes. That will put you ahead of the enemy. When you put up your periscope, look to the left!"

I calculated rapidly on my chart. Captain Orita was making a good move. The target and Furukawa would both be well away from us. The enemy, if he survived, would be unable to locate the source of this attack.

"Ready? . . . Go!"

Again, bubbles clouded my periscope. Mine was now the only *kaiten* remaining on I-47's after deck. When the bubbles cleared away I could now make out three empty *kaiten* racks ahead of me. The sight filled me with a deep loneliness, which must have been reflected in my voice a little later when I softly asked, "Are there any more of the enemy?"

My question was the first of many pouring into the conning tower. All reason had left my two remaining comrades. All we wanted to do now was fight! I clamored as loudly as the others to be next *kaiten* off. We kept it up for about twenty minutes, when we were all cut off by a voice from the tower.

"No more enemy sounds can be detected by our equipment," the conning tower telephone operator reported. "The remaining *kaiten* pilots will return to the submarine. We are now clearing your access tubes."

I cursed my luck. All that hope, and all that expectation, and now we could not go off. When the hissing sound of air ceased, I opened my lower hatch. Below, I saw the face of my maintenance man. "Please come out," he said, sliding up through the hatch and cramping himself into the small space behind my seat. "I will take care of everything for you."

Several crewmen were waiting as I re-entered I-47. "Welcome back!" they said, which shocked me at first. Then it made me feel good, because I realized they were actually happy that I had not been launched. A few faces showed the same kind of disappointment I felt, but the older crewmen, for the most part, were glad that one so much younger than they had not ended his life.

I strode past them and went to the wardroom. Maeda and Shinkai were already there, peering at their watches.

"It should have been time by now," said Maeda.

"How long has it been, Sir?" I asked.

"Thirty-eight minutes," Maeda said. "And there is no sound from the enemy, any more. He is out of range of our detection equipment."

"*Ah, so desuka?*" I said. "Is that so?" I became worried. Furukawa's course required a long run to get into position. Then he had to set his own intercept course from there. If he had any trouble controlling his depth, the destroyer might have seen him. It might now be running for its life, with him after it. Only a destroyer could approach a *kaiten's* speed, but with a good lead, it might get away.

Furukawa would blow himself up if he could not catch the enemy. I was sure of it. There was no way we could ever find him if he ran out of fuel. *Kaiten* sat too low in the water when surfaced to be seen from a submarine if there were any kind of waves at all. And Orita did not dare surface, anyway, in daylight, to look for him, especially when there were enemy ships around.

Suddenly we heard the sound operator call out. "I have an echo! Very faint! Degree of intensity is only one. It might be the *kaiten,* though." Our watches had ticked past forty minutes, then forty-five. Maeda's face had darkened. Our watches now showed that forty-seven minutes had elapsed. In thirteen more minutes the last of Furukawa's fuel would be gone. I prayed that the sound was that of his final rush at top speed into the enemy.

Then, before the sound operator could even announce it, we heard an explosion! It was not as big as the first two— they had been closer. But it was the sound of a *kaiten.* There was no doubt of it. No American destroyer could make that big a sound with a depth charge.

"*Banzai,* Furukawa!" I yelled. Tears ran down our cheeks.

"Petty Officer Furukawa has scored a direct hit!" the loudspeaker announced. No more cheers sounded through I-47, though. All suddenly became silent. I have never been able to explain why. The three ships credited to Orita's submarine for this mission, plus two credited to his torpedoes earlier, put I-47 ahead thirteen-nine in the competition with I-36. Crewmen should have been cheering hysterically and pounding one another on the back. Through my mind, in this intense silence, passed the words I had heard so often since joining the Imperial Navy. "In this crisis, you must stand ready to give your life, to save Japan!" Furukawa had given his, but the long wait during his attack seemed to take the steel out of all on board I-47. There was no feeling left in us to summon up more cheers. It had washed away during that forty-nine-minute wait.

Some time later, I don't know how much later, I returned to the crew's campartment. There, on two bunks, lay the small, carefully-stacked piles of belongings Yamaguchi and Furukawa had left beside their pillows. I fell into my own berth, sobbing endlessly. Death would be easier to take than this unendurable grief I felt at the loss of those two dear friends. Would Yamaguchi be able to get any beer in his new world? Would Furukawa, the true, staunch friend, be with him there, sitting quietly, and talking about his experiences in the Navy? I prayed for them between outbursts of weeping and sobbing, and for Lieutenant Kakizaki. "I will follow you, my dear friends," I said into my pillow, and asked them to welcome me with smiles when I came to the gate of Yasukuni.

The next day, May 3, found me somewhat recovered. My grief had been replaced by fatalism. All I yearned for now was to get the whole thing over with. But nothing was sighted during the day, and in the evening Captain Orita summoned Maeda, Shinkai and myself to him. "Because of our torpedo and *kaiten* attacks," he said, "our presence here is surely known to the enemy. He is sure to send air and surface patrols looking for us. So I am going to move my ship away, at once. We will cruise for a day or two, staying out of sight if at all possible. When he thinks we have gone, we will come back and try to find more targets. So you three may as well rest all you can. There will be no need for *kaiten* for, oh, perhaps three days."

Downhearted, we left his cabin and went to the wardroom. Lieutenant Kakizaki's belongings were still on his bunk. They made a very sad sight. I didn't know why they had been left there so long, and I hoped no one would neglect my belongings this way when I was finally sent off.

That evening and the following day passed without incident. On May 5, the navigator informed us we were now patrolling on a line between Guam and Okinawa. Nothing was sighted that day, either, and when I took my evening smoke in the conning tower I had a strange feeling. I could imagine that my companions were still with me, though there was no glow from their cigarettes in the darkness. As I puffed on my cigarette, it occurred to me that a man's emotions were more upsetting than anything else to him. Actually, I had no more to concern me at that moment than any other man on board I-47. The crewmen at all times were in as much danger as I. They were risking their lives. I was simply giving mine, and there was but a small difference. They might be giving theirs, too, at any moment, should an American destroyer trap us. Too much thinking was my trouble. I ought simply to go about doing what I had to do, as other men did.

The next morning, May 6, we had a *kaiten* drill. All went well, except for trouble with my telephone cable. Sometimes the voice at the other end would cut out, losing a word or two in the middle of a sentence, and at other times I would not hear anything at all for as much as thirty seconds. When the drill was over I told my maintenance man to check it.

"Without a good telephone connection I am useless," I said. "I cannot get instructions from the tower. I cannot learn where the enemy is, and what he is doing. Check that line thoroughly. Get a replacement for the receiver if necessary. I must have it in good working order!"

He said he would make the repairs. My maintenance man knew his business. He would stay on the job until repairs were made. If he could not put it in first class condition at once, he would work far into the night, then be up before dawn to finish the job.

Ironically, at 11:00 A.M., not long after *kaiten* drill ended, I-47's sound room reported a contact. Captain Orita sped to the periscope for a look around, and ordered battle stations manned at once. Shortly after that he ordered all three *kaiten* manned. He had decided to use us. The target must be a big one, I thought, as I raced through the engine room, otherwise he would be using conventional torpedoes.

"Petty Officer Yokota reporting!" I called from my lone position on the stern. "Number Three *kaiten* is manned!"

No answer.

I made the same report again.

No answer.

It was then I realized that my telephone line was completely dead. Water must have leaked into the connection, grounding it. Or perhaps the line had pulled loose somehow. I looked at the portion of the wire that was inside my compartment. It seemed all right. I examined the receiver again, and hit it with the heel of my palm a few times. Nothing could be heard.

Well, there's nothing to be done except prepare for take-off, I told myself. I went through the regular check of controls and gauges. Perhaps the telephone trouble was at the other end of the line. When they had it repaired and I could hear them again, I must be ready.

I was ready in a short while, and tried the line again.

No answer.

I waited, breathing a short prayer, and tried once more.

No answer.

I shouted into it.

No answer.

I went berserk. Cursing and screaming into the telephone, I demanded to be fired off. What if I didn't know what the target was, or where? "Turn me loose!" I shrieked into the transmitter. "I'll find the enemy myself!" I hoped the conning tower could hear me, even though I was not hearing them.

Still nothing. Since I could not get away until the two remaining hold-down cables were loosened, there was nothing to do but sit, and wait, and hope.

Soon I heard the noise of a *kaiten* motor up ahead. I listened closely and looked into my periscope, but could not tell whether it was on the port or starboard side. Was it Shinkai, or was it Maeda? I could not tell which, but another of my comrades was on his way to glory and death.

There were no more sounds for a while. My impatience grew and grew. Then I struck upon what I thought was an excellent idea. I would start my engine! Then Captain Orita would have to release me! He'd have to let me take my chances. I would go off without any instructions at all, of course. I'd have to search for the enemy alone. Perhaps I might not find him, and have to scuttle, and die in the ocean. But at least I'd be fired off. If I weren't, my *kaiten* would be lost. With all fuel used up, it would be useless. If I started the engine, Orita would either have to send me away or lose the worth of one weapon, perhaps lose the opportunity to sink one of the enemy.

I would do it! I reached back and was about to push the starting bar, when I heard air hissing into my access tube. *Kaiten* pilots were being called back. I gave up my plan in disgust, knowing there would be no more targets, and opened my hatch for return to the hull.

"Who went off?" I asked my maintenance man.

"Lieutenant Maeda."

"And Shinkai?"

"He had telephone trouble. His communications failed, like yours."

"How many enemy ships were there?"

"I'm not sure. Perhaps two." The mechanic looked sad. He felt he had failed me, with that telephone trouble. With a good line, I might have been sent off. I knew I would have been, since Shinkai's telephone wasn't working.

Shinkai was in the conning tower when I got there. The captain looked at both of us and shook his head. "You two had bad luck," he said. "I could not send you off without full information. The waves were too high. Visibility from a *kaiten* would be practically zero."

"But Lieutenant Maeda . . ." I began.

"He insisted that I let him go," said Orita. "And I think he may get a hit yet. Meanwhile, we will see that your telephones are repaired tonight for sure. You will yet get your chance."

"Sir," I asked then, "how many enemy ships were there?"

Orita looked at me a few seconds before answering. "Just one," he said, "a cruiser." His tone was a little angry, as though I were questioning him too closely. I didn't believe him, and I think he knew it.

"Well, Shinkai," I said, "there is no use just standing here, getting in the way of these people. Let's go."

As we stepped from the conning tower, we heard a great explosion. "Maeda has done it!" I told Shinkai. "He has hit a target, too!"

Again I experienced tears, running to the crew's compartment, and flinging myself into my berth. I was sadder at that moment then I had ever been in my life. I thought of what Captain Orita had told the six of us at Tanegashima when we had to go back to the base for repairs after being depth-charged. "To live, at times, is much more difficult than to die. A lot of patience is required to wait until the best possible moment for dying comes."

I was sure he had not told me the truth in the conning tower. He had said there was only one ship, but I felt there had been two or more. Cruisers did not often travel alone, at least enemy cruisers. They usually escorted something, or were escorted themselves, by destroyers. I was sure Captain Orita had lied, so that our spirits would not collapse, so that we would keep them up for when an enemy was sighted again.

I forgave him, in case he had not been telling the truth. I had great respect for Captain Orita. He had made us a promise at Tanegashima that his ship would take us out again after repairs had been made. He had kept that first promise. He had kept others, too, since we had moved out to sea on this mission. Now he had made another promise, that our telephones would be repaired before morning, so we would get a chance to go off after the enemy. I believed he would keep the promise.

Fate would not let him keep it, however. That night, while men were working hard passing a new telephone line to each of the *kaiten*, the wireless room received a message from home. "I-47's performance thus far is appreciated," it said. "Congratulations. Discontinue the rest of the operation. Return to base at once."

14 ◻ The Todoroki Group Is Formed

I must have made the world's most forlorn figure as I-47 steamed back through Bungo Strait. The four empty *kaiten* racks haunted my soul. My No. 3, at the stern, had turned a rusty red. It was nothing like the gleaming black weapon I had so proudly checked over at the beginning of the mission.

Shinkai felt as badly as I did. He, who had been always so jolly, was deep in gloom. We both felt like outcasts. We dreaded returning to our barracks. We were sure no one would speak to us. Six *kaiten* men had gone out, and four had been launched. Shinkai and I were now returning for the second time. People would think there was something wrong with us, we thought, and would turn their faces away.

As soon as we could be free of the submarine we went to our old room and stayed there, secluding ourselves as much as we could. We avoided contact with other people which possible. We hoped the earth would suddenly open and swallow us into its depths. To increase my own mental depression, too, there was the low physical feeling I had upon leaving the submarine. I had not had a bath in three weeks. I was covered with dried sweat, grease and dirt. Though I took many baths, I could never seem to cleanse myself of the filthy feeling that ran through me. I had the same kind of sensation that some people have when they are recovering from a long, serious illness—a deep lassitude, a complete unwillingness to do more than is absolutely necessary.

Four or five days passed this way after our return to Hikari. Then, on May 17, as I was lying on my bed, staring emptily at the ceiling, Lieutenant, junior grade, Tsubone burst into my room.

"Yokota, are you here?" he called.

In earlier days I would have sprung to my feet, come to attention and answered very briskly, "Yes, Sir!" This time the "Yes, Sir," came out of me reluctantly, as though spoken by a schoolboy who has been asked if he had committed some slight offense.

"You are to go to Otsujima at once!" Tsubone said. "Pack your things!"

"I, Sir?" I was stunned. Inside me the feeling had been growing that I might never again be selected for another *kaiten* mission. I feared the officers might think a man who had been out twice without success might not have enough determination for a third time. Of course my four friends, Kakizaki, Maeda, Yamaguchi and Furukawa were proof that this theory wasn't correct, but hadn't the Naval General Staff argued that a man could not sustain determination for death indefinitely?

"Of course you!" said Tsubone. "Petty Officer Irie died in training yesterday. He was supposed to go out in I-36 with a new mission. You have been ordered to take his place. Pack up!"

"But . . . but what happened to Irie?" I asked. Of our particular squadron at Tsuchiura, only Raita Irie and I had been selected for *kaiten* training. We had served together nearly all the time I had been in the Navy.

"He crashed into the target ship with Shoichi Sakamoto on board. Now get ready!"

Shinkai would be saddened to hear of those two deaths, I thought. The four of us had been good friends. Shinkai! I had forgotten him in my confusion. What would he say about my going to Otsujima? How would he feel? Lieutenant Tsubone had not mentioned anyone but myself. Only one man had been selected. My good friend Shinkai would have to remain at Hikari. It would break his heart.

"Report to Lieutenant Mitani as soon as you have packed, Yokota," said Tsubone, and left.

"Yes, Sir." I started getting into my uniform. Shinkai came into the room while I was finishing up. He saw that my things were packed, and cried out in an excited voice, "Are you leaving, Yokota? Where are you going?" He must have read the compassion in my eyes, for his suddenly became accusing. "You are leaving without me!" he said. "You were not even going to say goodbye!"

He was correct. In my mind, I had known I would not be able to bear parting from my friend. I had hoped to be gone from Hikari before he discovered I was leaving. I was sorry about Irie's death, but the truth was that it had changed my whole world for me. I was going out on a mission again. Now Shinkai, my friend in the face of death as well as in life, stood before me, his whole being charging me with desertion.

"What can I do, Shinkai?" I asked him. "They just gave me the order to leave a few minutes ago."

I didn't know what else I could say. I tried to console him. "They know how skilled you are in operating a *kaiten*," I said. "They need only one man right now, because of an accident. Raita Irie died yesterday, with Shoichi Sakamoto, during training. I am to take his place. When I get to Otsujima I will ask the leader if they need another man. I will tell them you are here, and very anxious."

"Never mind!" he shouted. "Go on! Leave! I don't care if I never go!"

"I'll be back in a few minutes, Kikuo," I said. "Wait here for me."

I rushed to Lieutenant Mitani's room, a little angry at Shinkai for delaying me. Friendship had flown off into the sky the moment Lieutenant Tsubone had given me my orders. I was concerned about my friend, but not so much that it lessened my inner happiness at being selected for this mission. Lieutenant Mitani answered my knock, a smile on his face.

"Well, Yokota, I guess you have received the news. You don't look very rested to me, but that cannot be helped right now. You are to board a launch for Otsujima in thirty minutes. Can you be ready by that time?"

"I am ready now, Sir," I answered. "But what about Shinkai? What will happen to him? Is it necessary that we be separated like this?"

Mitani's face was solemn. "Don't worry," said the maintenance officer, "we are keeping Shinkai in mind. It is just that they only need one man at the moment. One man must stay behind, obviously. Nothing can be done about that, can there?"

"That's true, Sir," I said, "but when I left our room just now, Shinkai was weeping. He is most unhappy."

Mitani patted my shoulder. He said no more time could be spent talking about it, and that I had to hurry. So I could do nothing more for Shinkai except look sympathetically at him as he stood on the pier, waving his cap over his head in farewell, while my launch steamed away toward Otsujima.

On arrival at Otsujima, I was in a great rush. They had

only given me an hour's notice at Hikari, I thought, so they must need me badly. I hurried to the officers' quarters and there met Lieutenant Commander Mizoguchi. He had been promoted one rank since I had last seen him and had relieved Lieutenant Commander Itakura as commanding officer at Otsujima.

"It is good to see you again, Yokota," he said. "I hear you have done very well in your training. That is a credit to this base, and we thank you. I'm glad to have you with us again."

I was more abrupt with him than an enlisted man should be with an officer. I cut short the formalities of greeting quickly, and asked him at once, "When does I-36 depart for action, Sir?"

"Oh, not for some time yet," he said. "She is having a short refit at Kure right now. She will come to Hikari to load *kaiten* later. Meanwhile, you will be having several sessions of combined training. You won't be leaving until the end of the month, I imagine."

The end of the month? I had expected to go on board the submarine as soon as I got to Hikari. How could Mizoguchi be so casual? Germany had surrendered to the Allied Forces a week before. Now America and Great Britain would be able to bring all their air and sea power to bear on Japan! We had already been driven from nearly every Pacific island. Our forces isolated in the Marianas, Philippines and New Guinea were being cut down to the last man. How could any kind of delay be tolerated?

My disappointment showed, but Mizoguchi offered no words to soften it. "You had better go to your quarters," he said. "The senior officer of your group will be looking for you, I am sure."

I returned to the pier, picking up my things and went to the barracks. Odd, I thought as I unpacked. My last mission had been on board I-47, the "never die ship." Now I was to go out in her rival, I-36. Would the crew be as friendly as the first had been? Would I feel as warmly toward them as I had toward I-47 men?

On the day of my arrival at Otsujima, a simple ceremony was held to bid a last goodbye to the souls of Petty Officers Irie and Sakamoto. Sakamoto, the judo champion, the raging tiger with whom I had joined in that famous horseback fight in the snow to give Ensign Toyama the beating he deserved, was dead. A sad thing, for a man of his great spirit to perish without getting into action. The two had been cramped into one *kaiten,* practicing, when they rammed into the side of a 10,000-ton transport they were using as a target. Their weapon sank at once. When their bodies were recovered, it was learned that sudden sea pressure had actually popped their eyes from their heads before they drowned. This I learned from other *kaiten* men who had helped bring up the lost weapon.

I learned that the submarines scheduled to go out for attack next were I-361, I-363 and I-36, my ship. I-165 was later included, but at the time I departed only the first three submarines were considered to make up the Todoroki Group. *"Todoroki,"* in Japanese, means "resounding," and can also be interpreted as the booming of great cannon. This second meaning applied to us. We were to have the effect of many great guns on the enemy. We would be a "great roar," a *"todoroki."*

I was lucky again, getting I-36, I thought. The other two ships were fat former transports, like I-368. They could only make thirteen knots on the surface, though they had great cruising range. If detected, such slow submarines would not have much of a chance against enemy destroyers. Nor could they successfully pursue ships, with their slow speeds. And the maximum depth they could dive safely was 240 feet. I-165, later included, had been hurriedly converted and would carry only two *kaiten* when she went out.

While I was at sea with I-47, another *kaiten* mission had gone out. It was called Shimbu, meaning "furtherance of the *samurai* way," a name given many times in Japan to organizations in which great spirit was sought. Organizations bearing this name sought to obtain members who were willing to make sacrifices, and to endure hardship. It was a very patriotic designation. The one ship which formed the Shimbu mission was I-367, which shows how badly off our submarine fleet was at the time. When she left on May 5, we had only four large cruising submarines, I-36, I-47, I-53 and I-58, left.

I-367 operated to the east of Okinawa, with five *kaiten.* Only one of these, manned by Petty Officer Masaaki Ono, could be fired. It was sent off on May 31, and officially credited with sinking a ship. The remaining four *kaiten* could not be fired because of mechanical failures.

More desperate measures were being taken in defense of our country. On May 4, a mass *kamikaze* attack was made on

Okinawa, in conjunction with a counter-landing by our forces there. While the planes were attacking, our island defenders would try to put out from shore and land again behind the enemy, catching them in a pincer movement. The strategy did not work. The Americans were much too strong for us. The planes were mostly shot down, and the counter-landing force was decimated.

My group this time was headed by Lieutenant, junior grade, Nobuo Ikebuchi. There were two other officers in it, Ensign Minoru Kuge and Ensign Ichiro Sonoda. For all three, this would be the third time out.

Ensign Sonoda had been with Ikebuchi in I-58, which was called back from the Tembu and Tatara missions before *kaiten* could be fired. Ensign Kuge had gone out with I-53 on the Kongo mission, but had mechanical trouble. He had similar trouble in I-36 with the Tembu Group, and was one of the two men not launched the day she made her big kill of four transports.

Petty Officer Eizo Nomura was, like myself, from Tsuchiura. He had been the second man not fired from I-36 on that fateful April 27. The other petty officer was Hidemasa Yanagiya, also a former cadet pilot from Tsuchiura. He had been with Ikebuchi and Sonoda on the two missions in I-58. He, too, had suffered the sadness of two returns.

So it can be seen why, with all these disappointments spurring us on, the spirit of eagerness was so high. We began our final training the next day, May 18, determined to make a good showing in front of everyone. The area of Tokuyama Bay was smaller than that used for training at Hikari, and it had been nearly a month since I had tried my hand at operating a *kaiten*. The attitude of the instructors showed that they expected a great deal of me. After all I had now been in *kaiten* training for over four months since that first day I put one in the water, so I exercised great care that day, and thought I made a fine run.

The seminar that night for us was very rough. Lieutenant Commander Tetsuaki Sugamasa, commander of I-36, was present, as were the commanding and executive officers of Otsujima base. It grieved us to learn they thought our performance of the day was not up to standards expected of men considered ready for a mission. My shot was graded as passing under the target ship's stern, they said. Ensign

Kuge's shot was sixty feet ahead of the target! Ensign Sonoda's missed the stern by sixty feet.

Petty Officer Yanagiya's timing must have been off. Instead of passing under the target ship, and staying deep until he was well clear of it, he made a mistake. When he surfaced he found himself directly in the ship's path! Only a sudden swerve by its captain saved Yanagiya from being knocked to the bottom of the bay and probably being killed. And Petty Officer Nomura's performance was worst of all. No one on the target ship could even see his *kaiten* at any time.

Our chief, Ikebuchi, was excused at the seminar. His torpedo stopped dead in the water, five minutes after launching. Its engine had failed, and he had to be towed back to the base. Kuge and Sonoda had, after all come close enough so that they would have sunk a big ship. They made good reports, and were excused. So was I, after a short report. My run was the best of the day, and was as good as an amidships hit, the instructors conceded.

But grief came upon Yanagiya and Nomura. Yanagiya's report was a poor one. He could not explain his mistake at all, and gave up. Nomura did not give up. He failed to admit his error quickly, and this enraged the chief instructor, who pounced on him at once.

"How long were you on board your *kaiten*, Nomura, from the start to the finish of your practice session?" he asked. This was Nomura's chance to make a guess at the time, and admit himself to have been at fault. But he made the mistake of hedging, and finally had to say he wasn't sure.

"What?" shouted one of the instructors. "You don't even take the trouble to keep track of your time underwater? Well, then, how far from the target were you when you made your final sighting?"

"About one thousand yards," said Nomura. "The waves were high. I could not see clearly. But I estimated about one thousand yards."

"So how could you be so far off from the target? Not one of the observers even saw you when you made your pass. You made a mistake in judging angles, Nomura. Admit it! That's why you did not come anywhere near the target!"

Nomura fumbled around, and was trying to say something

when an instructor shouted, "How many times have you been in *kaiten?*"

"Twenty-six, counting today's session, Sir," said Nomura. He couldn't say anything more. He looked so miserable that we hoped someone would take mercy on him and end the discussion. But I-36's commanding officer had something to add. "I was watching each *kaiten* depart, through my periscope," he said. "None of them made a smooth take-off from the submarine. And I also watched each man make his final run-in. The sixth one, Nomura's, was especially bad." He turned, and looked at us. "All of you looked like beginners," he said. "All of you used up too much time to aim for your final run-in. You will not have that much time when we finally face the enemy."

The new executive officer slammed his bamboo pointer down on a table. "You should be ashamed of yourself, Nomura!" he shouted. "As for the rest of you, it is no wonder that one or two of you come back from each mission, without being launched at a target. What is your *hachimaki* for? And your sword! Doesn't it mean anything at all to your spirits? And the big send-off given you by all hands when you leave on a mission. These things are not done so that you can turn around and come back again! Once at sea, you must overwhelm the enemy! If anything goes wrong with your *kaiten*, fix it! If the propeller won't spin, turn it with your bare hands! Crash into the enemy, no matter what! That's what the *kaiten* is for!"

I could not believe he was speaking such words! Was he serious? Did he think the six of us had come back because we wanted to? Perhaps he should have been on the various submarines when we were. He would then know that all of us had returned only in the hope that we would go right back out again, with *kaiten* in perfect condition. I did not think any of those officers understood what went on in the mind of a returned *kaiten* man. They must not have spoken with Lieutenant Commander Orita of I-47. A *samurai* could not live in shame and was always prepared to die. We had tried to be true to the *bushi do*, the way of the *samurai*. We were living now only so that we could die at the proper moment. These officers smiled and offered sympathy when we had to return dirty and grease-stained, from an unsuccessful mission. Now I could read hate in their faces. I felt that they considered us, in their hearts, to be cowards. Otherwise, why would they say such things to us? Or, if they did not say them themselves, let others say them without comment? Lieutenant Commander Sugamasa's words especially disturbed me. He could not possibly know anything about attack technique. He had never ridden in a *kaiten*. He could not know the many things that could go wrong, nor how much there was to concern a pilot once his weapon was freed from the chocks to which it was secured on a submarine's deck. In addition to that, he was a submarine man. And a submarine man who had taken *kaiten* out for attacks. He should have been sympathetic to us. He should have known the kind of feelings that filled us. He had experience with them, because he had to take back *kaiten* men from a mission, unfired. Surely he had known of their desires, and must have listened to their protests as he swung his submarine's bow for home.

I glanced at Ensign Kuge, a returnee from the Kongo and Tembu groups. His eyes were downcast, his face very red. Ensign Sonoda, who had also known disappointment, was worriedly chewing at his lower lip.

Nomura was rudely ordered to sit down, and the seminar ended soon afterward. I intended to rush to my room and stay there, unwilling to face Otsujima men again. Ikebuchi intercepted me at the door. "Everyone, to my room!" he shouted. "At once!" When the five of us were with him in his room, he spoke. "We cannot let them talk to us that way, men!" he said. "When we go out this time, we will make them choke on their words! This time we will die, no matter what! They will know we are not cowards. Would we be here, training to die, if we were cowards? They are too excited. They have let themselves forget that we are meant to strike at an enemy, not to die uselessly. They have let their chief concern be that we do not come back. Turn the propeller by hand, indeed! That statement shows you how ridiculous men can be when they forget our chief objective, overwhelming the enemy."

If someone had reproached me privately on returning from a mission, I might have been able to endure it. Or if someone had teased me, in a friendly way, I would have accepted it. But this public accusation leveled at myself and other men who had offered their lives, some more than once, was simply unjust! I wanted no more of Otsujima, the place I had once thought so highly of. All I wanted now was to get away to sea. I would never come back.

This feeling stayed with the six of us during the rest of our practice, even after we moved to Hikari, and all of us were more than ready when the day of departure finally arrived. I-361, armed with five *kaiten*, had left Hikari on May 23, under command of Lieutenant Masaharu Matsuura. I-363 followed five days later, captained by Lieutenant Commander Sakae Kihara. She also had five *kaiten* on board, including Petty Officers Shigeyuki Kobayashi and Teruyoshi Ishibashi. Kobayashi had been the petty officer who had given us all the word to report to the officers' quarters that long ago night we had received the beating. Ishibashi had been the straggler who'd caused the blows to come harder.

The day after I-361 left, American carrier aircraft made wide sweeps over our airfields on Kyushu, the islands which, with Shokaku and Honshu, form the Inland Sea. The enemy planes did much damage to our forces, and lessened the amount of help we would be able to summon if beset by attackers near our homeland. This made the passage out of Bungo Strait more dangerous than ever. Mines, destroyers and aircraft had to be averted before we could even get into clear water now. On the twenty-fourth and twenty-fifth great *kamikaze* attacks were launched on Okinawa, and this depleted our forces on Kyushu still further. The war picture was darkening more and more. And another submarine, I-12, was lost before we left port.

When I-36 made for Bungo Strait on June 4, we carried the twenty-fourth set of *kaiten* to be taken to sea. Up to that point our Sixth Fleet's official estimate was that more than thirty American ships had been sunk from our effort since the first sailing on November 8, 1944. These included aircraft carriers, battleships, cruisers, destroyers, tankers and transports. In return for this, we had lost six submarines. I-165, which was not in the Todoroki Group when I left port, was included later. She sailed with just a pair of *kaiten* on June 16. Two submarines of the four in Todoroki were fated not to return from this mission, and I-363 would come back to port without having found any targets. Only I-36, my ship, would meet with success.

I felt sorry for the men of I-36, and for men of I-47, I-53 and I-58. In June they manned the only first-class submarines left in the Imperial Navy. Because of the diminishing number of submarines, these men had to go out again and again with *kaiten*. They got no rest at all. When at sea, they stood watches or slept, spending many hours at their battle stations. When they came back to port they were dirty and exhausted, but had to go right to work, helping to refit their ship so it could turn around and go out again after picking up *kaiten*. Japan had more than seventy "iron whales" roving the Pacific at one point in the war. Now less than a dozen fit for fighting were left. Even the I-300 class, built for transport, had been pressed into *kaiten* service. Submarine sailors of the Imperial Navy probably saw more continuous cruising than anyone in the Pacific war. Long after the war had ended, I read that American submarine sailors were given special rooms at the famous Royal Hawaiian Hotel on Waikiki Beach in Hawaii between war patrols. They enjoyed fine quarters, plenty of the best food and lots of sunshine. When I learned this I realized more than ever how powerful were the forces against us, that they could give their fighting men such comforts and let them stay out of action for long periods.

Except for a few workmen and friends, the dock at Hikari was nearly deserted when we started out to sea. But it would not have made any difference if there had been a band, banners and cheering crowds. I might not even have noticed them. All I could think of that bright June 4 was, "You are getting another chance, Yokota. The third chance! This time you will be successful. After all, fate cannot cheat you forever!"

Our destination was an area to the east of Saipan, on the supply route from America to the Marianas. The line from Ulithi to Okinawa, it was estimated, would be heavily patrolled after the accomplishments of the Tembu Group. We knew, of course, that we would get no chance of hitting large warships. Nearly all of them would be far to the west of us as we cruised our area. We would have to settle for much smaller game. Still, any kill was important if it slowed the flow of fuel and ammunition to those mighty American task forces hammering the southern section of our homeland. Ammunition and fuel were their bones and blood.

The first two weeks on patrol in I-36 were very trying. We were often in danger of being detected by enemy patrols. But Captain Sugamasa was very skillful at dodging them, and we suffered no depth charge or bombing attacks. I had time to really know my new companions. Lieutenant, junior grade, Nobuo Ikebuchi, for instance, was the only married man ever to be a *kaiten* pilot and make an attack. All of us had been carefully screened when we volunteered, and married men were eliminated. Ikebuchi was single when he arrived at Otsujima, but he had a sweetheart from his days at Osaka College, whom he loved very much. Although a Reserve officer, he was thought by us at first to be an Etajima man, so military was his bearing and attitude.

Ikebuchi had much correspondence with his sweetheart and tried to be firm, saying that there was no point in marrying a man who might not have much longer to live, the way the war was going. But she broke down his resistance in a letter saying, "If I could be your wife for but one night, it would be happiness enough for me." That's all the wedded life Ikebuchi had. He was married wearing his uniform and returned to the base the following day, departing for sea soon afterward.

I grew to like him, and the others, especially Ensign Kuge, who was an expert card player. I could never defeat him. Yanagiya, from the remote northern islet Reibun, off Hokkaido, had arms thick as logs and was a shy man, but very intense in feeling. No doubt this was because he had lost a brother in the war and wanted to avenge him. He wanted to avenge Raita Irie, too, whose place I was taking. Irie and Yanagiya had been close friends.

Just after we sailed from Hikari, another submarine, I-122, was sunk in the Sea of Japan. The Americans were now so strong they could get right through our home defenses and attack shipping in that body of water, so sheltered and protected that we had long since come to think of it almost as another Japanese lake. Japan did enjoy some good luck, though. The day after we sailed, a typhoon caught the American fleet off Okinawa, inflicting great damage. After the war I learned that four battleships, eight aircraft carriers, seven cruisers and fourteen destroyers suffered much injury from this storm. But the "divine wind" was not enough. The enemy attack was quickly resumed, as fiercely as ever.

The good news about the typhoon hitting the enemy cheered us, but not for long. When Captain Sugamasa decided to have *kaiten* drill, every one of our six weapons refused to work! They were arranged in three side by side pairs, two *kaiten* forward of the conning tower, and four aft. Every one of them was pointed so that it faced the stern.

Starting near the bow, they were numbered as follows: Nomura's No. 6 was to port and Ensign Kuge's No. 5 to starboard. Yanagiya's No. 3 and my No. 2 were side by side, just aft of the conning tower. Near the stern sat Ensign Sonoda's No. 4 and Lieutenant Ikebuchi's No. 1. Ikebuchi's and my *kaiten* were on the starboard side of the deck.

Everyone that could get near the *kaiten* worked on them day and night. Finally, three of them were put into working order, Ikebuchi's, Kuge's and Yanagiya's. The rest of us gritted our teeth, cursed and fretted, to no avail. Sonoda and Nomura had rusted valves in their weapons. This prevented some of the controls from being operated. They had some chance still, though, and great efforts were made to free these sticking parts. I was almost certainly put out of action for good, however. My weapon had two cracks in the oxygen fuel lines. No one dared put an electric torch to them. One spark could blow up the oxygen, and possibly the warhead with it. If that happened, the submarine would be lost too. Still, we did not feel as badly as we might have on other occasions. Those accusations leveled at us back at Otsujima had made us completely fatalistic. We would take whatever came along. Sugamasa had seen with his own eyes what had happened this time. He could not make any unkind remarks about us. When the *kaiten* were ready, we would be ready also. If not . . . *shikata ga nai.*

We made our first contact about 5:00 A.M. on June 17, shortly after submerging for the day's run. We had been on the surface all night, mechanics trying to fix the remaining three *kaiten* so they could get into action.

"Ship, left, fifty degrees!" reported the sound room. "Degree of intensity is two."

I-36 came alive quickly. Battle stations were speedily manned, and Sugamasa's eye was at the periscope as we came up a little to periscope depth. Nothing happened after that until 5:40 A.M. when the sound room reported that the range to our target was increasing. "Degree of intensity has fallen off to one!" the operator reported to the conning tower.

"Stand by for *kaiten* action!" called out Captain Sugamasa. "Man Number One and Number Five!"

Ikebuchi and Ensign Kuge made dashes for their weapons, one on the bow, the other on our stern.

"There are two targets," the conning tower reported after a while, "one large transport and one cargo ship." All *kaiten* mechanics, even those of Sonoda, Nomura and myself, stood by access tubes, but no order came for other pilots to board their weapons.

I fidgeted in the wardroom, hoping Captain Sugamasa would order No. 2 to be manned. Even if the oxygen leaked, and prevented me from using high pressure to make full speed, I thought I still might be able to make an attack by being careful and not letting the enemy sight me. But it looked like he would use only No. 1 and No. 5, sending them off on a long chase. I-36's underwater speed was not enough for us to run fast and get into position ahead of targets that were distant from us. Only *kaiten* could catch such targets.

But a full hour more passed without any order being given to Ikebuchi and Kuge. Finally, Captain Sugamasa gave up. He ordered the two men back into the hull. "The targets had moved too far away to make any attack by us successful," he explained later.

Ikebuchi took this news in good spirit. He did not look at all disappointed, only tired from being cramped in the big torpedo for so long. "Things just don't always go the way we want them to go," he said, and grinned. "Maybe we'll sight a convoy later, and all go out together."

This didn't seem possible, because of those rusted valves in Nomura's and Sonoda's *kaiten* and my leaky fuel lines, but we caught the spirit from Ikebuchi. "I don't care if we only sight one ship," said Kuge, "so long as we can all go." A quiet man who neither drank nor smoked, Kuge was still smarting over the words spoken to us by the thoughtless officers at Otsujima.

"Take it easy," said Ikebuchi. "Let us have a game of *go*."

That relaxed the rest of us. It will be a most unusual day when you cannot obtain an opponent for Japan's most popular indoor game. We got out the tiles and board while Lieutenant Kuwabara, the chief engineer, produced a large bottle of beer and poured me a glass. I was so relaxed after the tension of the day that I poured it down my throat in one large gulp, drinking the full glass without stopping.

"Well done, Yokota!" exclaimed the chief engineer. "You

are a delight to the soul of an old beer-drinker like myself. You poured that down like a true veteran!"

I smiled, thanked him and left for the crew's quarters. There I spent the rest of the day and much of succeeding ones, reading and napping. Under Ikebuchi's calm leadership I no longer had a sense of urgency. When I-36 saw no enemy ships, it mattered little to me. Sooner or later, some would be sighted. The Americans had the ocean full of them. I would sink one, if my *kaiten* could be repaired in time. Meanwhile, there was nothing to do but wait.

15 □ Attack and Counterattack

Nothing more happened for nearly a week. Our lookouts saw nothing. Our radar picked up nothing. Meanwhile, anxious technicians worked with little sleep to repair our *kaiten*. They were in them much of the day, and again during the night, while we rode on the surface. Finally, while we were gathered in the wardroom one evening, the glad news came to us. All *kaiten* had been fixed, at least well enough to be usable if an attack came soon. Repairs could only be temporary ones, said the mechanics. If we were lucky, they would hold up. But if there was much delay, they could not guarantee them against further defects due to sea water and inside moisture.

An enemy ship was sighted in the evening of June 23. Lookouts shouted that it was a tanker. "Good!" we cried. This was the sort of target we were after. I-36 manned battle stations and ran hard on the surface toward the ship. Captain Sugamasa had estimated its course and speed and decided to rush on ahead of this fat prize. Then, in the morning, he would approach its path and ambush it.

During the start of this high-speed run. Lieutenant Ikebuchi went to the open bridge. "I want to see this target with my own eyes," he said. When he came down, he told us it was a tanker, of about fourteen thousand tons, and unescorted. It was making twelve to fourteen knots, and showed no sign of being aware we were near.

Excitement kept I-36 buzzing. Crewmen spoke hopefully to one another about chalking up another score and outperforming their rival, the submarine I-47. Our navigator hunched over his charts, dividers and pencils at hand, rising frequently to answer Captain Sugamasa's queries as to where we should be for greatest advantage in an attack, and what time we should be there. It was finally decided that the position we would reach by 4:00 A.M. would be the best one. On arriving at that point, we would submerge and await our prey.

208

The night passed, while I-36 raced ahead at her best speed. Ten minutes before four o'clock, we were on station and started to submerge. Shortly afterward our sound room reported screw noises. It now appeared to be two targets, the operator said, which made all hands more anxious than ever, especially the *kaiten* men. Two of us would be sent away now, instead of just one. I had a strong feeling that I would be one of these, and that my long waiting would be over.

At exactly 4:00 A.M. the order came. "Board your *kaiten!*" called the captain, and crewmen flattened themselves against the bulkheads as we raced past them. I had the telephone in one hand at the same time I was tightening down No. 2's lower hatch with the other.

"Number Two is manned and ready!" I reported.

I heard nothing for a while. The conning tower was taking reports from my five comrades. I checked all controls, and stood by for further word. It came after a short time.

"Number Five and Number Six! Stand by for launching!" I could hear this dimly through my phones, and my heart sank. Ensign Kuge and Petty Officer Nomura had been selected. Again I was left out. Still, I did not get excited about it. *Shikata ga nai.* It was fate, and I could not control fate. I merely slumped back in my seat. I was very relaxed.

After a while, I leaned forward and peered through my periscope. Never had I seen clearer water. It was as though I-36 were in a case, under glass. We were at periscope depth, and above me the dawn made things brighter by the minute as it broke over the broad Pacific Ocean. The submarine's hull was as sharply defined as if it were in a photograph, as were the *kaiten* of Ikebuchi, Sonoda, and Yanagiya. All four of us were facing the stern. The *kaiten* looked like great fish. I even imagined their sides were heaving as we rocked there gently beneath a slight swell.

I swung my periscope a full 180 degrees, and got slightly out of my seat, so I could look toward the bow of I-36. I could see its periscope clearly as it rose now and then above the surface, making scarcely a ripple. Captain Sugamasa certainly knew his business, I thought. It would take terribly sharp enemy eyes to sight that clue to our presence. It went up for a quick look and a swing around, then came back down almost at once. It put me in mind of how a leopard must stalk its prey through a jungle, relying mainly on scent and earlier experience with kills, and chancing a betrayal of its presence only occasionally and then very rapidly, by raising its muzzle for a scanning look.

"Angle is left, seventy degrees!" came through my phones. "Range is three miles. Target appears to be transport or tanker. *Kaiten* Number Five, stand by for launching!"

My neck was aching now, from straining around to see the forward end of the submarine. I was doing what was not normally expected of a *kaiten* man, looking directly behind my weapon. The conning tower blocked everything forward of it, but I wanted to see Ensign Kuge's *kaiten* pass as it raced off toward the enemy. Forcing myself to ignore the increasing pain in my neck and back, I gripped the periscope handles ever more tightly, to hold my awkward posture.

Minutes passed. Nothing happened. Then I heard a voice in the conning tower as it drifted into my talker's telephone. "Number Five is reported out of order. Number Six, stand by for launch!"

I almost wept for Kuge. This was his third disappointment. He had gone with the Kongo Group to Kossol Strait. There he felt a monstrous jar when the weapon of his friend, Lieutenant Hiroshi Kuzumi, mysteriously exploded right after being launched. A few minutes later when his turn came his *kaiten* failed to start.

He had gone out a second time, in this very submarine, I-36, with the Tembu Group, of which my I-47 had been a part. Operating to the east of Okinawa, he again sat idle in a defective *kaiten* while four of five friends roared off in attacks. Then, too, his weapon could not be started. And now he was to be left out again. No wonder Japanese are superstitious where the number three is concerned.

Well, we would see how Nomura did, now. I waited. Minutes later I overheard another report. "Nomura cannot get his propeller to turn over," a voice in the conning tower said.

I came to life then. "Rear *kaiten* are ready!" I shouted. It was rude of me to do this. Lieutenant Ikebuchi should have been the next logical choice for the captain. With that impetuous shout I classed myself as a vulgar person, with poor manners and no breeding, but I had seen a chance to take advantage of the situation. This enemy ship was over ten thousand tons. He was a fat target. I wanted to rip open his vitals. Good manners would have to be put aside for a while.

But no order came. A long silence followed, instead. My friends must have been shocked by my impetuosity, and embarrassed into quiet by it. I think I might have been about to apologize after no sounds came through my phones, but before I could phrase any statement a new order came.

"All *kaiten* wait!"

There was a short pause, followed by a voice on the general circuit. "We are making an attack with torpedoes."

Whoosh! I heard the first torpedo as it was sent away. It was quickly followed by three others. There was nothing I could do at that moment to make up for my poor behavior but pray. "Hit home!" I shouted. "Hit home!" I spoke to those Model 95 torpedoes as though they were living things.

Soon I heard an explosion. Then another! I could hear shouting in the conning tower. I was sure I-36 had made hits.

We *kaiten* pilots were ordered back into the hull. I felt good as I clambered back through the access tube. In one direction it was a road to death. In the other it was a road to life. How many times had I traveled it! How many more would I travel it? It did not matter. I-36 had struck a blow. One of the enemy had been downed.

We met with the capain in the wardroom. He told us that this ship was not the same one we had seen earlier in the night. That one had been a tanker. This one had definitely been a transport. When Nomura's and Kuge's *kaiten* proved defective, Sugamasa said, he had become disgusted. He had moved in to less than one and one-half miles and fired a standard spread of four regular torpedoes.

"Did we sink the transport, Sir?" I asked. I was positive we had done so, from the big sounds of those explosions.

Captain Sugamasa was disgusted. "No!" he said. "She listed a little when the torpedoes hit, but she was able to pick up speed and run away."

We didn't dare surface to chase her in these waters. And with our slow underwater speed, any ship could run away from I-36. I felt sorry for Sugamasa that the two *kaiten* proved defective. And that he had become disgusted. Otherwise he might have fired some of the rest of us. We could have chased that ship and caught her. Now we had to give up and retreat. We were fairly close to Saipan. Air patrols would be sent here, to seek us out.

This we found to be quite true. On the twenty-fourth and twenty-fifth we sighted enemy reconnaissance planes, but we dipped beneath the surface before they could approach us. Captain Sugamasa now decided to take no more chances. He did not want to risk another battle until he was sure his *kaiten* would work. So we began a long underwater run to the north, well out of Saipan patrol range. When we surfaced, in the darkness, each weapon was given a complete check. Again all six were found defective! Sugamasa could not have fired any of us! Hard work by the repairmen restored three of them to use again, but the temporary repairs on No. 2, No. 4 and No. 6 had not held up. We did not know whether they could be fixed again at all.

So the captain had to make a decision. Stay out of range and work on those three weapons, or move back in and fight with what he had available. He chose the latter. We would search for the enemy and do our best to get the three defective *kaiten* working again. On June 27, the dark hours found us steaming southward again, looking for the enemy.

Again and again I checked with the mechanics. They were making little progress with my *kaiten*. I urged them to greater efforts, though I knew they were doing their best. I was in a very low mood. At Otsujima, with the others, I had sworn to die, so that I would show those officers how wrong they were about us. I knew I could not go back again. Death would be simpler, and easier.

But death again refused to turn her head in my direction and hold out welcoming arms to me. I felt helpless, without strength. I discussed this with Ensign Sonoda.

"Sir," I asked, "what am I to do? I cannot possibly return to the base again. You know that."

All he could say then was, "You are right, Yokota." He was at a loss for words.

Then I had an idea. I remembered how sometimes, during training sessions, two men rode one *kaiten* together. "Why can we not double up on the *kaiten*?" I asked Sonoda. "We have done it before. Three *kaiten* are useless. Why must you, Nomura, and I have to suffer a fate far worse than dying, when there is a chance for us yet to die? We could go in the other three *kaiten* as extra riders, couldn't we?"

Sonoda's handsome face grew very serious. "I have already thought of the same thing, Yokota," he said. "In fact, I wanted to ride in Kuge's *kaiten* with him, and have actually asked Captain Sugamasa for permission to do so."

"What did he say, Sir?"

"He refused permission."

"He *what?*"

"He refused permission. He told me to wait for another chance. He also requested me to convince you and Nomura to do the same."

"Convince us to wait? After what happened at Otsujima?"

"Yes," Sonoda said. "Captain Sugamasa sees things somewhat differently now, I think. He knows we are not cowards, as some people hinted. He knows of our pride, and our willingness to die. But he told me that willingness to endure anything, even hints of cowardliness, is more important than pride. I admire the captain for his change of heart. I am going to obey his request. I want you to do the same."

His words puzzled me, especially since they came from the mouth of an Etajima graduate. Men from the Academy provided the great leadership of the Imperial Navy. They were the inspiration for other men to act. I knew that at Etajima men were taught that pride was more important than life itself. Pride and honor and consciousness of duty. I spent the rest of that day wondering if he had meant his words, and why a man with his background should give up on a promise the six of us made. True, what he said made sense. But there were still those people back in Japan who had intimated we were not true *kaiten* men. How were we going to prove them wrong now, if we returned once more? Such thoughts kept me restless through all of the night.

The next day was June 28, the twenty-fifth day of cruising since we had left Hikari. At 5:00 A.M. we were submerged after the night's surface run, our periscope poking up now and then to search for the enemy. It was quiet in I-36. There was no excitement, just the routine business of warfare, the dull monotony of going through the same tasks men had to perform daily. It was about that time we received a wireless telling us of I-165's fate. She was supposed to be coming out to join us, but she had been sunk the day before, without getting a chance to launch her *kaiten*.

I-361 had not been heard from either and was presumed lost. The ever-vigilant enemy, with his extensive surface and air patrols, had caught her, too. Our numbers grew fewer and fewer.

I-363 returned to base that day, too. On June 28, our submarine I-36 was truly an orphan of the Pacific. There was no friendly island, like Tanegashima, where we could pull in for shelter and protection. There were no friendly ships nearby, either, with whom we could communicate. What was left of the great Combined Fleet was bottled up at its main anchorage, in the Inland Sea. The remnants of our carrier and battleship force sat idle there, unable to sortie against the foe. Mines and the threat of air attacks like the massive one that sent *Yamato* to the bottom kept them bottled up, inert and helpless. But I-36 had to continue fighting, with no help whatever.

All fresh vegetables and meat were now gone. Only tinned food was available, and we hardly tasted it. It was as Petty Officer Tanaka, of I-47, had said—the longer you were out in a submarine, the less appetite you had. You ate less, and as a result grew tired more easily. Still, you could not eat. Dirty and weary, you could find no appeal in food. The medical officer was concerned about the state of health of all of us, and busied himself giving everyone vitamin and hormone injections. Excessive fatigue crept over all of us. When underwater, only a handful of men were on watch. The others slept like dead men. Even I, who had spent so many restless nights before, fell into my berth and was off to sleep, most times, in an instant.

At 11:00 A.M. on June 28, in spite of having had much sleep already, I was sitting in the wardroom, dozing, when I saw a petty officer from the conning tower watch dash past, heading for Captain Sugamasa's cabin.

The enemy! This thought flashed through my mind, and I stirred myself from my sleepiness. The next moment, Captain Sugamasa burst from his cabin and began climbing the ladder to the conning tower. Shortly after, his voice came over the loudspeaker.

"Enemy in sight! All hands to battle stations!"

More orders came, one upon another.

"Stand by for torpedo attack!"

"Load all forward tubes!'

"Stand by for *kaiten* attack!"

"Number One *kaiten* pilot, man your weapon!"

Lieutenant Ikebuchi was still asleep. Ensign Sonoda was shaking him by the shoulders. His voice was excited.

"Sir, we have an enemy in sight. You have been ordered to get aboard your torpedo!"

Ikebuchi had his clothes on, but they had been loosened to give him some comfort. He leaped to his feet instantly, fumbled with buttons for a few seconds, then ran toward the stern, shouting back to us, "Take care of everything for me!" He was dirty and sweaty.

I-36 had dipped down after sighting the enemy. Now Captain Sugamasa ordered her up again, to periscope depth. The sound room reported, "Target noises have intensity of two!" as I-36 began moving in to close torpedo range.

There was trouble in the conning tower, and in the wardroom we could hear part of the conversation. "We are in a bad position," Sugamasa said. "From here it is almost impossible to get a good angle for firing torpedoes. I am going to use the *kaiten*."

His voice came over the loudspeaker then, telling all hands of this. We could hear him also giving directions to Ikebuchi. "Target is right, ninety degrees. Range, three miles. Target is one ship, a large transport. Speed, twelve knots."

Then: *"Kaiten,* stand by for launching!"

"Ready?"

"Go!"

We could hear Ikebuchi's propeller turning over, as his tie-down clamps snapped open. He moved away. The sound room picked up the noise of his weapon receding. The time was exactly noon.

Quiet, staunch Ikebuchi was on his way. The man of the one-night marriage. The man who had so impressed us with his attitude that we had first mistaken him for an Etajima graduate instead of the Reserve officer he was. He had contributed greatly to the *kaiten* program. He had played a part in experiments at Otsujima that proved a submerged *kaiten* could stay down as much as twenty hours, if undamaged, during a training accident. Through him and others of equal courage, our planners were able to know just how much air purifier and emergency food to stock in each *kaiten*. He had been in at the very birth of the *kaiten* effort, being one of the first men to ride one in the water while they were still most unpredictable. I knew he would make a hit. Glory was sure to come to a man so devoted to his homeland and his countrymen.

Ten minutes passed. He should have nearly covered the distance to the target by this time, I thought. Then, though we were underwater, all of us heard the sound of many guns being fired.

The periscope was raised for a look.

"The enemy has discovered the *kaiten*!" we heard some-one shout. "The enemy has opened fire on it!"

Then came another report from above us. "The enemy ship has changed course! It is running away from the *kaiten*!"

"Get him, Ikebuchi!" I muttered fiercely to myself, though there didn't seem to be much chance of this. I guessed that Ikebuchi had been sighted when he made his final observation. That's when the enemy opened fire on him. Now he had to dip down again, so the shells could not hurt him. And he could not put up his periscope again, for fear of being seen once more. When his periscope went down, of course, the enemy changed course so as to dodge him. At this moment he might be racing at top speed to-ward empty ocean, while his target scampered off in another direction altogether.

Still, I had hope. No one I knew operated a *kaiten* with more skill than this man from Osaka College, except per-haps the dead Furukawa. And, on our last mission, Furu-kawa chased a destroyer for close to an hour before finally making his hit. I thought Ikebuchi could do the same. In any case, I knew he would never give up until his fuel ran out. The others with me felt the same way.

We *kaiten* men must have made a strange sight there in the wardroom. We had bunched together tightly and were all in a sort of crouch, facing to starboard, the direction from which the many gun sounds came. We were quiet, listening intently for the great explosion we wanted to hear. Minute after min-ute dragged by, and when I looked at my watch one time I was startled to see that a full forty minutes had elapsed since Sugamasa had given the command, "Go!" to our chief.

I was getting stiff now, from holding one posture so long, and was straightening up a little when the sound operator screamed, "New propeller noises! Very close! Degree of in-tensity is four!"

"Down periscope!" shouted Captain Sugamasa. "Emergency dive! Take her to 125 feet! Quickly!"

Our 3,000-ton ship dipped its bow almost at once, and began sinking downward as rapidly as skilled hands could make her go. Seconds later propellers passed directly over us. An enemy ship had tried to ram us!

"Stand by for depth charge attack!" shouted Sugamasa.

Well, it has come, I told myself. The death I welcomed. No longer need I worry about cranky *kaiten* No. 2. The enemy overhead would give the answer those critical officers back at Otsujima wanted. There would be no returnees from I-36 this time. None at all.

Then came the depth charges. They felt like a giant piledriver was smashing into the side of I-36. She shook and swerved, throwing me to my knees. The wardroom sofa leaped fully two feet above the deck and toppled over on its side. Every light I could see went out, and only about half of them came on again. The rest had been shattered in their mountings. The special anti-moisture coating on the ceiling above cracked and flaked, large pieces of it falling down upon our heads.

More than a dozen depth charges went off, in a string, close outside the hull. I-36's mammoth hulk was thrown to the right and then to the left, and rolled over so far I was sure we were capsizing.

That had to be a destroyer overhead. Where had it come from? How had it been able to surprise us so? Our positions were completely reversed now. The hunter had truly become the hunted. This thought flashed through my mind as a small statue of Buddha, placed in an alcove near the ceiling of the wardroom fell past my eyes and was dashed into two pieces on the deck. A bad omen, indeed! I was sure our fate had arrived.

What had happened was this. Two mistakes had been made. They could happen at any time in a submarine, but they were not supposed to happen. Our periscope was above the surface, but Captain Sugamasa was so intent on watching where Ikebuchi was supposed to be that he forgot to make the quick sweeps of the horizon that submarine captains make during an attack as an extra precaution. He was depending on our sound operators to warn him if anything else made its appearance on the surface.

But our sound operators were not sweeping, either. We had

two sets. One was directed at the target we were trying to sink. The other was trying to keep a bearing on Ikebuchi's *kaiten*, so we would know how he was doing. Not one person in I-36 was aware that an American destroyer had spotted our periscope and was racing in at high speed to ram and sink us. It was only by luck he was detected at the last minute. The operator who was tracking Ikebuchi could no longer hear him, and had started to make a sweep through a full circle, to help guard our rear, when he found this new enemy on our backs.

At this operator's shout, Captain Sugamasa had spun the periscope around. There, so big it completely filled his lens, was the high bow wave of an onrushing greyhound of the sea. Had that one sound operator not lost Ikebuchi from his equipment and decided to make a sweep, we would all be dead right now. Credit went to I-36's trained crew, too. Had they not gotten their ship down so suddenly, that grey bow would have knifed into our middle, engulfing all hands in sea water and sending I-36 straight to the bottom without a chance.

The destroyer's propeller noises receded, but quickly increased again. He was coming back for another try.

"Degree Four! Degree Five! He's directly above!"

Here they come again, I said to myself. I held my breath, and braced myself for more blows. I was especially fearful, I think, much more so than most men on the ship. All the submarine men had battle tasks. I had none. Nothing occupied my mind but fear. I had no work to busy my hands or fill my mind. All I could do was stand there with my comrades and take what came.

"Must I die by depth charges?" I called to heaven. My words were bitter. Ten months of training, hoping and being disappointed were being capped by the greatest disappointment of all, death without a chance to fight back.

More charges rained down on us. I-36 was buffeted about more.

"Water in the forward torpedo room!" The voice over the loudspeaker was calm, and I marveled at its even tones.

"Rudder control lost aft!" was the next report. "Shifting to manual rudder operation!"

Several men dashed past me, heading for the bow. They would help try to stop the leak up forward. Screw noises receded, then once more grew louder. More depth charges came down, this time near the stern instead of the submarine's sides. I wondered how Sugamasa's men had been able to spin us around. What force they must have used! Manual control of the rudder required much strength, and the control responded much more slowly than when it had electrical power.

"Leak in forward torpedo room now under control." The voice on the loudspeaker was flat, calm. Trained men were doing well the things they had trained to do, and my admiration for submarine men of the Japanese Navy rose to a new peak.

Sugamasa was doing his best to keep I-36's stern to the attacker overhead. If he could keep those explosions astern of us, at least one danger might be averted. Up near the bow were located the great batteries by which I-36's engines were turned when she was underwater. Excessive vibration near them might break some of them open. Then, if water got into them, the deadly chlorine gas every submariner fears would seep through the ship, killing us all very quickly.

The destroyer was now making its fourth run on us. Another dozen or so depth charges came down. These exploded below us, and to the rear, pushing I-36 up toward the surface as though a mighty arm was lifting it. The leak forward was stopped, but now we had another, near the stern, as the "thousand thunders" broke upon us. We were taking on water rapidly, and becoming tail-heavy. I-36 began sinking, sliding slowly backward.

Captain Sugamasa had to stop this. We had taken that first bunch of depth charges while at 125 feet, and had remained at that level during the succeeding attacks. Sugamasa's ship could dive safely to slightly more than three hundred feet, but instead he gambled.

A submarine, under attack, will usually dive as deep as it can, to keep plenty of water between it and its enemy. Knowing this, the attacking commander orders depth charges set for deep explosion. But Sugamasa had outguessed the enemy. That last group of charges had gone off well below us. So long as the enemy kept sending his charges that deep we had a chance of surviving. No wonder Sugamasa was the youngest submarine captain in our Navy, I thought. He knew what he was doing. He might yet bring us out of this.

But I-36's stern was becoming laden down with water. In spite of the engines, we were gradually sinking, because of excess weight aft. We had an angle of fifteen degrees on now, our bow much higher than our stern. It was time for another gamble, our captain thought, and he ordered a "small blow."

This was dangerous, and rarely done in the presence of the enemy. It meant discharging pressured air into our main ballast tanks, forcing some water out in order to lighten the ship. It had to be done very, very carefully. If not, air pushed into the main tanks might go right through and come out of the submarine. It would then bubble right up to the surface, marking our position clearly for enemy lookouts.

But we had to try it, so we did. Air was let carefully into one of the tanks, and water pushed out. I-36 came almost to an even keel, and stayed there. I felt she was gasping for breath, like a prize fighter who had taken too many punches. More than fifty depth charges had been sent at us so far. Thanks to Captain Sugamasa's skill, they had not killed us off. We were lucky.

But would we stay lucky? Like a boxer full of courage, we were still not out of the fight. But we, like a boxer who has taken fifty hard punches from his opponent, were wounded. Much damage had been done to us. At that moment we could do nothing but hang on. We were helpless to fight back. And we knew more hard blows were yet to come. Could we survive them?

16 □ Heroism and Survival

We five remaining *kaiten* men stood in the shambles of the wardroom. We looked at each other, our faces gaunt and pale. Each knew what the other was thinking. Would we die here? Would this be our answer to our critics? Had the design of fate been so woven that all our training, all our spirit, all our efforts were made to achieve this awful end, dying without a chance to help our homeland? I hope I will never again see in a man's eyes the hopelessness that was in the eyes of my friends as we leaned tiredly against whatever would support us and waited for the enemy's final, crushing blow.

Captain Sugamasa had another reason for not going too deep. He could go as low as 325 feet to evade this killer above us, were it not for the *kaiten*. The maximum depth they could withstand was 250 feet. And there was no guarantee they could do that, any more. The depth charge attacks must surely have damaged them some. A deep dive was sure to crack them open, even before we got as low as 250 feet. Those *kaiten* were meant for the enemy, not to be turned into scrap metal. This was one of his concerns at the same time he was fooling the enemy with the shallow dive.

Nevertheless, we were at that moment helpless. Reports throughout I-36 showed we had many leaks. We were losing electrical power, too, as connections were torn loose and instruments shattered by vibration. It would not take many more attacks before I-36 lost this battle. Those last depth charges were not as close as the others. They exploded well below us. But more charges did not have to be close, with the condition we were in. It would not take heavy blows to kill us off. Light ones, near-misses, could finish the job. Their vibrations could crack open our battery banks, loosing poison gas on us, or widen the holes in I-36, letting in sea water. The situation was hopeless.

221

At that moment Ensign Kuge, who had righted the wardroom sofa and was sitting on it, stood up.

"I will go!" he said.

He went to the conning tower and faced Captain Sugamasa. "My *kaiten* still works, Sir," he said. "Let me go off and get that destroyer."

"Thank you for your offer, Kuge," said the captain, "but it is impossible. Even if your weapon survived this battering, even if its engine still works, I'm almost certain its electrical equipment won't work. Look at what the depth charges have done to electrical appliances inside this submarine!"

"Let me go, Captain," Kuge kept urging. "Let me go!" He, like I, felt it was preferable to die in battle on his *kaiten* rather than like a whipped and helpless dog here in the hull.

"But suppose your electrical rudder control is demolished?" said the captain. "You could not possibly steer your *kaiten* by hand."

Those words! The officers at Otsujima should have heard Sugamasa now. Especially the one who said we should turn over our propellers by hand if necessary. Still, Kuge insisted he should be sent off. "We can't just wait here for the enemy to kill us!" he said.

Perhaps Sugamasa yet had hopes that his skill in maneuvering I-36 would get us out of this trap. Or perhaps that change of heart Sonoda spoke of made him feel his responsibility toward *kaiten* men more. Perhaps he interpreted Kuge's volunteering as simply a desire to die and prove those Otsujima officers wrong. In any case, he still refused permission.

Kuge's voice rose. He explained that he had plenty of training, and said he was confident he could stop this attacker. They were still arguing when the destroyer came back to make its fifth attack on us. The argument broke off as more depth charges exploded near I-36.

This set slammed the big submarine to one side so hard that every man was thrown to the deck, or against the opposite bulkhead. As the explosions died away I-36 rolled far to one side heavily, recovered slowly, and her fore-and-aft list increased. Our bow was now pointing upward much more than fifteen degrees. Walking through the ship was like climbing the steep side of *Fuji-san*, the sacred mountain only a few miles from my home in Toyko.

"All men not actually on watch," called out Sugamasa, "assemble in the forward torpedo room!" Dozens of men passed the wardroom, each one carrying some loose piece of heavy equipment. The stern had to be lightened and the bow made heavier, or else we could slip backward and keep slipping until we were at the ocean's bottom and dead. I joined the crewmen, and so did the other *kaiten* men. All of us struggled uphill with bags of rice from the submarine's provisions. We worked until we had filled most of the forward torpedo room, but it did not make one bit of difference in the ship's inclination. She still held that steep angle.

Most lights were gone now. In the pale glow of emergency lighting the crew's faces were gaunt and shadowed, smeared with grease and perspiration. So this is the way a submarine dies, I thought. This is how my friends had met their deaths. It was nothing like the attack I had endured in I-47 back near Bungo Strait weeks before. Here we simply sat, taking blow after blow, awaiting the final one that would put an end to us all. There was no respite from the assault. By the time I-36 stopped quivering, the enemy was back again, pouring down his deadly shower upon us.

This time we could plainly make out ourselves that there were two sets of screws above us. That first destroyer now had an assistant. Perhaps it was the one that dodged Ikebuchi's *kaiten*. Where was Ikebuchi now? Dead, no doubt. His fuel must have long since run out. He had probably used his short sword to commit *seppuku*. We had heard no distant explosion, as there would have been if Ikebuchi used his inside switch. He must have continued on until his fuel was exhausted, then disemboweled himself. What an end for a man so brave!

Each depth charge explosion made me think it would be the last one, especially when those two destroyers criss-crossed above us in the sixth attack. They knew exactly where we were. So far as they were concerned, I am sure, it was simply a matter of time. All they were waiting for was the telltale bubbling of black oil that would show our side was ripped open and that we were sinking. It puzzled me how we could take the punishment dealt out so far and survive.

Then came the seventh attack. Another dozen or so depth charges plummeted down toward us. They, too, exploded below us. This was luck. Had they realized what Captain Sugamasa was doing, the enemy destroyer commanders would set their depth charges for shallower explosions. On our deck, in the *kaiten* warheads, were fifteen thousand pounds of high explosives. If one of the warheads went, we would be finished. So, perhaps, would one of those destroyers, if it were overhead at the time. Its bottom could be ripped out.

Over ninety depth charges had come down at us by that time. Still I-36 staggered on. I had reached the point where every nerve end was ragged. I quaked constantly, and so did some others I could see. In my palm I held a celluloid container of potassium cyanide. I was sure the enemy would get us. Once they made their sought-after direct hit, and water came rushing into our hull, I was going to swallow the container's contents. I could not bear to think of death by drowning, or suffocation.

It was now 3:00 P.M. We had been subjected to seven separate depth charge attacks in two and one-half hours. Captain Sugamasa's voice came over the loudspeaker. It was desperate-sounding.

"*Kaiten* men, get ready! Man *kaiten* Number Five and Number Three!"

Kuge was getting his wish at last. Yanagiya was also being sent to his weapon. I shouted, "Good luck!" as they struggled along the slanted deck to their access tubes. I wasn't sure whether Captain Sugamasa put any hope in them, or whether he was simply giving them their wish, to die as *kaiten* men should. Maybe he knew his own life was short, and wished to close it with a grand gesture.

Mechanics had checked the *kaiten*. The electric rudder control was inoperative in each one. They were dry, though, a miracle after all that depth-charging. But Kuge and Yanagiya would have to employ manual rudder control. It would be very difficult for them to maintain a course for the enemy.

All of us had practiced using manual control of rudder in training. It made a *kaiten* zigzag terribly. If those destroyers were not close by when our *kaiten* were launched from I-36, there would be little chance of hitting them. The run-in would have to be short for success to be achieved.

The captain knew of this. It had made him reluctant to give permission when Kuge first asked for it, hours before. But now one last frantic effort had to be made to get the monsters off our backs.

There were no telephone connections to either *kaiten*. Both had snapped loose during the attacks from above. Kuge and Yanagiya would have no information from the conning tower on which to act. One hammer blow on the hull would be the signal for Yanagiya to go off. Two hammers blows would be the signal for Ensign Kuge.

Yanagiya's clamps were loosened, and a crewman swung a big hammer with all his might against the hull. Then we waited. A second passed. Then another. Then, welcome sound, we heard Yanagiya's propeller spin rapidly. He moved away, and was off in search of the enemy.

How would he handle his *kaiten*, I wondered? Would his meters and gauges give proper indications? At this moment we were at the 215-foot level, having slid down to it in spite of every effort made within the submarine, including the carrying of rice bags forward. Yanagiya would have to climb almost vertically if he were to remain near I-36's location and ambush the enemy.

Yanagiya's engine sound was still audible when a second crewman struck the forward part of our hull twice. We heard the securing bands for Kuge's *kaiten* snap open and fall on the deck, but there was no sound from his engine. Would he simply float to the surface? If so, the enemy would machine-gun his weapon. Could we survive the mighty explosion of his warhead if it went off directly above us? These questions passed rapidly back and forth among the group of men near me, and one said, "What difference? If those *kaiten* are lost, we are lost too!"

We waited, breathless, wondering what would happen. Then, about thirty seconds after Kuge's hold-down clamps had snapped, we heard a familiar sound. His engine had started! What a wonder! The *kaiten* was an unpredictable thing, I thought. In spite of scrupulous maintenance, those engines often did not start at Hikari and Otsujima. Now we had two weapons that had been exposed to the sea for twenty-five days, and had been beaten badly my many depth charges. Yet they worked. Some things are simply unexplainable.

The next few minutes were very quiet. The *kaiten* engines

faded, and no destroyer propellers could be heard. Another ten minutes passed. It was almost fifteen minutes since Yanagiya had been released. The two men must be steaming toward their targets, those two destroyers.

Quite suddenly we heard several small explosions, quite a ways off, followed by a giant one. A *kaiten* had detonated!

Hoarse cheers rose from our tired throats. "They did it!" we shrieked to one another. "One of them got an enemy!" A charge of 3,000 pounds had gone off, and we were sure in our minds one of the hunters above had been destroyed. Tears of sorrow and joy for my comrades welled into my eyes. One of them, at least, had fulfilled his destiny.

What of the other? Our sound room reported that only one destroyer could now be detected. He seemed to be heading toward the spot where the big explosion had occurred. He was dropping depth charges, the sound operator said. They were very far away from us.

More depth charges were fired. We in the hull could make them out faintly. We decided that this remaining enemy ship was pursuing the second *kaiten*. One of our friends was saving our lives for us. He was drawing off an attacker so I-36 could make an escape. How the enemy must have been surprised, we told one another. At one moment he was thinking he had a sure kill of a submarine. He was dropping depth charges as a hunter fires cool shots at fleeing game. The next moment he was faced with two giant, high-speed torpedoes, seeking to kill him instead.

More time passed. The sound of enemy screws disappeared completely. And no more depth charges could be heard. Both the *kaiten* and that destroyer must be somewhere far beyond the horizon. Captain Sugamasa changed course and crept away as quietly as he could. A returning enemy would have practically no chance of finding us now.

Thus did Petty Officer Yanagiya and Ensign Kuge save our submarine. Which one had hit the destroyer, and which had played the decoy? Had it been Kuge whose explosion we had heard? Had the shy Osaka man, who had written to his brothers and sisters daily, killed off that threat? How fierce had been his determination, this man who had suggested to Captain Sugamasa the idea of firing *kaiten* from the depths! How paradoxical did his behavior seem to people other than *kaiten* pilots, who knew him best? Kuge was so shy and bashful that he had to pretend he had a sweetheart when other men discussed the subject. On one occasion he showed us a picture of a lovely young girl in her school uniform, and told us it was his lover's. It was not until much later that we found out it was really a picture of his sister. Had this modest, retiring person been the one who'd struck that mighty blow?

Or was it Yanagiya, who had to stay at home, working in a fishery, while the rest of Japan's young men fought on far shores and distant seas? Growing furious at each bad turn of the war, he had finally overcome his parents' opposition and convinced them he had to fight for his country, even though they had already given one son in death. What a warrior he had been! At Tsuchiura this short, stocky man from the north had proven his aggressive spirit beyond doubt. A wrestling party was held, with 100 cadet pilots ordered to fight. Yanagiya was the only survivor, defeating all others after they in turn had defeated their opponents. More than a score of cadets were sent tumbling by his thick arms and body. Had it been this merry, honest man, who made no pretense about his being from a humble home, who had driven into the enemy's heart? Or had he foregone glory, to draw the second ship away and aid us to escape?

We would never know.

Captain Sugamasa spoke to us over the loudspeaker, his words interrupted by sobs.

"Attention, all hands!" he said. "I wish everyone to make their best efforts to repair the damages done to us. Ensign Kuge and Petty Officer Yanagiya have just died heroes' deaths, as did Lieutenant Ikebuchi. Do not let them die in vain! We will return to the base as quickly as we can, once the damages are repaired. We will refit, and come out to fight again. We will take our revenge for these three brave comrades. I give you my word I will lead that fight myself!"

All around me men were weeping. The only clean spots on their dirty, grease-smeared faces were where tears ran down them. I had wept on occasion before, but this time it was different. These were tears of true sorrow. They came up from the center of my being. This time I was not sorry for myself. I grieved for those brave men, and their honest, heroic acts. I actually wanted to return to port. I wanted to go to Hikari, get a new *kaiten*, and come back out with Sugamasa after the enemy.

After the captain stopped talking, we did not weep for long. We had no time for it. We were safe from the enemy, but not yet safe from the sea. We were badly damaged and slowly sinking. The electricians reported that the ship's batteries were nearly 90 per cent exhausted. We had only enough pressurized air left to make one attempt to raise the submarine. But we dared not use this until we had the ship as whole as she could be made. We had to stop every leak we could, so as not to waste what resources we had. We had to be sure no more water was coming into the submarine before we expelled any in order to rise.

All hands worked hard. I knew nothing about a submarine's workings. My contribution was to pass tools to men who knew how to use them in the correct manner, to hold portable lamps, and help move things. That is what I did. Continual progress was made in making repairs, and at 10 P.M., more than seventeen hours after we had first submerged for the day's underwater run, we made our attempt to rise. All hands were tense, holding their breath and silently trying to urge the ship upward with their minds. It was slow going, and there were times when there was doubt, but we made it. Shortly after ten o'clock in the black night of June 28, we were riding gently on the surface, hoping no marauding enemy had his radar turned toward us. If we appeared on his screen, we were lost. Our compressed air tanks had been emptied in making this ascent. If we had to go down again, we could not come up. The sea's surface, as we turned up our engines so they would recharge our great batteries and refill our air tanks, was like thin ice. All we had for defense if anyone appeared were two light machine guns. *Kaiten*-carrying submarines had no deck gun.

After all the day's bad luck, we had some good. There was no moon. Our radar antenna, which had suffered damage, was repaired, our batteries were charged, and we sucked air into storage tanks. Before long we were fit to make another dive, should it become necessary. The cool sea air refreshed our tired bodies. Faces brightened as air pressure and electrical charge gauge needles moved up. Though this area was supposed to be infested with enemy craft, we somehow felt the souls of our three dead friends were watching over us.

Several hours passed. Though there was no water for washing, all of us felt refreshed. The good air, welcome after the stale, did much for us. Then the radar room reported an enemy plane twelve miles away. Though we had completed only makeshift repairs we had to submerge.

This had to be done slowly. Nothing was working well enough to attempt a crash dive. I-36 slid under the waves in far more time than it would have taken her before that depth charge attack we had suffered. Apparently the plane did not sight us, and we hoped to get back up to the surface and the cool night air, but Captain Sugamasa had taken all the beating he wanted to take for a while. We stayed under the surface, and when he was asked when we would come up again, all he would say was, "Not for some time yet!"

During the long period of depth charge attacks we had been so full of fear that we did not notice the heat at all. Escaping death was the single thought we held. But now that we were out of danger, we realized the temperature of the submarine's interior was really oppressive. Our air conditioning system was damaged beyond repair. We had some electric fans, but all they could do was stir up the stale air. The entire crew was uncomfortable, made all the more so because of the loss of that cool air that had been coming into I-36 during the time we had been on the surface. The body of every man I could see was glistening with sweat, and even the ship's officers, who always wore their uniforms on even the hottest days, had stripped down to *fundoshi* like the rest of us.

We kept hoping Sugamasa would take the ship up soon, so we could cool off a little. I was dizzy with heat and fatigue, and headed for the crew's quarters. It was just a little less hot there, and I thought that if I lay down in my berth and kept perfectly still I might somehow feel cooler.

In the crew's compartment, near the bow, I found Petty Officer Eizo Nomura lying in his berth, weeping bitterly. Nomura was as tough in spirit as any man I had ever met in the Imperial Navy. I could expect him to cry whenever everyone else was crying in sorrow, but it startled me to see him weeping alone. He was just not that kind of person. I started to ask him what was the matter when I noticed a notebook lying on the berth beside him. I recognized it as Ensign Kuge's, entrusted to us the day before when Kuge mounted his *kaiten* to drive away the enemy above us.

"Here, Yokota," said Nomura, "read this."

He handed me the notebook, opened to a page near the end, and I saw that the officer had written down a testimonial, a memorial to leave behind him. I began reading.

"To all my friends at the base, from Minoru Kuge:

"Owing to maintenance trouble on our *kaiten*, three pilots will be forced to go back to the base again. We left port as a group of six. We had become good friends, and it grieves me that only three of us can meet the enemy.

"For Sonoda, Nomura and Yokota, this is not a first mission. They have been out twice before. Though they will have to return to you, I beg you not to look upon them with cold eyes. When told his *kaiten* could not be fired, Ensign Sonoda wept bitterly in the officers' quarters. I understood his feelings perfectly.

"Please send these three men out on a new mission as quickly as possible. They want to obtain perfect weapons, and strike the enemy with them.

"This is the final request of my life, and the only one I make of you as I await the order to go on my last mission."

When I read it, I joined Nomura in weeping. I wanted to cry Kuge's name aloud, and bless him, but did not do so because of crewmen being around us. Instead, I lay in my berth and prayed for our friend. He, like us, had gone out and known frustration by having to come back twice, from the Kongo and Tembu missions. So, in closing his diary, he was asking other *kaiten* men to have mercy on us.

"I will need no mercy, Kuge," I said. "I will go back and accept with calm whatever happens. If persons slander us behind our backs, so let it be. If they cannot understand how a *kaiten* man feels, I can do nothing to change that. You and Ikebuchi and Yanagiya understand, so nothing else is important. There will be some delay, but we will come out again. Wait for us. We will join the three of you before long."

I wiped the tears away. I had no more reason for them. Sleep moved over my sweaty body.

While I slept, Captain Sugamasa's crew kept I-36 moving slowly northward toward our home base. All hands wanted to surface the ship, but there was no chance to do so. Enemy patrols had grown intense. Every time the captain took the ship up far enough so the radar antenna could be raised above the surface, our operators saw enemy planes on the screen. So we kept running underwater, using up our batteries, knowing that it would be late at night on June 29 before we could have any chance of surfacing.

Everyone not on a cruising station was sleeping or dozing, trying to conserve what energy he had left, when at 9:00 A.M. a sudden explosion was heard. It was loud enough to wake everyone up, and we scrambled to the deck, clad only in filthy loincloths. We were puzzled, for no word came over the loudspeaker to tell us what was happening.

"Find out the source of that noise!" we heard Captain Sugamasa calling when Nomura and I reached the wardroom. The sound room reported it had nothing on its equipment.

"Try the radar!" said the captain.

The radar antenna was raised and swung around. "Nothing on the screen!" reported I-36's radar officer. Either our radar was not working correctly, or whatever it was that made the explosion had suddenly gone away.

There was a short conference in the conning tower, after which word was passed down to us. "We must be leaking oil," we were told. "An enemy plane has seen us. He has dropped a bomb to mark the spot. Ships will probably be coming to search for us now."

This was Captain Sugamasa's deduction. If it was correct, we were in worse trouble than before. We could not stop any oil leak from inside the sub. That black fluid would keep on escaping from our tanks until either we had no more fuel left or the enemy was upon us again. All hands moved to stations and rigged the ship to withstand depth charge attack. We were very frightened, for we did not know how much more damage our battered ship could sustain. It was certain we could not dive very deep, and we still had nine thousand pounds of high explosives clamped to our deck above. One good depth charge shot could mean the end of us all.

We waited, but no depth charge attack came. That made

Sugamasa positive that an airplane had only marked the approximate spot for ships. If he had been sure of our position, the pilot would have continued to attack with more charges. I-36 kept creeping northward. Perhaps by the time surface ships arrived we would be far enough away to escape them.

About thirty minutes later the sound room reported, "Propellers! Left, ninety degrees. Intensity of sound is two!"

The enemy was approaching! A plane had summoned him! He would find us before long, with a trail of oil to follow.

The thought sickened us. We had no defense at all. There were three useless *kaiten* on deck, and crewmen had all they could do just keeping I-36 on an even keel. We could not surface and fight. There were only two machine guns up there to use, and it was possible they wouldn't work, after all the ship had been through. Even if they did, they were no defense against five-inch guns. We would be blown to bits the moment we showed ourselves. There was only one thing for us to do, keep sneaking away and hoping the enemy would not find us. Once he did, it was the end.

Now we all could hear the sound of depth charges. But they were far away. What was the enemy doing?

"Intensity of propeller sounds is now three!" reported the sound room. The enemy was coming on. He was closer to us than he had been at the first report.

A few minutes later the sound room reported, "Intensity of sound is still three!"

This we could not understand. Why did he not come closer? Was he trying to lure us into speeding up I-36, so our screws would make louder sounds, and he could detect us more accurately? We heard the sound of a second barrage of depth charges. They were further away than the first group. It puzzled us, but I-36 kept course to the north, trying to steal away at about four knots. That speed would conserve our batteries longer, and it made little noise for enemy sound detectors to pick up.

We heard more depth charges, these still further away than any others. Then we heard more, but those were so far away that our sound room could not even hear propellers anymore.

"We are in luck!" said Sugamasa over the loudspeaker. "The sea above us is rough. It has helped us. I am sure we are leaking oil, and that is how the enemy airplane found us.

But the rough waves have scattered our leaking oil so that the enemy destroyer is not sure where to look for us. I am going to continue on this course, and hope he will continue to do what he is doing at this moment—drop his depth charges in the wrong place."

Temperature kept rising in the hull. Our oxygen supply was getting low, too. By evening we were gasping like fish left above the high-water mark by a great wave. At 6:30 P.M., Captain Sugamasa decided he had to take a chance. He had to get air, and recharge our batteries. We could not stay down much longer. The men would get too weak to control the submarine.

"Surface the ship!" he ordered, and everyone looked happily at one another. After this ordeal we were going to breathe clean air once more. We waited for the happy sound of air clearing water from our ballast tanks. But instead of that sound we got a different sensation. I-36 began sliding backward, and downward!

"Do shimashitaka?" we heard someone shout in the conning tower. "What happened?" One of the men on watch kept calling out depth readings. "150 feet!" we heard him say as we struggled to maintain our balance. "180 feet! 210 feet!"

The supposed safe depth for I-36 was around 315 feet. Lower than that she could not be expected to withstand the great pressure of the sea.

"240 feet!" shouted the watch. "270 feet! 300 feet! 330 feet!"

I had the sudden sensation that the sea was squeezing me as it was the hull of I-36.

"360 feet!" the voice droned on. "390 feet!"

"Oh, Lord Buddha!" I cried out. The watch called, "420 feet!" There was a screeching noise as though the submarine was being wrung like a face cloth. This is the end, I thought.

Then I heard the rushing hissing sound of air under pressure. The main tanks were being blown free of water. I-36 swerved this way and that for a few seconds, then rose steadily to the surface. Safe at last! I learned later that some petty officer, in his exhausted condition, had turned the wrong valve. It had taken only a few seconds to correct his mistake, but the enemy had nearly gotten us. He had weakened a highly-trained submarine man to the point where that person very nearly killed all his shipmates through a mistake.

We were still not out of trouble. Captain Sugamasa wanted to let Sixth Fleet know we were returning, but he knew the enemy would be listening for transmissions so they could pinpoint us for more attacks. You had to admire their fighting spirit. They were relentless. They never gave up. We ran on the surface and charged batteries. While this was being done, and air taken in, Sugamasa wrote a message and went over and over it many times, condensing it, making it as short as possible, so we would not have to use our wireless for very long. We had to minimize chances of detection.

When everything was ready for another dive, Sugamasa carefully instructed our best radio operator, and handed him the message. It was terse, and tapped out quickly.

"I-36 returning to base. Badly damaged by depth charges. Three *kaiten* expended."

As soon as it was transmitted, we slipped beneath the waves and stayed there. We ran underwater all through June 30, and surfaced late at night. While recharging the batteries this time, we listened in to enemy radio transmissions, many of which were in plain language. That's how confident the American fleet was at that moment. Sure that the Imperial Navy could not harm it, it did not even bother to code messages and hide what it was doing. Lieutenant Hagiwara, I-36's navigation officer, told us that the enemy's report on submarines to its far-flung units had our position calculated almost exactly. We stayed above water only the minimum time necessary, then submerged again. We came up again after dark on July 1, and repeated the process, as we did for the next four days. Only occasionally did we pick up enemy reconnaissance planes, and not once did we hear the sound of enemy propellers. Perhaps I-36, and not I-47, was the *shinanai* "Never Die ship."

Not long after midnight, in the early hours of July 6, we were in Bungo Strait, running on the surface. Home was not far away now. A few hours ahead there waited plenty of hot water and good food. Kyushu Island's silhouette rose darkly on the left, and Shikoku could be made out on the right. I had never expected to see either again.

But now, everything was all right, I told myself as I snatched a few minutes of fresh air on the open bridge. In a little while I would be ashore. Everyone would learn of Kuge's will, and Captain Sugamasa would speak for us. In a little while, perhaps two weeks, Sonoda, Nomura and I, together with three more *kaiten* men, would be steaming through this passage once more, heading southward in search of the enemy. Sugamasa had given all hands his word on that.

So, I thought, things were not so bad after all, and lapsed into happy reverie.

It was broken by a loud shout, and four great explosions. The bridge was cleared, and I-36's engines turned up to top speed. In the wardroom I exchanged many puzzled questions with others, for none of us had any idea of what had happened.

I-36's chief engineer came into the wardroom in a little while. "It is unbelievable!" he said. "After all we have been through, we are almost home when an American submarine tried to get us."

"An American submarine? Here, in Bungo Strait?" We knew the enemy submarines often patrolled off the southern end of the Strait, and had sunk ships there, but we were well into the passage when those explosions came.

"It's true," said the officer. "He fired four torpedoes at us. The nearest one passed only fifty feet behind our stern. The explosions you heard was when they detonated against the shoreline. How fortunate can one group of men be?"

Fortunate, indeed! And this was another sign of good luck, after all the bad luck we had. A few hours later I was on the deck of I-36 as she steered into the harbor at Hikari. The sun felt good, beating down on my back. It had been thirty-three days since I had seen it. Before it rose many more times, I would be going out again.

17 ◻ The Struggle's End, and My Dilemma

On July 6, 1945, when the wounded I-36 dragged herself back into port, I was low in spirits. I stayed that way for some time, remaining on board the submarine as long as I could. A check of damage done to the ship showed it to be fairly severe. She would go to Kure for repairs. No one knew how long it would be before she could be placed in a dry-dock. My training was to continue, meanwhile.

While I was at Hikari, plans were laid for the ninth *kaiten* mission to go out. There had so far been Kikusui, Kongo, Chihaya, Shimbu, Tatara, Tembu, Shimbu and Todoroki. The fourth and seventh groups, though sounding alike in English syllables, have slightly different ideographs in their spelling. The fourth Shimbu meant "God's Warriors," while the seventh meant "furtherance of the *samurai* way." This new group, called Tamon, would consist of six submarines, carrying a total of thirty-three *kaiten*.

Tamon was the name of one of our four Buddhist gods, the one charged with protecting Japan against her outside enemies. In addition, Tamon was the "youth name" of Masashige Kusunoki's son, Masatsura. The brave boy, who fought alongside his father in defense of the throne, used this name throughout his childhood, not taking another name until he reached eighteen, the age of manhood.

Only three first-line submarines, I-47 under Lieutenant Commander Shokichi Suzuki, I-53 under Lieutenant Commander Saichi Oba and I-58 under Lieutenant Commander Mochitsura Hashimoto, would go with this group. They were all that Japan had left, now that I-36 was put out of action. These ships would carry six *kaiten* apiece. The remaining three submarines would be I-363, I-366 and I-367, commanded respectively by Lieutenant Commander Sakae Kihara, Lieutenant Takami Tokioka, and Lieutenant Kunio Taketomi.

I-53 was the first to leave, departing from Otsujima on July 14. The last, I-363, left Hikari on August 8. On July 19 two submarines, I-47 and I-367, left port. Neither had any luck, and returned to port without making attacks. So did I-363. That eliminated sixteen of the thirty-three Tamon *kaiten*. Another five were eliminated by mechanical trouble, the curse of the *kaiten* effort. Only twelve, about one-third of those who had set out so bravely, were launched against the enemy.

I fussed and fidgeted at Hikari through the month of July, while most of these submarines set out. No one would let me ride a *kaiten*, and I needed practice badly if I were to go out again. I had not ridden one of the weapons for many weeks now, and needed much brushing up on technique in order to be proficient. I was given no chance for this during July, though. Other men were being rushed through training for "base *kaiten*," for use in Japan's final, massive defense plan. I didn't know about it until long after the war was over, but base *kaiten* were being considered an important part of the plan to halt the enemy attack at our shores.

I-53 sailed from Otsujima on July 14. None of her *kaiten* pilots, or her crew, had any way of knowing that our Emperor had already decided the war must be ended before complete catastrophe smashed our land. Two days before, he had told Prince Konoye to go to Moscow as his special emissary and ask the Russian government to act as intermediary in arranging peace terms between Japan and the United States. Neither of the two high leaders knew, of course, that Russia would avoid such a role because she was already planning to declare war on us herself.

Just before I-53 sailed, the fourteenth *kaiten* pilot to die in training perished at Otsujima. Lieutenant, junior grade, Yoshio Kobayashi hit an American-laid mine while making a practice target run, just as Petty Officers Taruhara and Kitamura had two months before. With Kobayashi in his weapon was the incredibly lucky Petty Officer Hiroshi Takahashi, who was riding double with him at the time. When they collided with this mine, the explosion popped open the *kaiten's* upper hatch. It blew, or perhaps pulled, Takahashi through this small opening. He landed some distance away in the water, stunned, but was able to keep himself afloat until a torpedo boat picked him up. Kobayashi, however, drowned.

I-53 was out for thirty-one days. She fired four of her *kaiten* and reported sinking three enemy transports, as well as one destroyer. I-366 was out only fifteen days. On August 8 she fired three *kaiten* and claimed three transports. I-47, I-367 and I-363, as I have said, had no luck at all. Among the disappointed men who had to return from Tamon, unfired, was my much-loved friend, Petty Officer Kikuo Shinkai, with whom I had trained for a mission long before. It was I-58, still under command of Hashimoto, which had the great good fortune. Though he used regular torpedoes for it, and not *kaiten*, Hashimoto sank a heavy enemy warship.

It was, as Lieutenant Commander Hashimoto later wrote, an unbelievable piece of luck. In the early morning darkness of July 30, while patrolling the Guam-Leyte line of travel, he downed this ship. It had been spotted just before midnight, almost by accident, as a small black blob on the eastern horizon. Hashimoto submerged to periscope depth, and through the night periscope watched this blob become a small triangle, then the shape of a large warship. He estimated it to be a battleship of the *Idaho* class. Its course was set so that it would, if continuing on it, pass directly across I-58's bows, and Hashimoto said to himself, "That ship is dead!"

All the submarine had to do was lie where she was, because the enemy ship did not appear to be following any zigzag course. As Captain Hashimoto continued to take ranges on her, however, he began to fear she would pass too close to him. If that happened, his torpedoes would not have enough range to arm themselves.

Japanese torpedoes, like many others, had to run through the water a certain distance before their detonators became mechanically cocked to explode on impact. He ordered right rudder, and made a long, slow circle. This put him back on the same course he was making when he sighted the target, but he ended the circle further away from the spot at which the enemy ship would pass him. Then, as she crossed I-58's bows at a range of only 1,500 yards, he let a spread of six torpedoes go.

"Four hits!" he shouted out to his crewmen before ordering deep submergence and a sharp turn to the right. He wanted to move ahead of the enemy and stay well under the surface while I-58 reloaded her torpedo tubes for a second attack. It took more than an hour to do this. When he surfaced, I-58's lookouts could see no sign of the big ship. Hashimoto searched for a short time, decided he had sunk the big ship, then dove and made his escape, fearing that its escort might find and sink him in turn. He did not know that this ship had no escort, nor that it was no battleship. After the war he was to find out very definitely which ship it was his torpedoes sent to the bottom.

Having already fired four *kaiten* on July 28, Hashimoto estimated a battleship had been added to the destroyer, tanker and two transports his human torpedoes had gotten earlier. On August 1 he fired his fifth *kaiten* and reported sinking a seaplane tender with it. His sixth *kaiten* had mechanical trouble and could not be launched. Petty Officer Ichiro Shiraki had to come back with the ship.

I-58 crewmen would have been amazed, when they sank this big enemy ship, if they had known it would give their commanding officer the strangest experience any naval officer ever had. After the war the Occupation authorities would fly Hashimoto to Washington, there to testify at the court-martial of the officer whose ship he had sunk. It was the heavy cruiser *Indianapolis*, which had carried atomic bomb parts from America to the Marianas.

By mid-July the American ships were coming very close to our shores, some of them even shelling Japanese cities and defense plants with their big guns. Waves of their carrier planes filled the skies. They hit Tokyo and our two biggest naval bases, Kure and Yokosuka. The last of our big fleet units were anchored at Kure, waiting to sortie as part of the master plan to defend Japan. American planes sank the aircraft carriers *Amagi* and *Kaiyo*, as well as the battleships *Haruna*, *Ise* and *Hyuga*. They also sank three cruisers, a destroyer and the submarine I-372. Japan had only a single battleship left now, *Nagato*. Badly damaged, she was the only Japanese battleship to survive the war.

While I fretted about not getting a chance to ride *kaiten*, Admiral Soemu Toyoda was counting up our remaining naval assets so he could urge the Emperor to continue the war. Toyoda knew the nation had more than 1,000,000 troops in the homeland, with plenty of guns and ammunition. He also knew that dozens of *kaiten* were being secreted along the coasts of Kyushi, Shikoku and Honshu. We had even sent six of them, led by Lieutenant Toshiharu Konada, to the island of Hachijojima, some 200 miles due south of Tokyo. The Americans would have to steam past this place in attacking central Japan. At that moment Konada would race out from the rocky shore and sink six of the enemy ships, preferably aircraft carriers.

Plans were drawn up in Tokyo for one final all-out assault, called Operation Decision, to be made on enemy forces near Okinawa. At the beginning of July, our armed forces still had over 10,000 planes. Some were obsolete, and some were only slow training planes, but all were judged useful for *kamikaze* attacks. A large number were hidden underground, and had been kept there for some time, to fool the enemy into believing we had very few aircraft left. The Japanese Navy also had over 100 newly-constructed five-man submarines, called *koryu*, and about 300 new two-man submarines, called *kairyu*. Both types carried two torpedoes each. The *kairyu* could carry, instead of torpedoes, a special warhead in its bow, weighing over 1,000 pounds, for crashing into ships as the *kaiten* did.

These "items of naval ammunition," so called because they were expendable, like bullets or big shells, had a potential, when added to over 100 "base *kaiten*," for sinking many hundreds of enemy ships. To back them up, we had still another weapon, called *shinyo*. These were small, light boats, about 15 feet long. Each carried a 550-pound explosive charge in its bow. They were intended to crash into enemy ships at night, at a speed of more than 20 knots. Some *shinyo* had been sent to Formosa and Okinawa, but there were still 2,000 of them scattered in coves and inlets along Japan's lengthy coastline. Some were deep inside our best harbors, where they could attack the enemy when he thought he was safest, anchored in a conquered port.

Our high command had estimated correctly, as was learned after the war, that the enemy would attempt his first landing on the southern island of Kyushu, then follow it with a second on the peninsula east of Tokyo. Our forces were disposed to take care of this, with about 3,000 *kami-*

kaze hidden on the southern island and 1,000 on the northern one.

It was early August before I got into a *kaiten* again. My days were finally brightened when I was ordered to go to Otsujima and train with men who had been assigned to Operation Decision, a mass aircraft and submarine assault on enemy ships near Okinawa. I was happy about this. Only a few *kaiten* pilots would make this sortie, due to lack of submarines to carry them. I was to be one of the lucky ones. I knew nothing about what was going on in Tokyo, nor anything about the great defense plan. All I knew, and all anyone else in the *kaiten* corps knew, was that we were still fighting, and would continue to fight to the death.

Before I left Hikari for Otsujima, another friend died in training, the fifteenth *kaiten* pilot to do so. He was Ensign Minoru Wada, who had gone out once, in I-363, with the Todoroki Group. His ship had cruised thirty-one days, sighting enemy vessels many times but never having the luck to be in good enough position for attacking them. It had to bring its five pilots back, and Wada died while practicing for a second mission. He had been launched for practice, and crashed into the bay's bottom near Hirao, the sad news of his death going almost unnoticed. On that day American airplanes had passed overhead on their way to attack Kure. There they inflicted great damage on our ships at anchor, and on shops and machinery so badly needed. Work on I-36 was slowed by this attack, and by another made July 28.

We at Otsujima set about preparing ourselves for another sortie against the enemy. There would be no send-off, of that we were sure. Times were too hard, and time itself too precious to waste in ceremonies. I had a *hachimaki,* and a short sword, so it didn't matter. What concerned me was only that I was going out again. This time, I swore to myself over and over again, I would not come back.

While we were at our tasks, boarding *kaiten* and making practice runs, great things were happening in Tokyo, events that came very close to dividing our nation forever. Two strong factions were doing their best to convince the Emperor of two different things. One faction wanted the war ended, no matter what the cost, before Japan was completely destroyed. They greatly feared a revolt among the people, who were suffering extreme shortages of food. The other faction wanted to fight on. They were willing to pay hundreds of thousands of Japanese lives to take hundreds of thousands of American lives. Loss of that many American lives, they insisted, would make the price of taking Japan so high that our enemies would sue for peace.

This latter faction had prompted the people in the farmlands to arm themselves with bamboo spears against enemy paratroopers. They had posted many *samurai* slogans in railroad stations and other public places, while also requiring radio and newspaper people to publish highly emotional patriotic appeals. But the men who wanted the war ended laid facts before the Emperor that could not be ignored. Over a million citizens had been killed in the home islands alone, from the terrible bombings and fires that followed them. Almost nine million were homeless, living in dugouts, caves and shacks. Nearly five million homes had been destroyed by the enemy, or pulled down by our fire fighters to create fire breaks. In Tokyo alone, right in sight of our ruler, two-thirds of the homes were gone. Our national wealth was greatly lessened, our great merchant fleet almost wiped out, and our Navy gone. Much of the population was truly destitute. Besides their homes, their places of employment had been bombed out, leaving them without shelter or the means to buy food.

We knew nothing of this. No one tried to give us special inspiration to fight on. At Hikari, Hirao and Otsujima we were a force unto ourselves. We had long ago made up our minds what had to be done. Whatever was happening elsewhere played no part in our thinking. It was our wish to destroy the enemy. We knew the war was going against Japan and hoped to turn the tide. Knowing the situation behind us could not have made us fight any harder. When a man has offered his life, that is all he can offer. No one can urge him to do more.

Emperor Hirohito had made up his mind that an arrangement with the enemy had to be worked out. He had made this decision even while I was out with the Todoroki Group in I-36, feeling that the awful suffering of his subjects must end. He was fixed in this decision weeks before August 6, the "day of double dawn," arrived. An atomic bomb was dropped on Hiroshima that day, making those who saw the tremendous ball of fire from it repeat ever afterward that "Hiroshima saw two sunrises." A second such bomb was exploded over Nagasaki three days later. Both caused wide destruction and a horrendous loss of lives. They helped convince the unconvinced that Japan no longer had any chance of winning.

I kept up my training at Otsujima, reveling in the thought that I would soon go out for the fourth time, and more than a little proud of the fact that I now had more time in the *kaiten* than any other pilot of the human torpedo force. I received no news from outside and, except for concern over whether my family was safe, thought of nothing but my coming departure. I knew nothing of the cabinet change the Emperor had made, nor of the posters threatening the lives of those who were trying to help our ruler work out an acceptable surrender plan. I had no inkling of a plot that was being hatched to seize the government "and protect it for the Emperor, who is receiving bad advice from traitors." I didn't know that, about midnight of August 9, our ruler had told his top advisors that "the time had come to bear the unbearable," that Japan would have to accept unconditional surrender rather than total annihilation. He listened to counter-arguments for four hours before using the ultimate weapon of his Imperial Presence to make all present agree that surrender was the only course to take.

On August 11 the government made a nation-wide announcement that the war had to be terminated. This did not have much effect on the people, because of the Imperial Army. Our Army was still trying to dictate national policies for Japan, even though General Hideki Tojo was out of power and in disgrace. General Korechika Anami, the War Minister, issued a statement of his own at the same time, and citizens had become accustomed to heeding the War Ministry's words. Anami urged the citizens to prepare for a fierce fight on Japanese soil. He cited the example of Iyeyasu Tokugawa, the mighty *shogun* whose line had been the actual rulers of Japan for 250 years, before it was overthrown by the Imperial Restoration movement in the nineteenth century. At one time Tokugawa, who conquered all Japan, allowing no one to rise against the Emperor, was besieged in his castle, fighting a hopeless battle against a mighty force of his enemies. He was almost out of food, water and arms when he had a sudden idea. Ordering the main gate of his castle thrown wide open, he strode outside it and stood there, beckoning his enemies to enter. Suspecting a trap, and giving Tokugawa credit for holding back some secret strength, they withdrew, and he later conquered them. War Minister Anami contended that the enemy would also retreat, if Japan appeared to be letting them come on and enter our homeland.

Certain Army officers in Tokyo completed planning a "temporary seizure" of our government that day. In spite of what General Anami said, they were reluctant to act, because of the official government announcement. But they soon took courage again, when an American broadcast carried a message from Secretary of State Byrnes, of the U.S. In it he said that "from the moment of surrender" our Emperor would be under the orders of the Allied Supreme Commander in the Pacific.

Those fiery officers would not consider such a possibility for one single moment. They spread a lot of talk about this being in violation of *kokutai,* our national system of the Emperor being all-powerful and subject to no one but the gods, and they spoke of *kunsoku no kan,* "the evil ones close to the throne." They also quoted General Anami, who had said the nation must fight on "even if we are forced to eat weeds, gnaw sand, and sleep in the hills!" They said only a traitor would accept the unconditional surrender demanded by the Potsdam Declaration, making our Emperor subservient to our enemies, and that those who agreed with the "evil advisers" should be shot.

I was taking water training in my weapon at Otsujima, waiting for I-36 to come and get us for Operation Decision when, on August 13, the Emperor summoned General Anami and Admiral Toyoda to his presence. He told them Japan would have to accept the terms of surrender, because there was no alternative. On that day American submarines even dared to shell our homeland, and the enemy forces were so strong that one of their flying boats landed right inside Tokyo Bay to pick up an American flier who had been shot down.

General Anami and his backers argued a long time, with some help from Admiral Toyoda, but the Emperor would not change his mind. The final draft of the surrender announcement was completed late on August 14, and just before midnight our ruler began making a phonograph record of it. This was locked up in a safe within the Imperial Palace, with only two men knowing where it was, for it was feared that rebels might try to seize the record and prevent its being broadcast.

By this time the *kichigai*, "the crazy ones," had begun to act. It was almost certain they had been told of the coming announcement by General Anami or someone close to him. Young Army officers killed Lieutenant General Takeshi Mori, commander of the Imperial Guard Division, which safeguarded the palace, when he refused to join their revolt. Then they forged an order from him, which told the Guard to seize the palace gates, letting no one pass in or out. They planned to do what others had done in Japan's history, make virtual prisoners of the Royal Family, then "return" the nation to its ruler when things were the way the rebels felt they should be.

Then they searched the palace, looking for the broadcast record. The Americans helped defeat this plan, however, because a Tokyo air raid alert required a full blackout. This darkened the palace and slowed down the hunt, because the rebels could only use flashlights. When dawn came, they still had not found the record. Not long after that General Shizuichi Tanaka, commander of the Eastern Army Corps, arrived at the palace gates. His troops had the defense of Tokyo as a responsibility. He had refused to join the insurrection, and had now come to halt it. He made an impassioned speech to members of the Imperial Guard and, at the end of three hours of continuous talking, finally convinced them the order from General Mori was a forgery. At that moment three of the rebel officers killed themselves on the spot, before General Tanaka's eyes. The general would kill himself a week later, in shame at not having stopped the rising when he first learned of it, but the personal threat to the Emperor was now ended.

At Atsugi Naval Air Station, however, there were more *kichigai*, Navy pilots led by their base commander, Captain Ozono. The captain had also learned of the forthcoming surrender broadcast. He quickly posted fifty men to guard his radio transmitter and began sending wireless messages to Navy ships and bases, beseeching everyone not to surrender, telling them that the planes and pilots at Atsugi would fight on to death. Nevertheless at 7:00 A.M. on August 15 the nation was stunned by startling news. For the first time in history, a Japanese ruler would address all of his subjects at the same time. *Tenno's* voice would be heard over Radio Tokyo at exactly twelve o'clock noon.

I learned of this while checking over my *kaiten* for a

water session. The commanding officer suspended all training. Everyone gathered near loudspeakers to hear what the Emperor would say. Exactly at noon, his voice came over the air. The terms of the Potsdam Declaration were to be accepted. All persons were to keep order and act honorably. All were to endure what suffering might come, for the sake of preserving our nation.

We gaped at one another when the broadcast was over. Was the war truly finished? Had we really lost? Was this the end of everything? Had all our efforts, all the lives lost, been in vain? Were my comrades Furukawa, Ikebuchi, Maeda, Yamaguchi and all the others resting in watery graves for nothing? The shock was so great that we simply could not absorb it. We *kaiten* men knew the war was not going well, but had no idea that the fortunes of war had gone so heavily against us that Japan might have to allow foreign troops on her soil. It was simply impossible for us, all dedicated men who had long ago offered to die for Japan, to accept the fact that our Emperor was now ordering us to live.

The base was complete confusion. No one knew what to say, or do. Dozens of *kaiten* stood ready, but that radio message prevented us from using them any further. What were we to do now? That was the main topic of conversation all afternoon. Up until the moment of the broadcast we had been full of fight. Now we were puzzled. That evening Lieutenant Yuasa, who had become executive officer of Otsujima, gathered all of us *kaiten* pilots around him.

"There seems to be something wrong about that announcement by the Emperor," he said. "We have received word that the surrender is the choice of the Emperor personally, and at the same time we have received word that it was not his own idea, but comes from bad advice given him by men who are suspected of being traitors to Japan. What the exact truth is, we do not know, so we are going to wait. We are not going to act on the announcement. The *kaiten* bases will continue as we have before. We will not stop unless an official order comes to us through the Commander-in-Chief of the Imperial Combined Fleet. He is the person who gives orders to us for the Emperor. So far we have not received any orders from him."

"*Banzai!*" A great cheer went up. That was what we needed to hear. It made our spirits soar once again. While

Army officers in Tokyo were entrenching themselves on hills near the city, and Navy planes from Atsugi were scattering leaflets over cities on Honshu, urging everyone not to surrender, we went about our training. We did not know that Vice Admiral Matome Ugaki had already led the final flight of *kamikaze* away toward Okinawa. Nor that Vice Admiral Takijiro Onishi, founder of the *Kamikaze* Corps, and General Anami had both committed *seppuku*.

I was launched the next day, August 16, from a torpedo boat. That day was no different from any other, except that the talk of all hands included a desperate note. Some *kaiten* men were ashore, getting instructions, others were at work adjusting and checking weapons on the dock. More were on board the torpedo boats, helping people like myself. And on the observer craft there were officers, as usual, grading our performance just like they always did. I-363 and I-367 returned from their fruitless sorties, and the last *kaiten* mission set out in search of the enemy.

This was the tenth, and last, *kaiten* sortie. It consisted of only one submarine, I-159, commanded by Lieutenant Takesuke Takeyama. This last ship departed from Hirao, carrying two pilots, Ensign Masashi Saito and Petty Officer Shinzo Imada, neither of whom had been out before. Captain Takeyama headed his vessel west and left the Inland Sea by way of Shimonoseki Strait. Bungo Strait was blocked by the enemy, so the submarine headed for the Sea of Japan. There the crew and *kaiten* men would lie in wait for the enemy. Just after they left Hirao the last *kaiten* man to die without going on a mission ended his life. Lieutenant Hiroshi Hashiguchi believed life should end for him if the war ended for Japan in defeat. He shot himself with a pistol.

On August 17, still eager to fight, I had another session of water training in my *kaiten*, launching for runs on a target ship. That evening we had a very severe seminar, with criticism heavy for those who did not do well in this grave time of deep crisis. I received no scolding, though, for I had done well. At that hour I was the most trained man in the entire *kaiten* force.

When the session ended, I went to bed, first straightening out all my belongings. I-36 was due to come and get us for Operation Decision, the August 20 attack on Okinawa. Instead of the submarine, however, Rear Admiral Mitsuru Nagai, Commander of Sixth Fleet, came to us from Kure.

All hands were assembled in front of the headquarters building to hear him speak.

"The news you received three days ago," he said, "is true. Japan has been surrendered unconditionally. Representatives of our government are at this moment on their way to the Philippines, where they will receive instructions to prepare for the landing of American and British troops in our land. It is His Majesty's wish that all of you lay down your arms. I herewith personally and officially give you that order!"

The ranks began murmuring. Several people shouted, "Never!" Others shouted, "No surrender!" and someone called out the slogan, "One hundred million Japanese die in honor!"

Admiral Nagai grew flushed and angry as the noise increased. He was disappointed, too, I know, because he had such strong feelings toward men of the *kaiten* force. He raised both hands in the air, and when the noise quieted down he spoke again.

"It is His Majesty's wish!" he cried out. "Do you think that you can disobey your Emperor and remain a Japanese one moment after that?"

He paused and allowed time for this to sink into our minds. He looked all around him for a long time, peering into the eyes of many men to see the effect his last statement had on them. Then his voice grew persuasive.

"Look at Germany!" he told us. "She was defeated before, and came back stronger than ever. She will do it again, too. Japan will come back, I tell you, stronger than ever before." At that point his voice became crisp and businesslike, as it must have been on the ships he commanded in his career. He was no longer trying to persuade people, just giving them orders he expected to be obeyed. "All of you are to depart from this place as soon as you can get ready!" he said. "But remember, you are members of the Imperial Navy. You will remain members of it, and are always to consider yourselves as such. You will be on indefinite home leave, that's all. It is possible that someday you will be recalled to duty again, when your country once more requires your service. Wait for that day! Thank you for all that you have done. Good luck, and goodbye."

Admiral Nagai stepped down then. In a short while he left the base. This was the third day after the surrender broadcast had been made from Tokyo. In spite of our determination to train as before, there had been a lot of talk about the Emperor's statement. A number of people who had been college students before putting on a uniform said that we should accept the inevitable. *"Shikata ga nai!"* they said, just as Japanese have always said after typhoons, floods, earthquakes or other disasters. "Nothing can be done!" They claimed that no one would dare advise our ruler to surrender unless it was necessary to do so in order that our country might survive and grow strong again.

But I and others like me, who had been *kaiten* men before these student officers, would not listen to such talk. We had gone out. We had seen our friends go off and die fighting the enemy. We felt that surrender was a betrayal of them. When planes from nearby bases flew over us, dropping "no-surrender" leaflets, we picked them up and read them. We had no thought at all of giving up. If no submarine came for us, we would have our *kaiten* towed to some cove and wait for the enemy there. It wasn't until Admiral Nagai, whom we loved and respected, spoke to us that our hot feelings cooled down. So strong was his influence that some men went straight to their barracks, packed, and were out of Otsujima base by nightfall.

I stayed at Otsujima. I wasn't going to go anywhere. There was no place, it seemed, for me to go. I had shut myself into a place of death. How could I emerge now, and enter a place of life? My soul belonged at Yasukuni, with those of my friends, not with my body. I would obey the admiral's orders, and give up my *kaiten*, but how could I give up my desire to live on in the memories of those who knew me best?

I-159 returned from the Sea of Japan, her *kaiten* unfired, the same day Admiral Nagai spoke to us. The war, so far as Sixth Fleet was concerned, had come to a close. The next day I realized that the admiral would have said anything to get us away from our weapons. Crews were already dismantling *kaiten* or draining fuel from them. Warheads were being locked up or disarmed. In other parts of Japan men were shooting holes in the fuel tanks of armored vehicles and taking the propellers from airplanes. High authorities were doing everything to prevent some incident against the Americans that would give them cause to continue the war.

With the return of I-159, the *kaiten* program ended. It

had cost 80 *kaiten* pilots killed in action, plus 8 more who had been on their way to be based ashore at Okinawa. Another 15 men had been killed in training accidents. I-37, I-44, I-48, I-56, I-165, I-361, I-368 and I-370, eight submarines, had gone down while seeking the enemy, their crews totalling more than 600 men. In exchange for these ships, weapons and lives, the Sixth Fleet estimated we had downed between 40 and 50 enemy ships, including a British cruiser of the *Leander* class.

More men left Otsujima. I stayed, suspended somewhere between life and death. I had been so fully consecrated to the idea of extinguishing my life that now I did not know what to do with myself. Many of my friends had achieved their goal of glorious death, but I had not. They were at the gate of Yasukuni now, waiting for me so we could all enter together. But the war was over, and I had no right to enter that sacred place. Nor could I again face the world, from which I had so completely withdrawn. I was miserable, and thought of committing suicide, but I was too proud to do it. My life had been measured as worth one large American aircraft carrier, I reminded myself. How could I surrender it now to a small pistol bullet?

I had no desire to go to Tokyo. It was one vast ruin, I heard. I had suffering enough, without viewing the suffering of others. My soul was in agony, so I stayed at Otsujima, doing little more than lie around for two weeks. I pondered the special Imperial Rescript issued after the surrender announcement to members of the military, in which the Emperor ordered us to "conquer a thousand difficulties, and endure the unendurable." That I could not do. Though I had decided not to die, I could not boldly enter life again. I became inanimate, waiting to see what the future would hold. I felt like one of our *bonsai,* the miniature trees that do not grow, but simply age.

But this phase of inactivity ended before long. On September 2, on board the American battleship *Missouri* in Tokyo Bay, the official surrender document was signed at 9:04 A.M. American troops were coming to occupy all naval and military bases. We who were still sleeping in the barracks were told we must leave.

I wondered and wondered what I should do, and finally decided to discuss in with my good friends, the Harada family. I went to Hikari and appeared at the door of their home, a suitcase in my hand.

"Welcome, Yokota-*san!*" said the lady of the house as she took my suitcase from me, her happy face, giving me the first moment of true pleasure I had known for some time. The wonderful lady was actually glad to see me and joyful to see me alive.

I explained my situation to her as best I could, though I had some difficulty in finding just the right words. I said I had no place to stay, that I didn't want to go back to Tokyo, and that I wanted no part of life at all, now that my friends were departed.

"Stay here!" she said, with the wonderful understanding I hoped my own mother would have had for me if she were alive. "Stay here as long as you like. Stay until you know what it is you want to do."

I moved into the Harada home. I was there during September, when the insurrectionists were convicted and sent to prison by Japanese authorities for failing to obey the Emperor's order. I was still there when chill fall came, writing many letters in October and November to my family, but getting none in return. I had no idea at all of where they were, or whether they were still alive. I sank deeper and deeper into gloom. I didn't even try to find employment, so that I could repay the Haradas for the food I ate. I didn't want to leave their home, for fear of meeting the enemy. It was not that I hated the Occupation people, but I could not bear facing the men who had defeated my country.

Then I received a letter from my sister Chiyoe. My entire family had been evacuated to an area near Mt. Fuji, but Chiyoe and her husband had just returned to Tokyo. Everyone was well, although there never seemed to be enough food available regularly. I packed my suitcase, thanked the Haradas for their extensive and uncomplaining generosity, and took a Tokyo train. On arriving in the capital city I saw something that horrified me. On the streets, people were begging! This numbed my heart; it was a worse sight even than people picking through garbage for food. How far Japan had fallen! Before the war there were no beggars. The streets of Japan were not like those of China and India. No one begged. It was too shameful a thing to do. Even our priests worn special baskets over their heads, to hide their faces, when they solicited alms for religious purposes. But such was the situation. So many people had lost those on whom they depended for support and protection that they had to beg, or starve.

I went to Chiyoe's house, and found her sympathetic. She was shocked to learn the truth about what I had been doing all these past months when the family thought I was flying airplanes. As I told her more and more about my friends and our philosophy, however, she began to understand my feelings. She left me to myself. Again I became a parasite, lying about, doing nothing, refusing to go out, retreating into my own mental world of the dead.

This continued for a month. Then, in January, 1946, a letter came from Mitsuo Takahashi, another *kaiten* pilot. He had been born in outlying territory of Japan, not in its main islands. He was forced to stay in Hikari and seek employment there, because the Allied authorities would not give him permission to travel homeward. His native place was being taken from Japan, along with other portions of the Empire.

"Dear Yokota," the letter said, "I want to tell of something that may interest you because of the feeling I know you had when the war ended and while you were at the Harada home."

It was a very long letter. It told of Admiral Nagai, who had became worried about *kaiten* men who seemed to have no desire to live. They had rejected the world on becoming human torpedo volunteers. Like myself, they could not bring themselves to re-enter it. So the admiral devised a plan for those men. He was forming a farming force. He had found a piece of land, and was donating some money. All *kaiten* men who wanted to retreat from the world, he said, could come to Hikari and join this force.

I answered Takahashi's letter at once. "I am willing," I said, "though I know nothing about farming." As I wrote the letter I kept telling myself, over and over, that this was the solution to my dilemma. I would neither have to live nor die. I would lose myself somewhere between them, in isolation. "I think I could be a farmer if I tried, Mitsuo," I wrote. "I will come at once."

Full of joy, I packed my suitcase once again. Chiyoe, her husband and their friends tried to convince me I should not go, but I rejected their protests and soon got a train back to Hikari. There I learned that our group leader would be

Lieutenant Shingo Takahashi. He had been executive officer for the group of midget submarines that had taken part in the attack on Pearl Harbor four years before. Takahashi was from Hiroshima, and a most grieved man. Already low in spirits when told by Admiral Nagai to put down all desire to fight any more, he started for his native city and found on arrival that his college professor father had been consumed in the atomic blast of August 6. Their home was gone, as well. It was while trying to console this lonely man that Nagai had gotten the idea for the farm corps.

At Hikari I also learned how another man had become sympathetic to the plan. He was Kichinosuke Nakao, who had a construction business. Mr. Nakao donated a large sum of money to help buy the land and to provide farming tools. The farm embraced about twenty-five acres and was outside the village of Mitsuo-mura, about twenty miles from Tokuyama, a city not very far from Otsujima base. The mayor there understood our feelings well, and cooperated in the purchase of the land.

There were eleven of us in the farm group, all emotionally unsettled. Six were midget submarine men and five *kaiten* pilots. We set out for our plot of land with the good wishes of our benefactors, and within a few days knew this was just what we wanted for ourselves. We were independent, and remote. No part of the world touched us. We tilled the land and planted crops. These included wheat, buckwheat, potatoes, sweet potatoes and several kinds of vegetables. We planted them, tended them, harvested them and sold them, all the while avoiding contact with other persons as much as possible.

At the months went on the hard work and sweat purified me. My body grew strong, and the dark cloud lifted from my mind. By the summer of 1946 we were a group of truly happy men. We felt like Buddhist priests, totally engaged in our own affairs and set apart from the affairs of others. While war criminals were tried, sent to jail or hanged, we worked on, oblivious to the world around us. As autumn passed and winter approached, I became more and more contented. I felt I would be perfectly content to spend the rest of my life like this. With no deep thoughts to disturb me, no other world disturbing my orderly routine.

Then, just before the end of 1946, a letter came from another *kaiten* pilot, a resident of Tokyo. He had gone straight home when Admiral Nagai told men to leave Otsujima. Now he was a student at Tokyo University.

"It has been wonderful, coming back here and resuming my studies, Yokota," he wrote. "The Allied Occupation authorities have completed their investigations. They do not bother anyone at all, so long as you make no trouble. I am very happy, and hope this letter finds you happy, too. School life is still just as enjoyable as it was before I interrupted my studies and entered the Navy."

Then his letter took a chiding tone. "Why don't you give up that fantastic idea of yours, Yokota?" my friend wrote. "You cannot shut yourself off from life and be a dead man. That is what you are now. You should come back to the land of the living. The life ahead of you is a long one. What is done, is done. You cannot dedicate yourself to foolish seclusion. You will want to make something of yourself in the many years that lie ahead of you, so that you can help Japan recover from this defeat. An education will be necessary for that. It is the first step toward a successful life. You were once willing to die for Japan. Are you now willing to work and study hard, so that you can help rebuild it? Come home, and come back to school!"

I read that letter many times. I found myself frequently dwelling on what my friend had said. My farming comrades were getting mail, of course. Some of it must have been like that letter. By the middle of January, 1947, our original eleven-man group numbered a half-dozen. Five had departed, making new lives for themselves. The more I thought about the letter, the more it made me feel like I was back at Hikari again, waiting to go out on a mission in my *kaiten*. The same old doubts began to assail me. I kept asking myself questions. Was I sincere in this farming effort? Was it really what I wanted to do? Did I really want to bury myself in farming? Or was this act of mine a way of leaving a will, something I had refused to do when I was a *kaiten* pilot because I realized I was just trying to impress someone with what a great and brave person I was? Was I hiding from the world because I wanted to, or was I doing something different just for the sake of being different?

Three months after getting the letter, I had searched my soul completely and found an answer. I packed my things, said goodbye to my old comrades, and started for the train station. Early in April,1947, I entered Kanagawa University at Yokohama, determined that I, like millions of my countrymen, would also build a new life. For Yutaka Yokota, nearly twenty months after it had ended for his Emperor, the war was finally over.

▣ EPILOGUE ▣

When World War II closed, the Japanese thought they had sunk some 40 Allied ships, including a British cruiser of the *Leander* class, through their *kaiten* effort. A check of all available sources reveals they sank only two U. S. Navy ships, the tanker *Mississinewa* in the *Kikusui* sortie, and the destroyer escort *Underhill*. This second ship was actually sunk by friendly forces on July 24, 1945, after being hit by a *kaiten*. Only one U. S. merchant ship, *SS Canada Victory,* was the victim of a *kaiten,* going down on April 27, 1945. These three vessels, measured against the 8 submarines and nearly 900 Japanese lives lost in the *kaiten* program, make the enemy's sacrifice seem fruitless.

Yet we can learn much from the *kaiten* story about a fine, intelligent, sturdy people. I believe that Japan, if her existence were threatened in the sixties, would have no more trouble mustering *kamikaze* and *kaiten* pilots than she did during the fevered war years, so deep-running and fervent is their love of country. I have seen tears in the eyes of so-called stoic Japanese when *Kimigayo,* the national anthem, is played, while at the same time aware that any of my fellow countrymen who suddenly cried out "God bless America!" in a crowd would probably be written off as a nut.

If one American, upon reading this book, comes to realize that a fuller knowledge of those who are pitted against us, whether it be in 1941 or 1962, is perhaps the best weapon we can have in our arsenal, I'll count my hours at the typewriter well spent.